THE BIAS OF PLURALISM

The Editor

WILLIAM E. CONNOLLY is Assistant Professor of Government at the University of Massachusetts at Amherst. He was awarded his bachelor's, master's, and doctoral degrees by the University of Michigan and has taught there and at Ohio University. Professor Connolly has held a Horace Rackham Graduate Fellowship and an Ohio University Research Grant. He now holds a Carnegie Fellowship to attend the Institute for Legal and Political Philosophy. He is the author of *Political Science and Ideology* (published by Atherton Press in 1967).

THE BIAS

EDITED BY

OF PLURALISM

William E. Connolly

ATHERTON PRESS

New York 1 9 6 9

The Bias of Pluralism
edited by William E. Connolly

Address all inquiries to:
Atherton Press, Inc.
70 Fifth Avenue
New York 10011

Library of Congress Catalog Card Number 69–19456

FIRST EDITION

Manufactured in the United States of America
DESIGNED BY LORETTA LI

Preface

The preoccupation of many political scientists with political taxonomy obscures the fact that "democratic pluralism" remains the dominant theory of politics for modern industrial societies with competing party systems. Taxonomies—such as structural-functional analysis, systems analysis, communications "theory," and decision-making analysis—provide schema from which political theories can be generated. But whichever taxonomy is employed by contemporary researchers, the theory that most often emerges is the theory of pluralism.

The purpose of this volume is to subject pluralist theory to critical examination. The authors do not claim that the theory is totally untenable; we do contend that conventional formulations of the pluralist interpretation are defective in several respects. As empirical theory, the conventional interpretation rests upon precarious and, often, unacknowledged assumptions. As normative theory, it projects impoverished ideals. As ideology, it fosters complacency among students of politics when creative reappraisal is needed.

The essays by David Kettler and myself are published here for the first time. Myron Hale's essay is a revised and enlarged version of an earlier publication. Arnold Kaufman has added an epilogue to his earlier published essay. The essays by Peter Bachrach and Morton Baratz, Andrew Hacker, Theodore Lowi, Marc Pilisuk and Thomas Hayden, and Brian Barry are reprinted here without revision. Acknowledgments are given at the beginning of each essay.

I would like to thank the contributors for suggestions about the format and content of this volume. Special thanks are due to Myron Hale, Arnold Kaufman, and David Kettler, who read and criticized an early draft of the introductory essay, and to Zillah Eisenstein, who helped prepare the index.

Contents

I : The Critique of Pluralist Theory

1 ⁘ *The Challenge to Pluralist Theory*

WILLIAM E. CONNOLLY

THE CLASSICAL THEORY OF PLURALISM

Pluralism has long provided the dominant description and ideal of American politics. As description, it portrays the system as a balance of power among overlapping economic, religious, ethnic, and geographical groupings. Each "group" has some voice in shaping socially binding decisions; each constrains and is constrained through the processes of mutual group adjustment; and all major groups share a broad system of beliefs and values which encourages conflict to proceed within established channels and allows initial disagreements to dissolve into compromise solutions.

As ideal, the system is celebrated not because it performs any single function perfectly, but because it is said to promote, more effectively than any other known alternative, a plurality of laudable private and public ends. Pluralist politics combines, it is said, the best features from the individualistic lib-

3

eralism of a John Locke, the social conservatism of an Edmund Burke, and the participatory democracy of a Jean-Jacques Rousseau.

The individual's active involvement in group life enables him to develop the language, deliberative powers, and sense of purpose which make up a fully developed personality. His access to a multiplicity of groups promotes a diversity of experience and interests and enables him to reach alternative power centers if some unit of government or society constrains him.

Society as a whole also benefits from pluralism. The system of multiple group pressures provides reasonable assurance that most important problems and grievances will be channeled to governmental arenas for debate and resolution. The involvement of individuals in politics through group association gives most citizens a stake in the society and helps to generate the loyalties needed to maintain a stable regime with the minimum of coercion. Stability is further promoted, in the long run, because public policy outcomes tend to *reflect* the distribution (balance) of power among groups in the society. Yet, the theory goes, innovation and change are also possible in pluralist politics. New groups, created perhaps by changes in economic processes or population distribution, can articulate new perspectives and preferences which will eventually seep into the balancing process, affecting the shape of political conflicts and the direction of issue resolution.

In short, pluralism has been justified as a system which develops individual capacities, protects individual rights and freedoms, identifies important social problems, and promotes a politics of incremental change while maintaining a long-term stability based on consent.[1]

THE LEGACY OF TOCQUEVILLE

The intellectual roots of pluralist theory reach back to Aristotle. But James Madison and, especially, Alexis de Tocqueville have provided the intellectual springboards from which many contemporary thinkers have constructed their own formulations.[2] Tocqueville, in describing and justifying American society of the nineteenth century, was careful to stipulate basic preconditions to the successful operation of pluralist politics. Some of these conditions persist today, for example, the universal suffrage, the competing parties, and the independent judiciary that Tocqueville celebrated. There are, however, notable discontinuities between many other conditions he specified and their contemporary equivalents. My purpose here is to ask to what extent twentieth-century society approximates the conditions for an ideal of pluralism formulated a century ago.[3]

A viable pluralism, Tocqueville believed, encourages among its citizens a widespread participation in politics "which originates in the lowest classes . . . and extends successively to all ranks of society." Such widespread involvement is necessary because "no one will ever believe that a liberal, wise, and energetic government can ever spring from the suffrages of a subservient people."[4] Students of twentieth-century politics, however, are unanimous in concluding that only a small minority of citizens, mostly from upper socioeconomic-educational brackets, participate actively in the political parties and interest groups of contemporary politics.

We need not remind contemporary readers that Tocqueville saw the "voluntary association" as a key agency for developing personality, protecting liberties, and channeling grievances to government. But the emergence of the large-scale, hierarchical organization has significantly altered the character of the voluntary association. It is at least questionable whether this contemporary institution serves as a medium for personality development. It advances the claims of some of its members more forcefully than it does those of others; and the individual's dependence on the structure within which he works may inhibit his opportunities to seek support from other units in times of stress. Moreover, the increased size and formalization required to make the "voluntary association" effective in contemporary politics alter the relationship between members and leaders envisaged by the classical ideal of pluralism. As C. Wright Mills has noted: "Voluntary associations have become larger to the extent that they have become effective; and to just that extent they have become inaccessible to the individual who would shape by discussion the politics of the organization to which he belongs."[5]

The old middle class, whose economic independence and work life encouraged its members to form and participate actively in civil and political associations, is increasingly displaced today by the dependent white collar class. The work life of this new (and allegedly still middle) class resembles that of Tocqueville's "workman" in many respects; it is doubtful whether, on Tocqueville's assumptions, such a work life will foster the breadth of mind needed for responsible citizenship.

> When a workman is increasingly and exclusively engaged in the fabrication of one thing, he ultimately does his work with singular dexterity; but, at the same time, he loses the general faculty of applying his mind to the direction of his work. He every day becomes more adroit and less industrious. In proportion as the principle of the division of labor is more extensively applied the workman becomes more weak, more narrow minded, and more dependent. The art advances, the artisan recedes.[6]

Tocqueville viewed the American frontier as a safety valve for social tensions which could ease the pressure on the balancing process and minimize temptations to supplement the politics of consent with a policy of suppression against discontented minorities. He also viewed the country's relative isolation from foreign concerns as a central factor allowing the system of "decentralized administration" to mute and tame the power of "central government." But the frontier has disappeared today; and the combination of deep involvement in world politics with national problems of economy management, transportation, communication, poverty, urban slums, and ghetto riots has produced a tightening and enlarging of political and administrative processes. Even from Tocqueville's perspective, the stakes of politics are higher today; the earlier safety valves are largely defunct; the contemporary means for the explicit and implicit intimidation of disadvantaged minorities are enhanced.

Tocqueville saw a widely dispersed and locally owned "press" as the most "powerful weapon within every man's reach which the weakest and loneliest of them all may use."[7] But such a press has been replaced today by centralized "media" remote from the individual and certainly more accessible to the privileged and the organized than to the "weakest and loneliest."

We can no longer say with easy confidence that "the American republics use no standing armies to intimidate a discontented minority; but as no minority has as yet been reduced to declare open war, the necessity of an army has not been felt."[8] And we might try to refute, but we can no longer consider irrelevant, Tocqueville's view of the probable relationship between a large military establishment and government:

> All men of military genius are fond of centralization, which increases their strength; and all men of centralizing genius are fond of war, which compels nations to combine all their powers in the hands of the government. Thus the democratic tendency which leads men unceasingly to multiply the privileges of the state, and to circumscribe the rights of private persons, is much more rapid and constant amongst those democratic nations which are exposed by their position to great and frequent wars, than amongst all others.[9]

If these structural changes have undermined some of the conditions specified by Tocqueville for the politics of pluralism, perhaps expanded educational opportunities and other new arrangements promote the needed conditions today; perhaps continuities in the electoral and judicial systems, more important in effect than the changes noted in the social and international context of politics, ensure that political pluralism remains fundamentally intact; or perhaps Tocqueville simply misread some of the most significant conditions of pluralism. Perhaps. On the other hand, in our eagerness to fit the comforting doctrine of an earlier period to the present system we might be prone to underplay the adverse ramifications of a new social structure and world environment; we might too easily assume that functions performed by old institutions in old contexts are still performed by those institutions in their new settings; we might quietly forget some of the functions celebrated in the classical ideal of pluralism and thereby fail to take full account of groups, concerns, and ideals which are not well served by the contemporary balancing process.

Tocqueville clearly realized that institutional evolution could undermine the politics of pluralism. His greatest fear, of course, was the emergence of "majority tyranny." Nevertheless, even while writing well before the period of rapid industrial growth in the United States, he could still point to that minority group which showed the greatest potential to gain ascendancy in the balancing process of the future:

> I am of the opinion, upon the whole, that the manufacturing aristocracy which is growing up under our eyes is one of the harshest which ever existed in the world; but, at the same time, it is one of the most confined and least dangerous. Nevertheless, the friends of democracy should keep their eyes anxiously fixed in this direction; for if ever a permanent inequality of conditions and aristocracy again penetrate into the world, it may be predicted that this is the gate by which they will enter.[10]

CONTEMPORARY PLURALIST THEORY

The dominant view among social scientists today is that some variant of pluralist theory provides the most adequate framework for understanding the contemporary political process. Two broad "types" of pluralist interpretation can be distinguished. The first, typically advanced by political scientists, views the government as the *arena* where major group conflicts are debated and resolved. The second, more often advanced by economists and sociologists, sees major social associations, especially organized labor and the corporation, involved in a balancing process which operates largely outside of government; the government acts more as *umpire* than as participant, setting rules for conflict resolution and moving in to redress the imbalance when one group goes too far. I will outline representative expressions of both the *arena* and *umpire* variants of pluralist theory. The summaries will be brief, identifying what I take to be the central thrust of these interpretations. Since relevant qualifications, hedges, and subordinate themes are necessarily given short shrift in a summary of this sort, the reader is referred to the works cited in the references for a more complete statement of both versions of pluralist theory.

The Arena Theory

Robert Dahl has formulated perhaps the most precise and persuasive interpretation of the arena version of pluralism.[11] Government is the crucial arena for the study of power, says Dahl.

> Government is crucial because its controls are relatively powerful. In a wide variety of situations, in a contest between governmental controls and other controls, the governmental controls will probably prove more decisive than competing controls. . . . It is reasonable to assume that in a wide variety of situations whoever controls governmental decisions will have significantly greater control over policy than individuals who do not control governmental decisions.[12]

There is no ruling class or power elite which dominates government over a wide range of issues. Rather, there are numerous bases for political power in American society—wealth, prestige, strategic position, voting power—and while each resource is distributed unequally, most identifiable groups in the system have and make use of advantages in one or more of these areas.

The competitive party system plays a major role in maintaining the system of pluralism. Since the "in" party's voting coalition is always threatened by the "out" party's attempts to create new issues which will shift marginal voters to its side, both parties constantly strive to increase their support among the major social and sectional groupings in the country. The result is a broad range of "minorities whose preferences must be taken into account by leaders in making policy choices."[13] Any "active" and "legitimate" group can usually "make itself heard at some crucial stage in the process of decision."[14] Or, as Dahl states the point in slightly more restrictive terms later: "few groups in the United States who are *determined* to influence the government—certainly few if any groups who are *organized, active*, and *persistent*—lack the capacity and opportunity to influence some officials somewhere in the political system in order to obtain at least some of their goals."[15]

Observation of issue resolution in the governmental arenas,

then, reveals a decentralized, fragmented bargaining process which involves numerous competing and overlapping minorities. But this bargaining is merely the "chaff" of politics; the social cement and constraints which make peaceful bargaining possible are found elsewhere.

> Prior to politics, beneath it, enveloping it, restricting it, conditioning it, is the underlying consensus on policy that usually exists in the society among a predominant portion of the politically active members. Without such a consensus no democratic system will survive the endless irritations and frustrations of elections and party competition. With such a consensus the disputes over policy alternatives are nearly always winnowed to those within the broad area of basic agreement.[16]

It is true, Dahl agrees, that only a minority of citizens actively participate in politics, but since the active minorities represent a large number of social groupings, since all organized, active, legitimate, and persistent groups have a "voice" in the process, and since the consensus which underlies and controls conflict resolution is a collective product of the whole society (at least of the politically active members), a pluralist system of politics exists.

What desirable functions does the pluralist system perform? Dahl emphasizes its contribution to a stable society based upon minimal coercion and the maximum protection of constitutional rights; it is a "relatively efficient system for reinforcing agreement, encouraging moderation, and maintaining peace in a restless and immoderate people."[17] The system's impact on personality—a central concern of pluralist theorists as diverse as Tocqueville and John Dewey—does not receive close attention from Dahl.

In a recent debate with Jack Walker, Dahl marshalled a series of quotations from his previous publications to show that he has been interested in expanding participation in politics, especially among the lower strata of society. But the statements quoted limit participation to government and view it primarily as a vehicle for channeling existing grievances to governmental arenas. Another tradition of pluralist thought, as we have seen, more directly links participation, the *development* of citizen capacities to translate problems into political issues, and the production of wise political decisions. It also argues that a viable political pluralism requires the expansion of participation beyond government to "the family, the church, business, and the school." Such a "social democracy" is necessary, in John Dewey's view, "from the standpoint both of the general welfare and the full development of human beings as individuals." These claimed linkages are clearly not at the focus of Dahl's analysis; he does not employ them as standards against which to appraise the performance of the pluralist system. He would not assert, for example, that "social arrangements which involve fixed subordination are maintained by coercion," or that "the very fact of exclusion from participation is a subtle form of oppression."[18]

The Umpire Theory

Adolf Berle is a representative spokesman for the "umpire" theory of pluralism. His modification of the arena theory flows from a recognition that the technological revolution of the twentieth century has generated massive organizations, especially the large-scale corporation, which initiate unilateral actions outside of the governmental process with important consequences for the society.[19] Berle was among the first in this country to perceive the separation of ownership and control in the large corporation and to ask: To whom or what are the corporate managers accountable today? To preserve the pluralist interpretation of American politics, Berle agrees, he must identify forces which effectively constrain and limit the exercise of corporate power.

The market economy, although not as important as it once was, exerts some constraint on corporate practices. Organized labor also exerts countervailing power in some areas. The corporate elites, implicated in the value system of the larger society, are developing a "corporate conscience" which provides a form of self-restraint on their actions. And if corporate managers step out of line, the government, responsive to the general public, will step in to constrain them. "There is," Berle asserts, "the State, through which action can be compelled.

There is the public, increasingly capable of expressing a choice as to what it wants and capable of energizing political forces if the system does not want it,"[20] Berle often slips into the rhetoric of majoritarian democracy when discussing the government as a regulator of the large-scale corporation. It is well to note also that he is speaking here primarily of public pressures upon government to change a status quo already achieved by unilateral corporate action, not a politics where the "public" vetoes corporate pressures to change governmental policy.

But how do we decide when the corporation is "out of line"? What are our standards of appraisal, where do they come from, and how do we ascertain whether the market, the corporate conscience, organized labor, and the democratic state are sufficiently constraining the corporation? Berle's answer is clear. Underlying and supporting all of the other constraints is the public consensus, "the body of those general, unstated premises which have come to be accepted."[21] The consensus determines the content of the corporate conscience; it emerges as public support for organized labor or other social groups when corporations push outside their appropriate limits; it provides the energy for citizen pressure upon the government when redress is required. Indeed, the consensus carries a heavier load for Berle than for Dahl; for it not only defines and limits pressures in the governmental arenas but also operates directly upon the corporate managers, constraining their extra-governmental activities.

But what groups shape these "unstated premises" and who activates the consensus when restraint is needed? All groups contribute to it, including the corporate interests themselves. But "of greater force are the conclusions of *careful* university professors, the *reasoned* opinions of specialists, the statements of *responsible* journalists, and at times, the *solid* pronouncements of *respected* politicians. . . . Taken together, this group, so long as its members are able to communicate their views, becomes the forum of accountability. . . . Collectively they are the developers of the public consensus."[22]

Berle's conclusions are still difficult to pin down. For what criteria determine which pronouncements are careful, reasoned,

solid, and respected? Which segments of society are most involved in bestowing "respect" upon those who develop and
defend the public consensus? What *concerns* are most prominent among the selected group of intellectuals, specialists, and
politicans? How does Berle decide that his "group" has more
influence on the consensus than, for example, businessmen and
corporate managers?

The "consensus," for both Berle and Dahl, is the most important force sustaining political pluralism. It is also a factor
which each theorist subjects to minimal examination.[23]

A CRITIQUE OF PLURALIST THEORY

Even the sharpest critics of pluralist theory agree that the politics of balance is a highly visible feature of American politics,
and most critics acknowledge that it plays some role of substance in the total system. Further, many of the critics believe
that pluralist principles must be included in any ideal of politics
relevant to contemporary society.

The critics see organized groups competing within governmental arenas; they typically agree that the mass media, although definitely biased, present a significantly wider range of
information and opinion than found in countries operating under a one-party system; they acknowledge that freedoms of
association, assembly, speech, and religion are comparatively
well protected here even after one has corrected for the gap
between official rhetoric and established practice.

On this view, the conventional pluralist interpretation is not
so much wrong as it is systematically misleading. For conventional pluralist theory focuses on the *competition of elites* operating within a "given" framework or context while the critics
believe that a more accurate picture results when one examines
the *biased context* or the "other face of power"[24] within which
elite competition occurs. The class structure which helps to
provide the social context for elite competition;[25] the "groups"
whose lack of organization, persistence, and legitimacy rules
them out of (or marginally in) the balancing process; the con-

cerns, potentially of interest to many or all segments of society, which are not carried by organized groups to the governmental arenas—these are the background features of pluralist politics which receive the attention of the critics. It is difficult to observe and weigh these factors, but as we have seen in our summary of pluralist theory, assumptions must be made at this level anyway. The critics, at the very least, refuse to shove these considerations into a residual category called the "consensus."

The late C. Wright Mills launched an early and polemical critique of pluralist theory, adopting a style and terminology which conveyed his outrage at the gap between the practice and promise of American politics. The polemical style, however, weakened the coherence of his formulations and opened his position to the kind of stereotyping which allows criticized scholars to ignore the challenge presented. Mills sought to call attention to the biased context of pluralist politics. He reminded us that "the goals for which interests struggle are not merely given; they reflect the current state of expectation and acceptance."[26] Many viable alternatives and potential issues, he contended, do not reach the governmental arenas and thus do not become part of the observable balancing process:

> Only one more point of definition: absence of public issues there may well be, but this is not due to any absence of problems. Impersonal and structural changes have not eliminated problems or issues. Their absence from many discussions—that *is* an ideological condition, regulated in the first place by whether or not intellectuals detect and state problems as potential *issues* for probable publics, and as *troubles* for a variety of individuals.[27]

Mills' view, stated in the terminology of Berle and Dahl, is that for some segments of society the prevailing consensus does not provide an adequate perspective or level of awareness with which to locate the structural causes of their vague feelings of anxiety, malaise, frustration, and resentment. As a result, undifferentiated "troubles" are not stated as clear-cut grievances; potential preferences are not organized as public issues; possible issues are not debated and resolved within governmental arenas. The linkages between private troubles and public is-

sues are highly biased: some segments of society, such as the
impoverished, the blacks, unorganized laborers, and many white
collar workers, have not even developed a "voice" which can
be "heard" on matters of great import for their lives; some
kinds of concerns, affecting most or all segments of society, are
not channeled to public arenas for debate.

Whose problems and claims does the system favor? Mills'
theory of the "power elite" is that corporate managers and
military leaders are developing a community of interests in
maintaining certain status quo arrangements. They effectively
protect, inside and outside of government, the prevailing distribution of wealth and income; corporate management's control over the organization of work life, price levels, investments,
expansion, and mergers; a tax structure favorable to wealthy
capital holders; the status and growth of the military establishment. Mills contends that policy modifications in these areas
are possible which would benefit wide segments of the society
psychologically and materially. But such possibilities are not
considered as viable options because of the power elite's influence over the "consensus" accepted by the vast majority of
American citizens.

Mills' positive argument for the power elite, as opposed to
his pointed critique of areas of analysis omitted from consideration in pluralist theory, is marked by unsupported gaps
covered by rhetorical flourish. One point is worthy of emphasis,
however. It is possible to combine elements from the "umpire"
theory of Berle and the "arena" theory of Dahl to support
Mills' view that the pluralist system is significantly biased
toward the concerns and priorities of corporate elites. Corporate managers (1) possess tremendous *initiating* power *outside* of government; (2) possess rather effective *veto* power
within government which can be used to protect their unilateral
initiatives in issue areas of greatest concern to them; and (3)
are beneficiaries of a *biased consensus* which lends legitimacy
to their initiatives and veto power while diminishing it for
groups which might otherwise seek to challenge prevailing
practices.[28] The interpretation supported by these considerations is not one of a hard line power elite "whose preferences,"

as Dahl expresses it, "regularly prevail in cases of difference in preference in key political issues."[29] Rather, they support an interpretation of a biased pluralism in which some concerns, aspirations, and interests are privileged while others are placed at a serious disadvantage.[30]

Other recent criticisms of conventional pluralist theory move along similar lines. Henry Kariel[31] points to the oligarchical tendencies within those large organizations which function both as interest groups affecting governmental policy and as agencies taking unilateral action of public consequence. Organizations such as the American Medical Association, labor unions, large corporations and The Farm Bureau achieve a quasi-official status within government as the legitimate representatives of physicans, blue collar workers, corporate managers and stockholders, and farmers. But in fact each unit speaks for a segment of its claimed constituency while presuming to speak for all. The government, in this interpretation, is not a neutral reflection of interests in the society, nor is it primarily a countervailing force acting for those interests and concerns which are severely disadvantaged. By co-opting legitimate interest group elites as the official spokesmen for broad segments of society, the government helps to freeze the status quo, making it difficult for "members" in these imperatively coordinated associations to challenge their "leaders" without risking legally supported internal sanctions.

In addition, the old constellations of interest groups take on a special legitimacy in the balancing process, and citizens with new problems and concerns encounter serious institutional and ideological obstructions to the formation of new organized groups which might express their aspirations. The middle level white collar worker and the unorganized blue collar worker, for example, are marginally represented by corporate and labor interests, yet they are classified under these categories. As Robert Paul Wolff observes: "The application of the theory of pluralism always favors the groups in existence against those in the process of formation."[32]

Critics such as Herbert Marcuse, Grant McConnell, and John Kenneth Galbraith join Mills and Kariel in stressing the extent to which pluralist politics today is "one dimensional."[33] Not only are the issues generated by competing groups constrained by established values and expectations (ideological constraints), but contemporary social structure encourages groups to organize around occupational categories while inhibiting effective political organization on the basis of other considerations. These structural constraints reinforce rather than mitigate existing ideological constraints.

The highest priority claims of each occupational group aim at enhancing the status and economic position of its core membership. Even if all occupational categories were well represented in the pressure system, the balancing process itself would tend to focus on the government's allocation of economic security and benefits while relegating to the periphery of attention other dimensions of private and public life affected by the decisions and nondecisions of government. Thus a bias in the very slicing of "groups" contributes to a "pattern of *one dimensional thought* and *behavior* in which ideas, aspirations, and objectives that, by their content, transcend the established universe of discourse and action are either repelled or reduced to terms of this universe."[34]

One-dimensional pluralist politics suppresses exploration of alternatives by proliferating issues within a narrow range of concerns. The impact on personality of a stultifying work life, the ugliness of our cities, the inadequate provisions for public transportation, the limited opportunity for most individuals to participate in the decision-making processes of the localities and organizations within which they are implicated, the societal consequences of planned obsolescence—these "issues," affected by the decisions that are made and could be made, are not among the high priority issues generated by the "clash and clang" of effectively mobilized groups.

Similarly, military, corporate, and labor interests press for defense expenditures to maximize the income and status of their particular constituencies. But where are the groups of comparable stature which press to ensure that total defense expenditures are maintained at the minimum level needed to protect national security? It is admittedly difficult to judge the minimal level of defense expenditures needed, but the point is that this very question is not readily incorporated into the balancing process; an "answer" emerges which reflects more the aggregation of particular interests than a debate over the question itself.[35] Mitigating forces are at work here, we hope. But the example illuminates a point too often overlooked by the celebrants of pluralist practice: the aggregation of organized interests does not always ensure that the public interest is well served.[36]

These critiques of pluralist theory, then, tend to converge around a small cluster of themes. Since there is some confusion about the kinds of claims the critics are advancing, it may be useful to list them in a formal way here, starting with those which point to gaps between pluralist rhetoric and pluralist practice and building to those which imply the need to revise some features of the pluralist ideal itself.

1. The prevailing system inhibits some segments of society from efficacious involvement in the balancing process while bestowing cumulative advantages upon other segments.

2. The process of interest aggregation ignores some concerns explicitly shared by many citizens because persistent, active, and legitimate "groups" fail to define these concerns as high priority interests. This condition could persist even if every citizen belonged to at least one politically effective group.

3. Many *latent concerns*—those which might well interest wide segments of society if they were publically articulated as issues—are not identified or sharply defined by the prevailing system of issue formation.

4. Work life and decision-making processes within those territorial and functional units which underpin modern pluralism are often not conducive to that personality development which both enhances life for the individual and enables a political system to avoid the potentially debilitating effects of widespread apathy underlaid by simmering hostility and resentment.

5. The status quo biases in the prevailing system of issue-formation and conflict-resolution discourage efforts within recognized channels to (*a*) increase "out" group involvement in the balancing process, (*b*) and (*c*) bring unorganized and un-

articulated concerns to political arenas, and (d) initiate reforms *within* organizations designed to foster personality development. Thus, as a rapidly expanding technology promotes equally rapid social change, ideological and institutional constraints in the political system inhibit efforts to cope with the accompanying dislocations.

These claims, clearly, can be formulated as empirical hypotheses and subjected to at least partial test. The relative lack of such efforts suggests that skilled methodologists have seldom been excited by these questions while interested critics have only recently begun to move beyond general criticism to the task of conceptual clarification and empirical verification.

THE CRITICAL TEMPER

The disparities among the critics of contemporary pluralist theory should be clear enough. Mills and Marcuse, when compared to Galbraith, Kariel, and McConnell, are more thoroughly critical of the existing system, more pessimistic about the prospects for generating desired reforms, probably more permissive in their acceptance of violence as a vehicle of change, and perhaps ultimately committed to a political vision which transcends any variant of the pluralist ideal.[37] These differences are important; sorting them out can serve as a useful prelude to developing one's own position.

Yet, when contrasted to the dominant orientations and research priorities which undergird conventional pluralist theory, certain unifying commitments can be discerned among the critics. A definable "critical temper" finds increasing expression within the "left wing" of political science (and allied disciplines) today and I seek here to identify and support the main thrust of that temper. More specifically, recognizing that some individuals may not fit neatly into this or that category, my aims are: first, to suggest that the ongoing controversy over pluralist theory is linked to fundamental questions about the nature and proper functions of political inquiry; second, to summarize the central concerns which orient the critical temper; and, third, to catalogue some recent efforts and suggest some new tasks within this latter framework.

The Approach to Political Inquiry

If "behavioralism" means the formulation of hypotheses about political phenomena, an effort to be clear in the concepts used to state those hypotheses, and an effort to locate observable indicators which can reliably test the formulated hypotheses, then most critics accept the behavioral revolution. If it means, further, an effort to establish a system of universal or probability laws which, when applied to specified conditions, can promote the prediction and control of events,[38] then many critics (with a few more dissents) accept this as one of the legitimate goals of political inquiry. But acceptance of these methodological ideals does not necessitate commitment to the professional role definitions and research priorities of many practicing political scientists.[39] Several points need attention here.

First, the critics place normative concerns at the center of political inquiry. Some believe that values can be grounded objectively, others that "ultimate" values cannot be.[40] But, whichever view is taken, it is clear that correctly structured empirical inquiry is essential to informed value decisions. Normative considerations, in this view, should play a primary role in defining the questions asked in empirical inquiry. Considerations of methodological convenience or of "theory" building where the theory to be built is not explicitly linked to normative clarification, are at best secondary concerns. For these considerations usually result in inquiry serving unexamined ends; they force us to make normative decisions on the basis of information which is unnecessarily incomplete.

Thus one of the cutting edges in the current controversy involves the *aims* guiding inquiry into pluralist politics. The principal aim of conventional pluralist theory is to ascertain the relationship between the existing system of conflict resolution and the maintenance of stability. It is not that proponents of this view will accept as desirable any system which is stable. It seems to me, at least, that the proponents largely *assume* that the values generally thought to be served by pluralist democracy are fairly well served by the existing system. They then *ask* whether the system also promotes long-run stability.

The critics have higher aspirations for the system and begin inquiry at a different point. The system is relatively stable: thus it can afford reasoned criticism; it can aspire to higher achievement; it can tolerate militant pressure for institutional change. Assuming a background of system stability and a highly developed economy the critics ask: How effectively does the balancing process cope with problems generated by rapid social change and by a complex, volatile international environment? What is the impact of the prevailing decision-making processes and distributive outcomes on the lives of individuals in various social positions? These questions require conceptualization and standards of appraisal which are only partially provided by conventional pluralist theory.[41]

Finally, in examining the structure of pluralist theory, the critics have become impressed by the extent to which conceptual and operational decisions have prejudged the outcomes of inquiry. Conventional conceptualizations of "group" (Hale), "interest" (Barry and Lowi), "power" (Bachrach and Baratz), "decision" and "politics" (Hacker), draw attention to those features of the system favorable to the pluralist interpretation while shoving unfavorable features to the background.[42]

We have not reached the "end of ideology" in political inquiry, but we have, until recently, seen a justifying ideology dominate the field.[43] Responsible political inquiry requires the researcher to become more aware of how and where deeply rooted commitments shape his methodological moves. The task is not easy, however. It involves a continued effort to ascertain the congruence between one's rhetorical and actual commitments; it requires a clear statement of the aims of inquiry; it probably requires immersion in opposing theoretical systems to see if one's operating conceptual apparatus screens out phenomena relevant to the questions formally asked; and it requires specification of the "contrast-model" against which one's selective descriptions are developed.

The Search for a New Contrast-Model

Description precedes explanation, and in any given context there is no such thing as a "complete description." In a highly structured theory, it may be possible to state exacting criteria which can control the selective process of description.[44] No contemporary political theory has, however, achieved the level of precision required. Description in these interpretations is selective; but the exact standards of selection, even in comparative analysis, have not been specified.

In describing the work process in nineteenth-century America, Tocqueville used the phrase "divided labor," meaning that each worker in the manufacturing process makes one small contribution to the finished product rather than making the entire product himself. Tocqueville could have emphasized other features of the situation observed: the work is arduous, perhaps; there is an interesting rhythm in the workers' activities induced by the assembly line; the finished product is durable. But Tocqueville's description draws immediate attention to the difference between *labor* in manufacturing society and *craftsmanship* in feudal society.

Because of background and predilection, Tocqueville's descriptions of American society usually focused on features which contrasted that system with an idealized version of aristocratic society. His contrast-model was his version of aristocratic society. His descriptions of the "equality of condition," the "voluntary association," the "trading mentality," the citizens "lost in the crowd," and the new "manufacturing aristocracy" are more understandable both in meaning and in our appreciation of considerations governing Tocqueville's selective emphases when we relate them to the contrast-model of aristocratic society.[45]

Conventional pluralist theory is developed against a varying mixture of authoritarian, totalitarian, and pluralistic arrangements in other societies. In the first chapter of his study of power in New Haven, Dahl discusses the ruling oligarchy which dominated the city in the early nineteenth century:

By almost any test it seems safe to infer that the elite of New Haven, like the Standing Order in Connecticut, *completely* dominated the political system. They were of *one* common stock and *one* religion, *cohesive* in their *uniformly conservative* outlook on all matters, *substantially unchallenged* in their authority, successful in pushing through their own policies, and in *full* control of such critical social institutions as the established religion, the educational system . . . , and even business enterprise. Both they and their opponents took their political supremacy as a fact.[46]

Now this is not the only contrast-model employed by Dahl, but it is the central one. Its primary function is to rivet our attention to what the contemporary system is *not*: it is not dominated by a tightly knit ruling class. New Haven, for example, has moved from "the old patterns of oligarchy based upon cumulative inequalities to new patterns of leadership based upon dispersed inequalities."[47]

It is undeniable that contrast-models drawn from authoritarian regimes and from other pluralistic societies perform a valuable service. They accentuate dangers to be avoided and call attention to desirable conditions already achieved here. But the critical temper contends that such contrast-models are currently used too exclusively. Inquiries couched in those terms fail to emphasize problems and dislocations we share with these other systems; they fail to dramatize future possibilities here which are not presently in practice somewhere else. Descriptions defined exclusively against these contrast-models foster complacency and suffocate reformist impulses.

The critical temper seeks to describe and appraise American pluralism against a reflectively developed vision of a better society. Yet, to be persuasive, the empirical and normative commitments embedded in such a model must be spelled out clearly, and its proponents must insist that the model need not be fully attainable in practice (i.e., "realistic") in order to provide a useful standard of comparison, a set of goals to be sought, and a spur to persistent political activity.

Efforts in this direction are already evident. David Kettler has constructed a typology of "political rationality" which can help to organize this kind of inquiry.[48] The concept of human "needs" suggested by Christian Bay and that of "public interest" formulated by Brian Barry and Richard Flathman are beginning attempts to develop criteria against which the successes and failures of existing practice can be appraised.[49] Peter Bachrach, Arnold Kaufman, and Robert Pranger have contended that participation in group decision processes is an important condition of personality development and have begun to ask how to implement these goals in industrial society.[50] Grant McConnell has explored the relationship betwen constituency size and issue-formation in an effort to discover how important problems shuffled out of pluralist politics today might be reinstated as issues.[51] Theodore Lowi seeks ways to raise suppressed issues by promoting interest group *confrontation* within governmental arenas; his proposals are designed to reduce occasions where the wide public effects of particular group claims are protected from debate.[52]

Michael Reagan has explored the implications of giving corporations national rather than state charters; and, more generally, he has asked how to institute tighter political controls over these increasingly political institutions.[53] Henry Kariel suggests that the scope of political rights be extended to include activity within the large-scale organization in order to protect internal dissent and to reduce the organization's constraints on its members' external political life. He joins others in seeking means to diffuse the control and biases of mass media more widely.[54] Finally, some social philosophers have displayed a resurgent interest in the question of distributive justice; we can expect efforts to ask how the distributive outcomes of pluralist politics measure up to reasoned norms of justice.[55]

The list could be extended, but the point is clear. The critics are moving beyond mere criticism and toward the statement of positive alternatives. Such a shift will help to make all researchers alert to the role played by contrast-models in guiding inquiry; it also promises to bring the critical temper into sharper focus.

WILLIAM E. CONNOLLY : 25

Demarcation of the Political

Andrew Hacker and Theodore Lowi, among others, have made it clear that the age of the large-scale organization allows us no longer to limit the "political" to what goes on in government.[56] But once we move beyond government, what standards can we employ to sift "political" aspects from the rest of social life? The question is perplexing. Its perplexity helps to explain why, as Peter Bachrach has noted, even political scientists who formally state broad definitions of the "political" tend to shy away from the implications of those definitions in research practice.[57]

David Easton has offered perhaps the best-known definition that transcends government. Politics, he says, involves the "authoritative allocation of values for society." But this formulation does not fit the needs of the critical temper. For "authoritative" seems to imply that decision-makers intend the politically relevant effects of their actions, that those affected know who makes the decisions, and that the implicated parties accept the process and outcomes as legitimate. But many structured relationships have important distributive consequences which are unintended by decision-makers and unrecognized by those affected; and processes and outcomes considered nonauthoritative by some segments of society might still have important allocative effects. The term "authoritative" is useful for Easton whose interest in questions of allocation is manifestly subservient to the goal of understanding the "basic processes through which the political system . . . is able to persist in a world of either stability or change."[58] The concept and its limits, however, are not appropriate for those concerned with appraising the variable impact on personality of the prevailing system of issue formation and resolution; nor is it appropriate for those who ask how closely the operating principles of "value allocation" coincide with justifiable principles of distributive justice.

Furthermore, most demarcations of the political settle first the arenas and range of issues to be included and then ask who is *actively involved* in deciding those issues. Thus, studies of political "decision-making" ask how organizational settings, social backgrounds, time factors, and personalities influence the perceptions and choices of those actively involved in the governmental decision process.[59] But a political analysis seeking to go beyond description of ongoing processes by tapping possible levers of change cannot remain satisfied with this approach. How do the deciding agent's perceptions of options compare to the range of options actually available? Why are some alternatives ignored and what kinds of infusions might bring more desirable options to the surface? A political analysis oriented to the possibilities of change asks not just who is involved in policy and how they perceive those possibilities; it also asks which possible options are not perceived and *where* new moral perspectives, alternatives, and pressures can be most effectively introduced. It may well be, for example, that pressure is sometimes most effective when applied to inactive agents of potential power rather than only to active agents of demonstrated importance.

No developed focus for "political" inquiry keyed to the concerns of the critical temper is presently available, but in my view John Dewey's distinction between the "public" and the "private" is likely to provide the most fruitful starting point.[60] Dewey refuses to limit the political by reference to the institutional source or legitimacy of "transactions." The focus is on the consequences of recurrent transactions; consequences are to be considered "public" (or political) if their scope is broad, their importance for specified values is great, and their direction is potentially subject to intelligent control. By thus extending the conventional limits of "politics," the critical temper points to new arenas where decisions of consequence must be exposed and contested if the practice of pluralist politics is to approach the pluralist ideal.

Strategies of Change

Conventional pluralist theory, perceiving a minimal gap between existing arrangements and desired alternatives, fosters only a marginal interest in strategies of institutional change. Indeed, Myron Hale suggests that the "cosmology" of group theory encourages inquiry into processes of "partisan mutual adjustment," but discourages exploration into possibilities of inducing significant social change.[61]

For those, however, who perceive a significant gap between the processes of a biased pluralism and more desirable alternatives, the problem of strategy becomes central. Many questions are involved here, including identification of places where new information, moral considerations, and pressure are likely to be most effective; development of tactics which promise the most long-run success; location of those societal segments whose position renders them actually or potentially interested in challenging prevailing practice; mobilizing the potential forces, and maintaining pressure over a long haul. The problem of strategy is the most difficult question faced by the critical temper.

Yet, for all its importance, the problem has not received much systematic attention. C. Wright Mills mentioned the "intellectuals" as a possible agency for "radical change." John Kenneth Galbraith has exhorted the "educational estate" to use its increasingly strategic position to challenge existing priorities in the industrial system. Arnold Kaufman has recently explored the range of strategies open to the "radical liberal," seeking to escape the twin dangers of the "realist's" anticipatory surrender to the status quo and the "self indulgent" radical's refusal to use established "pluralist" structures to effect significant change.[62] David Kettler has found the strategies of the responsible party, Presidential leadership, and partisan mutual adjustment to have inherent weaknesses as well as objectives only partially congruent with the critical temper. He seeks to supplement these conventional strategies with new infusions of "outside" pressure which expose privileged elites to the substratum of groups and concerns presently ignored by the prevailing pressure system.[63]

These recent investigations display an awareness that the question of strategy cannot be left to "historical forces" or resolved by simple recourse to conventional political strategies. They reveal, further, a serious effort to cope with the well-known obstacle stated by Roberto Michels: that the organization required to channel inchoate discontents and unstructured idealism into coherent pressure also tends to generate conservative leadership and to dilute original objectives.

Much more work is needed here, certainly. But it should be noted that the emergence of the critical temper itself can be a contribution to strategy. The articulated temper helps to educate a larger public to the deficiencies of a biased pluralism and to the promise of future achievement; it reopens forgotten debates among social scientists, challenging the complacency of some and activating the latent concerns of others; it exerts constructive pressure on liberals in and around government.

The actual and potential impact of the critical temper is hard to locate precisely. Indeed, it is possible that its positive impact will be swept away amidst the society's repressive reaction to ghetto riots, student unrest, and the uncertainties of international politics. The pluralists are right in contending that no single group can control the shifting sentiments and forces which emerge in times of stress.

But individuals and groups can make *some difference*. Whichever way the pendulum threatens to swing and whatever *amount* of influence the critical temper promises to have, its reasoned articulation of criticisms, alternatives, and strategies shows some promise of mobilizing disaffected groups, of driving wedges in the prevailing system of balances, and of undermining attempts to justify a politics of suppression. This is no mean contribution in a period when the politics of complacency has failed to speak to those groups and aspirations balanced out of the pluralist system.

REFERENCES

1. There are several variations of "the" pluralist ideal. James Madison emphasized the role of constitutional limitations in promoting political stability and protecting minority rights. Tocqueville focused more on the social preconditions of political pluralism and added personal development through group association to the Madisonian objectives of stability and rights. The ideal sketched above draws more from Tocqueville than Madison; it also reflects strands from John Stuart Mill, John Dewey, and G. H. Mead. When the ideal is

stated in the most optimistic terms, those who believe that technological imperatives or other necessities require its revision are challenged to discuss explicitly why and by whom these costs are to be paid.

2. For example, in his recent text, *Pluralist Democracy in the United States: Conflict and Consent* (Chicago: Rand McNally, 1967), Robert Dahl quotes Tocqueville extensively and favorably. In *Political Man: The Social Bases of Politics* (New York: Anchor Books, 1960), Seymour Martin Lipset devotes the first chapter to a review of the perspectives of Marx, Tocqueville, Michels, and Weber. His summary statement: "Essentially this book suggests that the sociology of politics return to the problem posed by Tocqueville: the social requisites and consequences of democracy. And I think it shows that any attempt to deal adequately with such a problem forces us to the method he employed so successfully: comparative analysis" (p. 24).

3. During the period covered by Tocqueville's work the beneficial effects of pluralism were not universally shared. Slavery, sweatshops, draft riots, child labor, savage treatment of Indians, and the absence of female suffrage, were part of the less visible underside of the political balance then existing. Tocqueville was not oblivious to these conditions (or to most of them); the statements noted here are intended to convey his views about those social conditions which enhanced the *possibility* of a fully developed pluralism and which showed the greatest promise of protecting the future against the twin dangers of "majority tyranny" and "harsh" minority rule.

4. Tocqueville, *Democracy in America*, Richard D. Heffner, ed. (New York: Mentor Books, 1956), pp. 109, 306.

5. *The Power Elite* (New York: Oxford University Press, 1959), p. 307. See Chapters 11 and 13 for discussions which parallel many of the points developed here.

6. *Democracy in America,* pp. 217–218. The proper comparison here is not of the absolute "breadth of mind" of the old middle class with its contemporary counterpart but of the relative gap in the two periods between the consequences of political decision and the level of awareness approximated by each "middle class." When the effects of political decisions have deepened and broadened, the new group's level of awareness must be correspondingly extended and enriched if an equivalence of function is to be achieved. Recent studies which apply the Tocqueville thesis to the white collar worker should be read with this point in mind. See José Ortega y Gasset, *The Revolt of the Masses* (New York: Norton, 1932); C. Wright Mills, *White Collar* (New York: Oxford University Press, 1951); Robert Presthus, *The Organizational Society* (New York: Vintage Books, 1962).

7. *Democracy in America,* p. 308.

8. *Ibid.,* p. 65.

9. *Ibid.,* p. 299.

10. *Ibid.,* p. 220. Tocqueville visited the United States in 1831. According to W. W. Rostow the "take-off" period of the industrial economy was 1843–1860; rapid industrial growth first occurred from 1868– 1893. *The Stages of Economic Growth* (Cambridge: The University Press, 1962).

11. The interpretation is sketched in the last chapter of *A Preface to Democratic Theory* (Chicago: University of Chicago Press, 1956). The same general view is applied to the politics of New Haven in

Who Governs? (New Haven: Yale University Press, 1961); and the sketch of pluralist politics at the national level is filled out in some detail in his recent text, *Pluralist Democracy in the United States.*

12. *A Preface to Democratic Theory,* pp. 48–49.

13. *Ibid.,* p. 32.

14. *Ibid.,* p. 145.

15. *Pluralist Democracy in the United States,* p. 38 (my emphasis).

16. *A Preface to Democratic Theory,* pp. 132–133. Herbert McClosky reveals the importance of Dahl's qualifying phrase, "among a predominant portion of the politically active." Political elites, he argues, provide greater support for the procedural norms of democracy than does the rest of the population, reveal "more affirmative attitudes toward the political system," and have somewhat more favorable views toward existing economic inequalities. They are distinguished from the general public by "education and economic status, . . . greater public interest and awareness, and . . . access to the command posts of community decision." "Consensus and Ideology in American Politics," *American Political Science Review,* LVIII (June 1964), 361–382, at p. 373.

17. *A Preface to Democratic Theory,* p. 151. For a discussion of the implications of this statement, see Christian Bay, "Politics and Pseudo-politics: A Critical Evaluation of Some Behavioral Literature," *American Political Science Review,* LIX (March 1965), 39–51. The Bay article, along with several others which bear on the themes developed here, is reprinted in Charles A. McCoy and John Playford, eds., *Apolitical Politics: A Critique of Behaviorism* (New York: Crowell, 1967).

18. The quoted statements are from John Dewey, "Democracy and Educational Administration," *School and Society* (April 1937), 457–458. The issues raised here are slippery, but pervasive. Terms like "coercion," "freedom," "oppression," "power," and "consent" are imbued with different shades of meaning by investigators who start with different views about such questions as the empirical connections between social democracy and political democracy, the most important questions to ask of a political system, and the kinds of change possible in the system. Issues which at first appear easily subject to empirical test turn out to be conceptual disagreements rooted in different normative priorities and assumptions about societal possibilities. See the debate between Jack Walker and Robert Dahl in the *American Political Science Review,* LX (June 1966), 285–325. Dahl's position appears to be shifting. In *Who Governs?* he is critical of the "dogma" that "democracy would not work if citizens were not concerned with public affairs . . ." (280). In "The City in the Future of Democracy," *American Political Science Review,* LXI (December 1967), 953–970, the need for participation is emphasized. For an exceptionally clear discussion of the issues here, see Arnold Kaufman, "Human Nature and Participatory Democracy," this volume, Chapter 8.

19. Berle's theory of pluralism is best stated in *Power Without Property* (New York: Harcourt, Brace and World, 1959). John Kenneth Galbraith's *American Capitalism: The Concept of Countervailing Power* (Boston: Houghton Mifflin, 1952) is an earlier formulation of a similar position. Note, though, the significant shift in Galbraith's position in *The New Industrial State* (Boston: Houghton Mifflin, 1967). For a discussion of the kinds of actions of public consequence

initiated by corporations, see Andrew Hacker, "Power to Do What?" this volume, Chapter 4, and Hacker, ed., *The Corporation Takeover* (New York: Anchor Books, 1965).

20. *Power Without Property,* p. 138.
21. *Ibid.,* p. 111.
22. *Ibid.,* p. 113 (my emphasis).
23. I discuss this question further in Chapter 2 of my *Political Science and Ideology* (New York: Atherton Press, 1967). A very useful analysis of the question is found in Peter Bachrach, *The Theory of Democratic Elitism: A Critique* (Boston: Little, Brown, 1967), esp. Chapter 4.
24. See Peter Bachrach and Morton S. Baratz, "The Two Faces of Power," this volume, Chapter 3.
25. "The flaw in the pluralist heaven is that the heavenly chorus sings with a strong upper-class accent." E. E. Schattschneider, *The Semi-Sovereign People* (New York: Holt, Rinehart & Winston, 1960), p. 35. See also William Domhoff, *Who Rules America?* (Englewood Cliffs: Prentice-Hall, 1967), for a recent summary of the class context for pluralist politics. He contends that the "upper class" (1 per cent of society) receives a highly disproportionate share of wealth and income from the society while holding a highly disproportionate share of strategic positions in the executive branch of the government, the industrial and financial corporations, the mass media of communication, and major universities and foundations. Domhoff does not, though, establish the cohesiveness of this "group."
26. Mills, *The Power Elite,* p. 246.
27. Mills, in I. L. Horowitz, ed., *Power, Politics, and People: The Collected Papers of C. W. Mills* (New York: Ballantine Books, 1961), p. 253.
28. Berle supports (1) and Dahl provides support for (2) when he acknowledges that on issue areas of great concern for organized, active, legitimate, and persistent groups, "it is easier to veto a change than to initiate one, easier to preserve the *status quo* than to change it." *Pluralist Democracy in the United States,* p. 386. For (3), Dahl mentions a bias in the American consensus: "Most Americans also display complacency about their economic institutions. Proposals for extreme reconstruction do not enjoy much support. The great corporations, it appears, have gained widespread acceptance. . . . The trade unions are somewhat more unpopular than the corporations: many would like to see them more severely regulated by the government, but few would say that they would like to see trade unions done away with altogether." *Ibid.,* p. 331.
29. Dahl, "A Critique of the Ruling Class Model," *American Political Science Review,* LII (June 1958), 464. It seems clear, furthermore, that very few of the ruling elite theories argue the view which Dahl wants to test. For the best available discussion of the elitist doctrines of Mosca, Pareto, and Michels, see James H. Meisel, *The Myth of the Ruling Class* (Ann Arbor: Ann Arbor Paperback, 1962).
30. For a critique and refinement of Mills' theory of a military-industrial coalition, see Marc Pilisuk and Thomas Hayden, *"Is There a Military-Industrial Complex?"* this volume, Chapter 6.
31. Henry Kariel's critique is best developed in *The Decline of American Pluralism* (Stanford: Stanford University Press, 1961). Among political scientists this book, probably more than any other single

work, has encouraged critical scrutiny of conventional pluralist theory. See also Kariel's *The Promise of Politics* (Englewood Cliffs: Prentice-Hall, 1966).

32. Wolff, "Beyond Tolerance," in Wolff, Barrington Moore, Jr., and Herbert Marcuse, *A Critique of Pure Tolerance* (Boston: Beacon Press, 1965), p. 41. All three essays in this book bear on the themes of the present volume.

33. Herbert Marcuse, *One Dimensional Man* (Boston: Beacon Press, 1964); Grant McConnell, *Private Property and American Democracy* (New York: Alfred A. Knopf, 1966); Galbraith, *The New Industrial State*.

34. *One Dimensional Man*, p. 12. See further, Myron Hale, "The Cosmology of Arthur F. Bentley," this volume, Chapter 2, for a discussion of the meaning of group "interest" in the Bentleyite "cosmology."

35. See Marc Pilisuk and Thomas Hayden, this volume, Chapter 6.

36. See Brian Barry, "The Public Interest," this volume, Chapter 7, for an analysis of the "public interest"; see also Richard Flathman, *The Public Interest* (New York: Wiley, 1966).

37. Even these distinctions are too crude to be fully accurate. Marcuse, for example, is surely more pessimistic than Mills about the possibilities for effecting meaningful change: "The critical theory of society possesses no concepts which could bridge the gap between the present and its future; holding no promise and showing no success, it remains negative. Thus it wants to remain loyal to those who, without hope, have given and give their life to the great Refusal." *One Dimensional Man*, p. 257. For a critique of Marcuse, see Allen Graubard, "Herbert Marcuse: One Dimensional Pessimism," *Dissent* (May–June 1968), 216–228.

38. Or, in the case of probability laws, the prediction and control of "mass events." See May Brodbeck, "Explanation, Prediction, and 'Imperfect' Knowledge," in May Brodbeck (ed), *Readings in the Philosophy of the Social Sciences* (New York: Macmillan 1967).

39. The editors of *Apolitical Politics* suggest that a deficiency in the logic of behavioral methodology stands behind existing inadequacies in pluralist theory. It sems to me, however, that not logical or methodological necessity but the role definitions and ideological commitments of political scientists are crucial here. These factors cut across methodological orientations.

40. The view of values as merely "emotive" expressions is rejected by most ethical philosophers in the analytic tradition today. See Henry D. Aiken, *Reason and Conduct: New Bearings in Moral Philosophy* (New York: Knopf, 1962); Richard Brandt, *Ethical Theory* (Englewood Cliffs: Prentice-Hall, 1959); Richard Flathman, *The Public Interest;* Alasdair MacIntyre, *A Short History of Ethics* (New York: Macmillan, 1966).

41. It should be noted that too narrow a focus on institutional stability might fail to detect personal discontents which will eventually explode into violence. And groups which adopt expectations that the system cannot meet could help to undermine a stable system. Few theories completely ignore either the question of stability or the question of system impact on individual lives, but different theories do distribute their emphases differently.

42. Hale, this volume, Chapter 2; Barry, this volume, Chapter 7; Lowi,

"The Public Philosophy," this volume, Chapter 5; Bachrach and Baratz, this volume, Chapter 3; Hacker, this volume, Chapter 4.

43. For the "end of ideology" thesis see Daniel Bell, *The End of Ideology* (New York: Collier, rev. ed., 1962). For a discussion of the problem of ideology in political inquiry, see Kenneth Boulding, *The Image: Knowledge in Life and Society* (Ann Arbor: The University of Michigan Press, 1956); William Connolly, *Political Science and Ideology;* and the classic analysis of this problem, Karl Mannheim, *Ideology and Utopia* (New York: Harcourt, Brace & World, 1936). As the term is used here, a "justifying ideology" is marked by: (1) its emphasis on desirable aspects of those areas subjected to empirical inquiry, e.g., stating that active, organized, persistent, and legitimate groups have some voice in the system without emphasizing the reverse side of that contention; (2) its tendency to make comforting assumptions in those areas where empirical claims cannot in practice be brought to careful test, e.g., the view that most politically relevant "troubles" are organized as group preferences and raised as issues; (3) its tendency to *label* the system studied in ways which promote complacency among the audience, e.g., "pluralist democracy" or "economic democracy" rather than, say, "restrictive elite competition." A critical ideology makes opposing moves at each of these points.

44. For a discussion of this problem see William Dray, *Philosophy of History* (Englewood Cliffs: Prentice-Hall, 1964), pp. 27–39. See also *Language, Thought, and Culture,* William Henle, ed. (Ann Arbor: University of Michigan Press, 1963).

45. Full elucidation of the notion of contrast-model would include not only what we see but how we see. What analogies do we employ to convey our observations? Mechanistic, organic, geometric, energy system, and cybernetic analogies have been adopted by various thinkers as vehicles for expressing their observations. These choices are not neutral in their effects. Once made, they influence our judgments about the possibilities and consequences of change; they exert an impact on the research methods we find appropriate. For discussions impinging on these questions, see Ralf Dahrendorf, *Class and Class Conflict in Industrial Society* (Stanford: Stanford University Press, 1959); Karl Deutsch, *The Nerves of Government* (New York: The Free Press, 1963); Arnold Rose, "The Relation of Theory and Method," in L. Gross, ed., *Sociological Theory: Inquiries and Paradigms* (New York: Harper & Row, 1967), pp. 207–219.

46. *Who Governs?* p. 15 (my emphasis). See Berle, *Power Without Property,* Chapter V, "A Long View of People's Capitalism and Soviet Communism," for a similar comparison. Dahl in *A Preface to Democratic Theory* devotes a chapter to the ideal of "polyarchy," emphasizing certain procedural requirements of an ideal pluralist system. But it is not at all clear to me that Dahl used this ideal very extensively as a contrast model against which to appraise American politics. Deane Neubauer (a former student of Dahl's) does in "Some Conditions of Democracy," *American Political Science Review,* LXI (December 1967), 1002–1009. The United States is ranked 16 out of 23 democracies in his analysis.

47. *Who Governs?* p. 54.

48. Kettler, "Political Science and Political Rationality," in *Political*

Theory and Social Change, David Spitz, ed. (New York: Atherton Press, 1967) pp. 59–89.

49. Bay, "Politics and Pseudo-politics"; Arnold Kaufman, "On Alienation," *Inquiry,* VII (Summer 1964), 1–25; Flathman, *The Public Interest;* and Brian Barry, this volume, Chapter 7.

50. Bachrach, *The Theory of Democratic Elitism,* Chapter 6; Robert Pranger, *The Eclipse of Citizenship* (New York: Holt, Rinehart & Winston, 1968); Kaufman, this volume, Chapter 8.

51. *Private Power and American Democracy,* especially Chapters 4 and 10.

52. Lowi, this volume, Chapter 5.

53. "Restructuring the Corporate System," in Irving Howe, ed., *The Radical Papers* (New York: Anchor Books, 1966), pp. 175–189. Several of the essays in this volume bear on questions considered here. See also Michael D. Reagan, *The Managed Economy* (New York: Oxford University Press, 1963).

54. *The Decline of American Pluralism,* esp. Chapters 14 and 15.

55. See for example, Brian Barry, *Political Argument* (New York: The Humanities Press, 1965). Richard Brandt (ed.), *Social Justice* (Englewood Cliffs: Prentice-Hall, 1962); Stanley Benn and Richard Peters, *The Principles of Political Thought* (New York: The Free Press, 1965), pp. 123–200. W. G. Runcimun, *Relative Deprivation and Social Justice* (London: Routledge and Kegan Paul, 1966).

56. Hacker, this volume, Chapter 4; Lowi, this volume, Chapter 5.

57. Bachrach, "Corporate Authority and Democratic Theory," in David Spitz, ed., *Political Theory and Social Change,* pp. 257–273.

58. Easton, *A Framework for Political Analysis* (Englewood Cliffs: Prentice-Hall, 1965), p. 25. See Hale, this volume, Chapter 2, for a discussion of the connections between "systems theory" and Bentley's theory.

59. For an inventory of recent literature in decision analysis, see James A. Robinson and Richard C. Snyder, "Decision-Making in International Relations," in Herbert C. Kelman (ed.), *International Behavior: A Social-Psychological Analysis* (New York: Holt, Rinehart and Winston, 1965), pp. 433–463. See William T. Bluhm, *Theories of the Political System* (Englewood Cliffs: Prentice-Hall, 1965), pp. 53–65, for an insightful comparison between the decision-making approach of Thucydides and Richard Snyder which bears on the discussion above.

60. Dewey, *The Public and Its Problems* (New York: Holt, 1967), esp. Chapters 1–3. Similar considerations are found in Michael Reagan, *The Managed Economy,* esp. pp. 207–210.

61. "The Cosmology of Arthur Bentley," this volume, Chapter 2. The phrase "partisan mutual adjustment" is Charles Lindblom's. He justifies this process as the most rational method of conflict resolution in a pluralist system. *The Intelligence of Democracy* (New York: The Free Press, 1965).

62. Kaufman, *The Radical Liberal: New Man in American Politics* (New York: Atherton Press, 1968).

63. Kettler, "The Politics of Social Change," this volume, Chapter 9.

2: *The Cosmology of Arthur F. Bentley*

MYRON Q. HALE

"Realism" in systematic political science in this country began to emerge, in a reaction against the inadequacies of legal and institutional description, early in this century. David Easton,[1] remarking the change, cites in evidence Arthur F. Bentley's attempt "to fashion a tool." By midcentury, it may be said, Bentleyism is tooling the fashion. A recent commentator, deploring the current emphasis on methods and measurements, declares the new orthodoxy has left its mark on the profession no less than on the world and is partially responsible for our failure to identify and solve social problems.[2] Yet, for all the talk about Bentley's influence, and despite the social significance of his ideas, there has been too little study of his theory of politics. I propose to examine his writings as those of a "realist" and to show how his search for both "realism" and a "science of politics" may lead to a surreptitious sanctification of the actual.

This article, which appeared in the *American Political Science Review*, LIV (December 1960), 955–961, has been slightly enlarged.

Bentley's political work had an ulterior end; it was not pure curiosity. "My interest in politics," he said, "is not primary, but derived from my interest in the economic life, and . . . I hope from this point of approach ultimately to gain a better understanding of the economic life than I have succeeded in gaining hitherto."[3] The terms of his solution, expressed first in *The Process of Government*, reflected his understanding of the early twentieth-century midwestern social and economic structure. Influenced by social Darwinism and sociological realism, and rejecting legal and judicial formalism, Bentley advanced what could be called a "functional" theory, based upon what he later called the "transactional approach."

His friend John Dewey remarked upon the profound intellectual revolution that Darwin introduced. Before Darwin, Dewey explained, species had been Aristotelian forms: "Only changes which lead to some definite or fixed outcome of form are of any account and can have any account—any *logos* or reason— made of them."[4] Darwin destroyed the rigidity and the permanence of species: "And change rather than fixity is now a measure of 'reality' or energy of being; change is omnipresent."[5] The philosophy of pragmatism grounded itself on mutability rather than the immutable. Horace Kallen expressed this by saying that attention shifted from the noun to the verb.[6]

Darwin rested his thesis on the evidence of nature. But Durkheim later argued that ideas about nature are projections of social ideas upon the outer world,[7] and Ashley-Montagu has since written that Darwinism was a transfer of the savagely competitive economy of Victorian England to biology.[8] Pragmatism has not escaped a similar attribution. Jerome Frank pointed to the early interest of another pragmatist, Charles Peirce, in legal subjects, and suggested that his attitude toward nature was an expression of his social views.[9]

In Arthur Bentley, a Darwinian of sorts with close intellectual ties to pragmatism, we have a striking example of the projection of a social outlook onto the cosmos, so that J. R. Kantnor quite accurately characterized his system as a "socio-cosmological dialectic."[10] Like all cosmologies, it had implications for human values; it could be projected back on society and when so projected would resolve questions of validity and conduct. Perhaps Bentley's cosmology was temperamentally unsuited to the man. Sharing with conservatives their distrust of reforms,[11] he was nevertheless a reformer if not a radical. He produced an unpublished manuscript on the domination of the United States by business, called "Makers, Users, and Masters in America,"[12] and in 1924 he was chairman of the Indiana state committee of the LaFollette party. He was sympathetic to the farmers and desired their organization as an interest group. Nevertheless, the implications of Bentley's cosmology are conservative.

It is this underlying character, I think, rather than the persuasiveness of the system as such, that accounts for his widespread popularity in the period after World War II. The past fifteen years have seen a revival and proliferation of many varieties of conservative thought. Some have subscribed to the "New Conservatism." Others have embraced a theology. Still others, whose commitments to science will not permit them that relief, have found that they can avoid the larger issues of our day by renouncing problems of substance and giving their attention solely to methods—Hence, perhaps, some of the vogue of statistics and game theory, a retreat from politics which has been called "the New Scholasticism."[13] Even more satisfactory for such a purpose is Bentley's cosmology. Systematized godlessness, will do as well as God to justify the social order, and godlessness enjoys the prestige of science. There is, of course, one drawback: cosmologies are inherently unscientific. The operational logic to which Bentley subscribed is usually considered by its sponsors, such as Percy Bridgman[14] and John Dewey[15] to be a tool which by its very nature excludes finalities. The philosophical achievement of Bentley might therefore very accurately be said to consist of placing the fluid and provisional logic of Dewey in an absolute and closed cosmos.

Bentley, as we have noted, began as an economist, and indeed he considered himself an economist for most of his career. But he soon discovered that economic problems were political, and this led to *The Process of Government*. It is all the more interesting to speculate, therefore, on why he apparently gave so little attention to institutional economics, for this discipline also assumes that economic factors seek political expression. It may be that the implicit acceptance of the inevitability of change in institutional economics was what repelled him, for from the beginning he sought a closed and definitive system.[16] And it is perplexing, for instance, that he gave no attention to the equilibrium theory of Leon Walras, for Bentley's social philosophy was also an equilibrium theory—although he never gave it that name—and his epistemology reduced all philosophy to social philosophy.

Bentley's method of analysis was influenced by sociological and anthropological writers, primarily Marx, Simmel, Durkheim, and Brooks Adams, and the result was a kind of economic and sociological realism that he called "a statement of what is." But *The Process of Government* can hardly be called an empirical work. Although Bentley turned to the random, everyday contemporary milieu in its sociological context to discover the materials of politics, in *The Process of Government* he only cited observed raw data suitable to his system and then announced an exclusive formula—much as Marx adduced the economic data of the hungry forties to support a philosophy which in fact rested upon assumptions independent of the data. There are, of course, two major differences. Whereas the philosophy of Marx was historically oriented and rested on the assumption of change, Bentley's was ahistorical and changeless. And whereas Marx turned away from philosophy—indeed, he never clearly formulated his purely philosophical views[17]—and gave himself up to close empirical studies, Bentley abandoned merely factual disciplines for the study of meaning and knowledge.

In his first work Bentley claimed that local data have an independent existence apart from the general environment.[18] But in *The Process of Government* he attempted to see all social facts and values in operation, and to discover social laws. He based his analysis on "functional observation of full system," and concluded that a science of politics is possible. In 1926 appeared *Relativity in Man and Society;* in it he denies that local data have independent existence: their meaning always derives from their setting in an environment.[19] His next two books were in the field of logic, and led to his collaboration with John Dewey in writing *Knowing and the Known,* which was published in 1949.[20] Like Bentley's last book, *Inquiry into Inquiries,*[21] published in 1954, it emphasized the character of knowledge as an experience which involves not only the knower but the whole context of the event. Knowledge does not occur inside the skin of the observer: it is a "transaction" between him and the outside world, or, more accurately, it is a total event which is mangled if one breaks it into parts, observer and observed.

Dewey and Bentley described successive formulations of the process of knowledge:

> *Self-action:* where things are viewed as acting under their own powers. *Inter-action:* where thing is balanced against thing in causal inter-connection. *Transaction:* where systems of description and naming are employed to deal with aspects and phases of action, without final attribution to "elements" or other presumptively detachable or independent "entities," "essences," or "realities," and without isolation of presumptively detachable "relations" from such detachable "elements."[22]

Apparently this three-stage understanding of cognition was intended to mirror the history of science. The first view, that of innate powers of action, is attributed to the Greeks.[23] The second, mechanical causation, was displayed in Newtonian physics. The third, said Bentley, is modern scientific theory, and he asserted that the transactional method was the method of Einstein.

But the third method is vaguely phrased. One may conjecture that it meant something more to Bentley than to Dewey. Dewey was preoccupied with the problem-solving process, and one can say with confidence that for him the transactional approach was significant because it took account of the interdependence of organism and environment—the local, reciprocating process by which the environment presents a problem to the organism and the organism successfully modifies the environment. Dewey's point of departure is the need of the organism, the incompleteness of the situation in which the organism finds itself. Bentley's conception is the completeness of the system which fulfills itself by imposing conduct upon the organism. The system functions: whatever occurs is functional. Nothing is or can be dysfunctional for Bentley.[24] In an early essay he called for a cosmology, a theory "that shows knowledge as a function not merely of symbioplasm, but of the cosmos in its aspects of the greatest symbiotic phenomena."[25] That theory proved to be the transactional approach, and Bentley called it a "floating cosmology."[26]

The point of Bentley's agreement with Dewey is limited to the notion of the interdependence of phenomena, and this Percy Bridgman would not object to. Bridgman, however, rejected as anthropomorphic "any attempt to set up any theory applicable to the entire universe,"[27] and perhaps it was Bentley's metaphysical bias that prompted him later to an attack on Bridgman, whom he had once so much admired. At any rate, we have the extraordinary spectacle of Bentley's applauding Bridgman for his operational logic, and attacking him for making epistemological inquiry into the foundation of that logic.[28] For Bridgman, knowledge is relative to the knower. For Bentley, it was relative to the cosmos.

At the level of social theory, the difference between Bentley and Dewey is this: Dewey kept the universe open toward the future; he believed that new goals could be set and achieved by human effort.[29] For Dewey, meaning was human aspiration. For Bentley the universe was the contemporaneous struggle which was the boiling equilibrium of a closed total social system. Meaning, then, was merely a social event within this struggle. The transactional approach yields this cosmic view. This involves an extreme form of what has come to be called the sociology of knowledge, a view which reduces ideas to factual responses of interests to the environment. Bentley embraced the sociology of knowledge in *The Process of Government*. He said:

> When a man writes a book to advance some particular theory about society, he reflects in it a certain phase of the social process. . . . The reflection of a phase of the social process is the same

thing as the reflection of some group interest or set of group interests. His "theory" is such a reflection.[30]

We may ask what group interest these words reflect, and the rest of the book tells us. Society is always in a state of balance —it would be more convenient to say equilibrium—in which certain groups occupy a position of dominance.[31] Now, the sociology of knowledge equally disarms the critics and the defenders of the *status quo*, intellectually. It transforms the issue between them into a practical contest of power, and so amounts to an endorsement of the position of the present possessors of power. To be sure, it is impartial, and will accept as willingly any new regime. It renders allegiance to any *de facto* power. Indeed, Bentley's ethical neutrality was evident when he suggested that no interest was more justified in dominating than any other. This attitude, though implicit in Bentley, may be called "cynical conservatism."[32]

Bentley's theory of knowledge is a faithful reflection of the theory of society described in *The Process of Government*. The subsurface layers, "the process of social life" and "political facts," can be seen in motion, through social activity and political action, and can be dealt with as social fact. Ideas have reference to nothing other than social life; they are observable as social fact. Ideas are surface, not subsurface, forms. The sole question is, what interests or factors of social life express themselves through the ideas? Answering this question forces one to break away from the individual as the unit of explanation of thought or of society, and to point instead to the more substantial social element, the group. Thus, says Bentley, the units of society are not individuals but groups. But the group, too, is not a solid unit. Bentley makes it clear that what he calls groups are processes rather than collections of persons. They are ongoing activities which swirl in the social cauldron. Since activities are interlaced in a moving process and one has significance in terms of others, all phases of all activities are related. A group is a cross-section of such an activity. Like any cross-section of a process, it omits motion, and thereby introduces a falsification of the data. But the process itself is not properly an isolable phenomenon. It is an activity within a context which produces it and gives meaning to it. The real transaction, the proper study of political science, therefore, is the entire system, according to Bentley. We may observe that it is precisely at this point that the analogy to equilibrium theory in economics, with its account of balance and redress through the whole system, leaps out.

It is too much to ask us to entertain a picture of all of society as a single transaction, and Bentley accordingly supplies us with tools of understanding which presumably point toward the complete picture. For purposes of description he reifies groups. He gives us the conflict groups of Simmel and Gumplowicz, but not the classes of Marx. But what underlies the groups is, as with Marx, economic interest, rather than race as with Gumplowicz. Economic interests, the "lower-lying" activity and the raw material of politics, are the substructure upon which groups are erected. Not government, but the "group adjustment process" behind the government should be the object of examination. If adjustment in society is carried on by groups beneath the political level, economic groups are the keys to the system. Economic factors are not only the determinants of political events but the creators and controllers of ideas. Ideologies—but he does not use the word—are mere rationalizations of the interests of the group.[33] All social behavior, indeed, is conflict behavior, meaningful only as a function of underlying economic interest.

But, as Socrates demonstrated to Thrasymachus, interest is an ambiguous term. May not a man or a group mistake its interest? An affirmative answer would destroy the cosmology; it would admit the existence of a standard of judgment outside the universe of overt behavior. Accordingly, Bentley embraces the negative. The interest of a group is its course of behavior: the activity is the group and the interest simultaneously.[34] This deprives the word "interest" of any explanatory value, and banishes the economic substructure from the system. We are left with the picture of multifold processes which can be described only in terms of the contemporaneous system of which they are a part.[35]

Viewed one by one, Bentley says, groups are in conflict, and some dominate others. But in terms of the whole system, dominance and subordination are misleading terms. These are merely ongoing activities of groups comparable to other ongoing activities of other groups. Slaves also are a group, and carry on an activity; and this activity is their interest and in their interest.[36] Indeed, the "functional observation" of the "full system" comprises all the "facts" and "activities" and their development within the system. Everything is functionally related in the system. In cross-section each group occupies its natural—i.e., inevitable—position, and society is a natural— i.e., inevitable—order, dominated by a natural—i.e., inevitable —aristocracy.[37] On this teaching, all must be for the best in this best of all possible worlds.

If interest has no subjective content and can be defined only as overt behavior, it follows that "need" also is a description of what exists rather than a report of a disparity between what exists and some independent standard of reference. In his first work, a study of *The Condition of the Western Farmer*, Bentley suggested that the debtor needs the creditor; farmers need the bankers.[38] In *The Process of Government* he universalizes this conception. Need is not an emptiness but an activity. The activity may include a clamor, but this clamor is merely a part of the ongoing activities which make a balanced system. It orchestrates with all the other clamors into the music of the spheres.[39] It seems that Bentley is willing to pay a high price for the satisfaction of a closed system.

Institutions of government, Bentley tells us, are ongoing activities which express the dominance of groups. But the equilibrium of the system will prevent the domination of a single group through government, he says, for the group process in government is balanced by the group process outside of government. But if interests are manifested solely through groups, and there are no interests which are not so manifested, there is no essential difference between what Bentley calls the "representativeness" of interest groups and the structural organization of government. All social phenomena have pressures connected with government, and government is nothing more than an organization of interests combined into a single system. Indeed, the essence of his functional theory of the state is that all interests and all potential interests are a part of the governing process, since each interest is represented in proportion to its pressure.[40]

It follows that government also is open to no reproach for maladjustment, inefficiency, or frustration of interests. Complaints against government mean nothing more than that other groups besides the dominant ones engage in activity. Bentley also describes this phenomenon. Government generates opposition,[41] an activity which may institutionalize itself formally. The study of government is the study of the groups pressing on one another and new groups pushing old from the various agencies. And Bentley undertakes to classify governmental forms in terms of the group structure of society. Differences in government are not differences of principle, but rather of "techniques for the functioning of interests."[42] By watching the groups that secure organized methods of access to political power and comparing group processes, we can classify forms of government. But regardless of the form the process is always the same, for the existing political structure can only reflect groups which are "freely combining, dissolving, and recombining in accordance with their interest lines."[43] It is perplexing that at one point Bentley suggested that contemporaneously American government was "out of adjustment," out of balance with its group base.[44] On his principles this is impossible.

One of the most striking things about this system, as we have seen, is its contemporaneity. It does not aim at the future, it does not express the past. Of course, Bentley takes account of the past. He mentions "habit-background" and "custom," but these are assimilated to the system.[45] They enter into the substantive content of present interests. Since the idea of interest has no content save activity, no meaning except occurrence,[46] it is hospitable to anything that can be said to enter into occurrence. But this does not give him a time-oriented system. The real is always here and now. All of the system lies before the observer and can be understood fully in terms of immediate contemporary observation. Time, for Bentley, is a dimension of the present.[47] The relation between Bentley's theory and his method should now be apparent. Through his transactional approach, the observation of the full functioning of the system, he asserted that it was possible to grasp the inner aims and purposes of any system characterized by stability. He conceived the particular (interest) as an integrated and reciprocating part of this "dynamically" changing system. His methodology was based, therefore, upon the concept of equilibrium or balance. It made possible a science of politics. He concluded:

> One might work out a picture of the adjustment, "normal" for the given society . . . in terms of the adjustment of the actual strengths . . . a process that every interest forcing itself beyond the point of endurableness to the remainder of the interests would be checked before its excess has provoked violent reaction.[48]

So Bentley's science of politics ended in a science of control within a closed system.

We may suppose that a political scientist who announced, without more, that political science could dispense with history and psychology would win few followers. But apparently it is possible to contrive a system which attributes no significance to psychology and history and win converts to the system. This has only recently been true. The first edition of *The Process of Government*, in 1908, was rather uncharitably received and had limited influence. The second, in 1935, was published by friends at a small press as a kind of reflex of interest in his more important work in logic. But in 1949 it had a third edition, and in 1955 a fourth; in 1957 a *Festschrift* was presented to Bentley. Formal studies have acknowledged indebtedness and sometimes professed adherence to his principles.[49]

One, who acknowledged his indebtedness, has attempted to fill some gaps in Bentley's theory. The most important of the analytical pluralists, whose book, *The Governmental Process,* has inspired many contemporary group theorists, is Professor David B. Truman.[50] Like Bentley, Truman maintains that governmental decisions are determined by conflicting group pressures. He tells us why group needs and interests result in organized political pressures when he says, following Bentley, that they emerge when necessary because of the identity of interest and activity—every group has its interest and these interests always result in organized group action. As new interests that small groups cannot handle begin to emerge, large groups or voluntary organizations will arise to deal with those interests. The results of this pressure-group activity are benign, because groups are checked by counter-groups. The equilibrium of the system prevents the domination of a single group through government. It is "potential groups" that limit government. Truman's model is based upon Bentley's equilibrium theory and his group theory of politics.

Speaking generally, pluralists in the Bentley tradition failed to take into account the political and economic structure within which the group process takes place. "Realism" would seem to dictate that the most powerful or privileged groups in society "limit" government, and that a "pluralist" political system requires a conflict of values, not just conflicting groups. Failing to recognize this, many of Bentley's followers overlooked the fact that the group theory of politics became the basis of a modern pluralism which is no longer concerned with efforts to change the system. Bentley's "habit background" and Truman's "rules of the game" in fact operated not only to increase the power of the powerful, but to maintain existing institutional arrangements.

Another of Bentley's followers has attempted to fashion a "new tool." David Easton is searching for a general theory of politics through a unifying conceptual framework for political analysis. Like Bentley, Easton's model rests on a functional theory of politics and his methodology upon equilibrium theory. Bentley charged that "the real transaction, the proper study of political science is the entire system." Easton's "systems approach to politics" is a variant of Bentley's transactional approach and the "functional observation of the full system."

In his first work, *The Political System,* Easton offered his definition of politics as the "political interactions" that are "predominantly oriented toward the authoritative allocation of values for society." Because of the nature of the exchanges and transactions that take place between a political system and its environment, he tells us that the political system is adaptive. He also tells us how to combine the concept of equilibrium and system along with his observation on the interdependence of phenomena in the total process or function. His structure of systems analysis is left for future research.

In his later work, Easton tells us his main concern is to "develop a logically integrated set of categories, with strong empirical relevance, that will make possible the analysis of political life as a system of behavior." But he is concerned with a particular aspect of system behavior: "The basic process through which the political system regardless of its generic or specific type, is able to persist in a world of either stability or change." And, he concludes that the task of behavioral science is to "put kinds of questions that reveal the way in which life processes or defining functions of the political system are protected."[51]

Easton's definition of politics, i.e., "the authoritative allocation of values," suffers not only because values cannot be allocated, but because it raises the boundary question, i.e., whether "private" governments' decisions are authoritative beyond the membership of the group, etc. But his underlying concern is systemic persistence and the processes of regulating stress. In attempting to deal with developments that may drive the essential variables of the political system beyond their "critical ranges," Easton focuses on the regulatory responses the system can make and the functional consequences for the system.[52] Qualitative, large-scale, or fundamental changes in the system are not his concern, but rather the maintenance of systemic equilibrium or balance. Indeed, little attention in his work is given to concrete allocation or distributive questions concerning who gets what, nor is there any real emphasis on specific human behavior patterns. Like Bentley, Easton's systemic focus contributes no significance to psychology or history.

What is the explanation of this recent popularity of Bentley? In 1957, the Marxist economist Paul A. Baran attributed the vogue of equilibrium theory in economics to the current failure of capitalism to solve the problem of growth.[53] Equilibrium theory studies transactions in a closed system and until lately it implicitly denied the goal of growth. But the economic problem of most of the world is growth.

Equilibrium theory in politics also studies transactions in a closed system and still assumes the sempiternity of the system. It is ironical that the current fashion should insist upon the perpetuity of group struggle and group conflict, while the socialist sector of the world makes the point that cooperation rather than conflict may be the basis of social life, and many of the uncommitted countries seek such a solution. I submit that the teachings of cynical conservatism are inadequate. Those of us who are interested in developing a more adequate theory of politics must look closely at the tendency for Bentley's cosmology to persist in contemporary frameworks for political analysis.

REFERENCES

1. *The Political System* (New York, 1953).
2. Arnold A. Rogow, "Comment on Smith and Apter, or Whatever Happened to the Great Issues," *American Political Science Review*, 51 (September 1957), 771.
3. *The Process of Government, A Study of Social Pressures* (Chicago, 1908), p. 210.
4. John Dewey, *Reconstruction in Philosophy* (New York, 1950), p. 64.
5. *Ibid.,* p. 67.
6. See his article on "Functionalism," *Encyclopedia of the Social Sciences* (Edwin R. A. Seligman, ed.), VI, 523–525.
7. Emile Durkheim, *Elementary Forms of the Religious Life* (New York, 1915).
8. Ashley-Montagu, *Darwin, Competition and Cooperation* (New York, 1952).
9. Jerome Frank, "A Conflict with Oblivion: Some Observations on the Founders of Legal Pragmatism," *Rutgers Law Review*, Winter 1954, pp. 425–463.
10. Quoted by Sidney Ratner in Richard W. Taylor, ed., *Essays in Honor of Arthur F. Bentley: Life, Language, Law* (Yellow Springs, 1957), p. 53.
11. *The Process of Government*, pp. 1–18. It could be argued that Bentley belonged among the anti-formalists whose influence for decades was not conservative.
12. See Ratner, in Taylor, *op. cit.,* p. 35.
13. See Barrington Moore, Jr., *Political Power and Social Theory* (Cambridge, 1958), pp. 90–110.
14. *The Nature of Physical Theory* (New York, 1936).
15. *Logic: The Theory of Inquiry* (New York, 1938).
16. See *The Process of Government*, pp. 208, 465–482, for his statements on socialism, Marx, and a class analysis of society. Bentley

claims that Marx's analysis lacked validity because the class did not possess unity as the group did.

17. Engels in his *Anti-Dühring* undertook this task; see Frederick Engels, *Herr Eugen Dühring's Revolution in Science* (New York, 1939).
18. *The Condition of the Western Farmer as Illustrated by the Economic History of a Nebraska Township,* Johns Hopkins University Studies in History and Political Science, Vol. II (Baltimore, 1893), p. 10.
19. *Relativity in Man and Society* (New York, 1926), pp. 205–206. "Let the test of every phase of society be in terms of some other phase or phases."
20. *Knowing and the Known* (Boston, 1949).
21. *Inquiry into Inquiries: Essays in Social Theory* (Boston, 1954).
22. *Knowing and the Known,* p. 108. On pp. 72–74, the authors defined the transactional approach as "functional observation of the full system, actively necessary to inquiry at some stages, held in reserve at other stages, frequently requiring the breaking down of older verbal impactions of naming. . . . Inter-action is presentation of particles or other objects organized as operating upon one another. Self-action is pre-scientific presentation in terms of presumptively independent actors, souls, minds, selves, power, or forces, taken as activating events. . . . If we confine ourselves to the problem of the balls on a billiard table they can be profitably presented and studied interactionally. But a cultural account of the game in its full spread of social growth and human adaptation is already transactional."
23. Francis Cornford, *The Laws of Motion in Ancient Thought* (Cambridge, 1931).
24. "Knowledge and Society," in *Inquiry into Inquiries,* pp. 12–24. On page 20: "Our task now is to take the Dewey theory of knowledge as arising at crises of action and broaden it out, so that it will be explicitly stated in terms of more than individual lives." Bentley does this by reducing the individual to a segment of "taxioplasm," an inseparable part of a society which can be properly comprehended only within a system which embraces also the physical environment. On page 18: "The wolf fighting with the pack over the too-limited quarry is as much symbiotactic as when previously it was running down the prey." Symbiotaxis is the total process or function; it follows that the prey is symbiotactic too.
25. *Ibid.,* p. 25.
26. Arthur F. Bentley, *Behavior, Knowledge, Fact* (Bloomington, 1935), p. 183.
27. Bridgman, *The Nature of Physical Theory* (Princeton, 1936), p. 183.
28. *Inquiry into Inquiries,* pp. 113–140.
29. Dewey, *Reconstruction in Philosophy.*
30. *The Process of Government,* p. 429.
31. *Ibid.,* p. 215.
32. I am indebted to Professor Arthur W. Macmahon for this epithet. He suggested that American political scientists who since 1946 have become interested in responsible party government and the issues of politics should have discredited, not resuscitated, Bentley.
33. *The Process of Government,* p. 241: "Each group . . . will bolster up its claim on an elaborate structure of reasoning and assertions. . . . When we go down to the group statement we get down below mere reasoning to the very basis of reasons."
34. Bentley put no limitations on the validity of the transactional approach and group theory as a methodology to understand politics,

since he had to his own satisfaction reduced political phenomena to processes in a system and groups. See *The Process of Government,* pp. 208–209: "When groups are adequately stated, everything is stated. When I say everything I mean everything. The complete description will mean the complete science, in the study of social phenomena, as in any other field. There will be no more room for animistic 'causes' here than there."

35. It is just at this point that many behavioralists begin their analysis.

36. Bentley, *The Process of Government,* p. 271. "No slaves, not the worst abused of all, but help to form the government. They are an interest group within it." This is hard to reconcile with his refusal to admit Marx's classes as groups.

37. *Ibid.,* pp. 219–254.

38. *Op. cit.,* p. 46.

39. See *The Process of Government,* p. 443: "all of the groups . . . have value in terms of each other, just as have the colors in a painting, or sounds in music. . . . There is not a bit of the process that does not have its meaning in terms of other parts."

40. See *Relativity in Man and Society,* pp. 119–120: "The term state indicates a great complex of closely coinciding activities, which hold together, and get enough representative process for stability. The state is fundamental not as a mystic being but only in the sense of this stability, this durational extent, this relative permanence."

41. See *The Process of Government,* pp. 234–38. Bentley contends that a group representing subgroups and reflecting a common economic interest transforms itself into a hierarchically organized aristocratic machine of government, and the group struggle follows: a natural aristocracy opposed by a natural demagogy. A natural aristocracy generates a natural demagogic group movement.

42. *Ibid.,* p. 443.

43. *Ibid.,* p. 358.

44. *Ibid.,* pp. 301, 358–59, 449–58. Not only did he feel that government or the American Republic was "out of adjustment," but that we had not modeled a system of government to meet our needs, and that democracy or representative democracy was a "structural arrangement" which would prevent groups from obtaining a "disproportionate power of functioning through government."

45. See *Inquiry into Inquiries,* p. 344: "Behavioral pasts and futures— histories and goals, habits and purposings—are before us descriptively in behavioral presents."

46. See *The Process of Government,* pp. 192–93, where Bentley said that if a comparison of group activity were made, "we shall have the human nature and the environment comprised in our very statement of the activities themselves—the actual happenings."

47. See *Relativity in Man and Society,* pp. 139, 205–206; also *Inquiry into Inquiries,* p. 24.

48. *The Process of Government,* p. 458.

49. Not all "group theorists," however, have been bound by his system.

50. This is not to say that there are not important differences between Bentley and Truman. Bentley claimed to have the only possible general theory of politics.

51. *A Framework of Political Analysis* (New Jersey, 1965), p. 78.

52. For Bentley nothing could be dysfunctional for the system. This is not true for Easton.

53. *The Political Economy of Growth* (New York, 1957).

3: *Two Faces of Power*

PETER BACHRACH
MORTON S. BARATZ

The concept of power remains elusive despite the recent and prolific outpourings of case studies on community power.[1] Its elusiveness is dramatically demonstrated by the regularity of disagreement as to the locus of community power between the sociologists and the political scientists. Sociologically oriented researchers have consistently found that power is highly centralized, while scholars trained in political science have just as regularly concluded that in "their" communities power is widely diffused.[2] Presumably, this explains why the latter group styles itself "pluralist," its counterpart "elitist."

There seems no room for doubt that the sharply divergent findings of the two groups are the product, not of sheer coincidence, but of fundamental differences in both their underlying assumptions and research methodology. The political scientists have contended that these differences in findings can be explained by the faulty approach and presuppositions of the

From *American Political Science Review*, LVI (December 1962), 947–952.

sociologists. We contend in this paper that the pluralists themselves have not grasped the whole truth of the matter; that
while their criticisms of the elitists are sound, they, like the
elitists, utilize an approach and assumptions which predetermine
their conclusions. Our argument is cast within the frame of
our central thesis: that there are two faces of power, neither
of which the sociologists see and only one of which the political
scientists see.

I

Against the elitist approach to power several criticisms may
be, and have been leveled.[3] One has to do with its basic
premise that in every human institution there is an ordered
system of power, a "power structure" which is an integral part
and the mirror image of the organization's stratification. This
postulate the pluralists emphatically—and, to our mind, correctly—reject, on the ground that

> nothing categorical can be assumed about power in any com-
> munity. . . . If anything, there seems to be an unspoken notion
> among pluralist researchers that at bottom *nobody* dominates
> in a town, so that their first question is not likely to be, "Who
> runs this community?," but rather, "Does anyone at all run this
> community?" The first query is somewhat like, "Have you stopped
> beating your wife?," in that virtually any response short of total
> unwillingness to answer will supply the researchers with a "power
> elite" along the lines presupposed by the stratification theory.[4]

Equally objectionable to the pluralists—and to us—is the
sociologists' hypothesis that the power structure tends to be
stable over time.

> Pluralists hold that power may be tied to issues, and issues can
> be fleeting or persistent, provoking coalitions among interested
> groups and citizens, ranging in their duration from momentary
> to semi-permanent. . . . To presume that the set of coalitions
> which exist in the community at any given time is a timelessly
> stable aspect of social structure is to introduce systematic in-
> accuracies into one's description of social reality.[5]

A third criticism of the elitist model is that it wrongly equates reputed with actual power:

> If a man's major life work is banking, the pluralist presumes he will spend his time at the bank, and not in manipulating community decisions. This presumption holds until the banker's activities and participations indicate otherwise. . . . If we presume that the banker is "really" engaged in running the community, there is practically no way of disconfirming this notion, even if it is totally erroneous. On the other hand, it is easy to spot the banker who really *does* run community affairs when we presume he does not, because his activities will make this fact apparent.[6]

This is not an exhaustive bill of particulars; there are flaws other than these in the sociological model and methodology[7]—including some which the pluralists themselves have not noticed. But to go into this would not materially serve our current purposes. Suffice it simply to observe that whatever the merits of their own approach to power, the pluralists have effectively exposed the main weaknesses of the elitist model.

As the foregoing quotations make clear, the pluralists concentrate their attention, not upon the sources of power, but its exercise. Power to them means "participation in decision-making"[8] and can be analyzed only after "careful examination of a series of concrete decisions."[9] As a result, the pluralist researcher is uninterested in the reputedly powerful. His concerns instead are to (a) select for study a number of "key" as opposed to "routine" political decisions, (b) identify the people who took an active part in the decision-making process, (c) obtain a full account of their actual behavior while the policy conflict was being resolved, and (d) determine and analyze the specific outcome of the conflict.

The advantages of this approach, relative to the elitist alternative, need no further exposition. The same may not be said, however, about its defects—two of which seem to us to be of fundamental importance. One is that the model takes no account of the fact that power may be, and often is, exercised by confining the scope of decision-making to relatively "safe" issues. The other is that the model provides no *objective* criteria for distinguishing between "important" and "unimportant" issues arising in the political arena.

II

There is no gainsaying that an analysis grounded entirely upon what is specific and visible to the outside observer is more "scientific" than one based upon pure speculation. To put it another way,

> If we can get our social life stated in terms of activity, and of nothing else, we have not indeed succeeded in measuring it, but we have at least reached a foundation upon which a coherent system of measurements can be built. . . . We shall cease to be blocked by the intervention of unmeasurable elements, which claim to be themselves the real causes of all that is happening, and which by their spook-like arbitrariness make impossible any progress toward dependable knowledge.[10]

The question is, however, how can one be certain in any given situation that the "unmeasurable elements" are inconsequential, are not of decisive importance? Cast in slightly different terms, can a sound concept of power be predicated on the assumption that power is totally embodied and fully reflected in "concrete decisions" or in activity bearing directly upon their making?

We think not. Of course power is exercised when A participates in the making of decisions that affect B. But power is also exercised when A devotes his energies to creating or reinforcing social and political values and institutional practices that limit the scope of the political process to public consideration of only those issues which are comparatively innocuous to A. To the extent that A succeeds in doing this, B is prevented, for all practical purposes, from bringing to the fore any issues that might in their resolution be seriously detrimental to A's set of preferences.[11]

Situations of this kind are common. Consider, for example, the case—surely not unfamiliar to this audience—of the discontented faculty member in an academic institution headed by a tradition-bound executive. Aggrieved about a long-standing

policy around which a strong vested interest has developed,
the professor resolves in the privacy of his office to launch an
attack upon the policy at the next faculty meeting. But, when
the moment of truth is at hand, he sits frozen in silence. Why?
Among the many possible reasons, one or more of these could
have been of crucial importance: (a) the professor was fearful
that his intended action would be interpreted as an expression
of his disloyalty to the institution; or (b) he decided that,
given the beliefs and attitudes of his colleagues on the faculty,
he would almost certainly constitute on this issue a minority
of one; or (c) he concluded that, given the nature of the law-
making process in the institution, his proposed remedies would
be pigeonholed permanently. But whatever the case, the central
point to be made is the same: to the extent that a person or
group—consciously or unconsciously—creates or reinforces
barriers to the public airing of policy conflicts, that person or
group has power. Or, as Professor Schattschneider has so admirably put it:

> All forms of political organization have a bias in favor of the
> exploitation of some kinds of conflict and the suppression of
> others because *organization is the mobilization of bias*. Some
> issues are organized into politics while others are organized out.[12]

Is such bias not relevant to the study of power? Should not
the student be continuously alert to its possible existence in
the human institution that he studies, and be ever prepared to
examine the forces which brought it into being and sustain it?
Can he safely ignore the possibility, for instance, that an individual or group in a community participates more vigorously
in supporting the *nondecision-making* process than in partici-
pating in actual decisions within the process? Stated differently,
can the researcher overlook the chance that some person or
association could limit decision-making to relatively non-con-
troversial matters, by influencing community values and political
procedures and rituals, notwithstanding that there are in the
community serious but latent power conflicts?[13] To do so is,
in our judgment, to overlook the less apparent, but nonetheless
extremely important, face of power.

III

In his critique of the "ruling-elite model," Professor Dahl argues that "the hypothesis of the existence of a ruling elite can be strictly tested only if . . . [t]here is a fair sample of cases involving key political decisions in which the preferences of the hypothetical ruling elite run counter to those of any other likely group that might be suggested."[14] With this assertion we have two complaints. One we have already discussed, viz., in erroneously assuming that power is solely reflected in concrete decisions, Dahl thereby excludes the possibility that in the community in question there is a group capable of preventing contests from arising on issues of importance to it. Beyond that, however, by ignoring the less apparent face of power Dahl and those who accept his pluralist approach are unable adequately to differentiate between a "key" and a "routine" political decision.

Nelson Polsby, for example, proposes that "by pre-selecting as issues for study those which are generally agreed to be significant, pluralist researchers can test stratification theory."[15] He is silent, however, on how the researcher is to determine *what* issues are "generally agreed to be significant," and on how the researcher is to appraise the reliability of the agreement. In fact, Polsby is guilty here of the same fault he himself has found with elitist methodology: by presupposing that in any community there are significant issues in the political arena, he takes for granted the very question which is in doubt. He accepts as issues what are reputed to be issues. As a result, his findings are fore-ordained. For even if there is no "truly" significant issue in the community under study, there is every likelihood that Polsby (or any like-minded researcher) will find one or some and, after careful study, reach the appropriate pluralistic conclusions.[16]

Dahl's definition of "key political issues" in his essay on the ruling-elite model is open to the same criticism. He states that it is "a necessary although possibly not a sufficient condition that the [key] issue should involve actual disagreement in preferences among two or more groups."[17] In our view, this is an inadequate characterization of a "key political issue," simply because groups can have disagreements in preferences on unimportant as well as on important issues. Elite preferences which border on the indifferent are certainly not significant in determining whether a monolithic or polylithic distribution of power prevails in a given community. Using Dahl's definition of "key political issues," the researcher would have little difficulty in finding such in practically any community; and it would not be surprising then if he ultimately concluded that power in the community was widely diffused.

The distinction between important and unimportant issues, we believe, cannot be made intelligently in the absence of an analysis of the "mobilization of bias" in the community; of the dominant values and the political myths, rituals, and institutions which tend to favor the vested interests of one or more groups, relative to others. Armed with this knowledge, one could conclude that any challenge to the predominant values or to the established "rules of the game" would constitute an "important" issue; all else, unimportant. To be sure, judgments of this kind cannot be entirely objective. But to avoid making them in a study of power is both to neglect a highly significant aspect of power and thereby to undermine the only sound basis for discriminating between "key" and "routine" decisions. In effect, we contend, the pluralists have made each of these mistakes; that is to say, they have done just that for which Kaufman and Jones so severely taxed Floyd Hunter: they have begun "their structure at the mezzanine without showing us a lobby or foundation,"[18] i.e., they have begun by studying the issues rather than the values and biases that are built into the political system and that, for the student of power, give real meaning to those issues which do enter the political arena.

IV

There is no better fulcrum for our critique of the pluralist model than Dahl's recent study of power in New Haven.[19]

At the outset it may be observed that Dahl does not attempt in this work to define his concept, "key political decision." In asking whether the "Notables" of New Haven are "influential overtly or covertly in the making of government decisions," he simply states that he will examine "three different 'issue-areas' in which important public decisions are made: nominations by the two political parties, urban redevelopment, and public education." These choices are justified on the grounds that "nominations determine which persons will hold public office. The New Haven redevelopment program measured by its cost —present and potential—is the largest in the country. Public education, aside from its intrinsic importance, is the costliest item in the city's budget." Therefore, Dahl concludes, "It is reasonable to expect . . . that the relative influence over public officials wielded by the . . . Notables would be revealed by an examination of their participation in these three areas of activity."[20]

The difficulty with this latter statement is that it is evident from Dahl's own account that the Notables are in fact uninterested in two of the three "key" decisions he has chosen. In regard to the public school issue, for example, Dahl points out that many of the Notables live in the suburbs and that those who do live in New Haven choose in the main to send their children to private schools. "As a consequence," he writes, "their interest in the public schools is ordinarily rather slight."[21] Nominations by the two political parties as an important "issue-area," is somewhat analogous to the public schools, in that the apparent lack of interest among the Notables in this issue is partially accounted for by their suburban residence—because of which they are disqualified from holding public office in New Haven. Indeed, Dahl himself concedes that with respect to both these issues the Notables are largely indifferent: "Business leaders might ignore the public schools or the political parties without any sharp awareness that their indifference would hurt their pocketbooks . . ." He goes on, however, to say that:

> the prospect of profound changes [as a result of the urban-redevelopment program] in ownership, physical layout, and usage of property in the downtown area and the effects of these changes

on the commercial and industrial prosperity of New Haven were all related in an obvious way to the daily concerns of business-men.[22]

Thus, if one believes—as Professor Dahl did when he wrote his critique of the ruling-elite model—that an issue, to be considered as important, "should involve actual disagreement in preferences among two or more groups,"[23] then clearly he has now for all practical purposes written off public education and party nominations as key "issue-areas." But this point aside, it appears somewhat dubious at best that "the relative influence over public officials wielded by the Social Notables" can be revealed by an examination of their nonparticipation in areas in which they were not interested.

Furthermore, we would not rule out the possibility that even on those issues to which they appear indifferent, the Notables may have a significant degree of *indirect* influence. We would suggest, for example, that although they send their children to private schools, the Notables do recognize that public school expenditures have a direct bearing upon their own tax liabilities. This being so, and given their strong representation on the New Haven Board of Finance,[24] the expectation must be that it is in their direct interest to play an active role in fiscal policy-making, in the establishment of the educational budget in particular. But as to this, Dahl is silent: he inquires not at all into either the decisions made by the Board of Finance with respect to education nor into their impact upon the public schools.[25] Let it be understood clearly that in making these points we are not attempting to refute Dahl's contention that the Notables lack power in New Haven. What we *are* saying, however, is that this conclusion is not adequately supported by his analysis of the "issue-areas" of public education and party nominations.

The same may not be said of redevelopment. This issue is by any reasonable standard important for purposes of determining whether New Haven is ruled by "the hidden hand of an economic elite."[26] For the Economic Notables have taken an active interest in the program and, beyond that, the socio-economic implications of it are not necessarily in harmony with the basic interests and values of businesses and businessmen.

In an effort to assure that the redevelopment program would be acceptable to what he dubbed "the biggest muscles" in New Haven, Mayor Lee created the Citizens Action Commission (CAC) and appointed to it primarily representatives of the economic elite. It was given the function of overseeing the work of the mayor and other officials involved in redevelopment, and, as well, the responsibility for organizing and encouraging citizens' participation in the program through an extensive committee system.

In order to weigh the relative influence of the mayor, other key officials, and the members of the CAC, Dahl reconstructs "all the *important* decisions on redevelopment and renewal between 1950–58 . . . [to] determine which individuals most often initiated the proposals that were finally adopted or most often successfully vetoed the proposals of the others."[27] The results of this test indicate that the mayor and his development administrator were by far the most influential, and that the "muscles" on the Commission, excepting in a few trivial instances, "never directly initiated, opposed, vetoed, or altered any proposal brought before them. . . ."[28]

This finding is, in our view, unreliable, not so much because Dahl was compelled to make a subjective selection of what constituted *important* decisions within what he felt to be an *important* "issue-area," as because the finding was based upon an excessively narrow test of influence. To measure relative influence solely in terms of the ability to initiate and veto proposals is to ignore the possible exercise of influence or power in limiting the scope of initiation. How, that is to say, can a judgment be made as to the relative influence of Mayor Lee and the CAC without knowing (through prior study of the political and social views of all concerned) the proposals that Lee did *not* make because he anticipated that they would provoke strenuous opposition and, perhaps, sanctions on the part of the CAC.[29]

In sum, since he does not recognize *both* faces of power, Dahl is in no position to evaluate the relative influence or power of the initiator and decision-maker, on the one hand, and of those persons, on the other, who may have been indirectly instrumental in preventing potentially dangerous issues from being raised.[30] As a result, he unduly emphasizes the importance of initiating, deciding, and vetoing, and in the process casts the pluralist conclusions of his study into serious doubt.

V

We have contended in this paper that a fresh approach to the study of power is called for, an approach based upon a recognition of the two faces of power. Under this approach the researcher would begin—not, as does the sociologist who asks, "Who rules?" nor as does the pluralist who asks, "Does anyone have power?"—but by investigating the particular "mobilization of bias" in the institution under scrutiny. Then, having analyzed the dominant values, the myths and the established political procedures and rules of the game, he would make a careful inquiry in which persons or groups, if any, gain from the existing bias and which, if any, are handicapped by it. Next, he would investigate the dynamics of *nondecision-making,* that is, he would examine the extent to which and the manner in which the *status quo* oriented persons and groups influence those community values and those political institutions (as, e.g., the unanimity "rule" of New York City's Board of Estimate[31]) which tend to limit the scope of actual decision-making to "safe" issues. Finally, using his knowledge of the restrictive face of power as a foundation for analysis and as a standard for distinguishing between "key" and "routine" political decisions, the researcher would, after the manner of the pluralists, analyze participation in decision-making of concrete issues.

We reject in advance as unimpressive the possible criticism that this approach to the study of power is likely to prove fruitless because it goes beyond an investigation of what is objectively measurable. In reacting against the subjective aspects of the sociological model of power, the pluralists have, we believe, made the mistake of discarding "unmeasurable elements" as unreal. It is ironical that, by so doing, they have exposed themselves to the same fundamental criticism they have so forcefully levelled against the elitists: their approach to and assumptions about power predetermine their findings and conclusions.

REFERENCES

1. This paper is an outgrowth of a seminar in Problems of Power in Contemporary Society, conducted jointly by the authors for graduate students and undergraduate majors in political science and economics.
2. Compare, for example, the sociological studies of Floyd Hunter, *Community Power Structure* (Chapel Hill, 1953); Roland Pellegrini and Charles H. Coates, "Absentee-Owned Corporations and Community Power Structure," *American Journal of Sociology,* 61 (March 1956), 413–19; and Robert O. Schulze, "Economic Dominants and Community Power Structure," *American Sociological Review,* 23 (February 1958), 3–9; with political science studies of Wallace S. Sayre and Herbert Kaufman, *Governing New York City* (New York, 196); Robert A. Dahl, *Who Governs?* (New Haven, 1961); and Norton E. Long and George Belknap, "A Research Program on Leadership and Decision-Making in Metropolitan Areas" (New York, Governmental Affairs Institute, 1956). See also Nelson W. Polsby, "How to Study Community Power: The Pluralist Alternative," *Journal of Politics,* 22 (August 1960), 474–84.
3. See especially N. W. Polsby, *op. cit.,* pp. 475f.
4. *Ibid.,* p. 476.
5. *Ibid.,* pp. 478–79.
6. *Ibid.,* pp. 480–81.
7. See especially Robert A. Dahl, "A Critique of the Ruling-Elite Model," *American Political Science Review,* 52 (June 1958), 463–69; and Lawrence J. R. Herson, "In the Footsteps of Community Power," *American Political Science Review,* 55 (December 1961), 817–31.
8. This definition originated with Harold D. Lasswell and Abraham Kaplan, *Power and Society* (New Haven, 1950), p. 75.
9. Robert A. Dahl, "A Critique of the Ruling-Elite Model," *op. cit.,* p. 466.
10. Arthur Bentley, *The Process of Government* (Chicago, 1908), p. 202, quoted in Polsby, *op. cit.,* p. 481n.
11. As is perhaps self-evident, there are similarities in both faces of power. In each, A participates in decisions and thereby adversely affects B. But there is an important difference betwen the two: in the one case, A openly participates; in the other, he participates only in the sense that he works to sustain those values and rules of procedure that help him keep certain issues out of the public domain. True enough, participation of the second kind may at times be overt; that is the case, for instance, in cloture fights in the Congress. But the point is that it need not be. In fact, when the maneuver is most successfully executed, it neither involves nor can be identified with decisions arrived at on specific issues.
12. E. E. Schattschneider, *The Semi-Sovereign People* (New York 1960), p. 71.

13. Dahl *partially* concedes this point when he observes ("A Critique of the Ruling-Elite Model," pp. 468–69) that "one could argue that even in a society like ours a ruling elite might be so influential over ideas, attitudes, and opinions that a kind of false consensus will exist—not the phony consensus of a terroristic totalitarian dictatorship but the manipulated and superficially self-imposed adherence to the norms and goals of the elite by broad sections of a community. . . . This objection points to the need to be circumspect in interpreting the evidence." But that he largely misses our point is clear from the succeeding sentence: "Yet here, too, it seems to me that the hypothesis cannot be satisfactorily confirmed without something equivalent to the test I have proposed," and that is "by an examination of a series of concrete cases where key decisions are made. . . ."
14. *Op. cit.,* p. 466.
15. Polsby, *op. cit.,* p. 478.
16. As he points out, the expectations of the pluralist researchers "have seldom been disappointed" (*Ibid.,* p. 477).
17. Dahl, *op. cit.,* p. 467.
18. Herbert Kaufman and Victor Jones, "The Mystery of Power," *Public Administration Review,* 14 (Summer 1954), 207.
19. Robert A. Dahl, *Who Governs?*
20. *Ibid.,* p. 64.
21. *Ibid.,* p. 70.
22. *Ibid.,* p. 71.
23. *Op. cit.,* p. 467.
24. *Who Governs?,* p. 82. Dahl points out that "the main policy thrust of the Economic Notables is to oppose tax increases; this leads them to oppose expenditures for anything more than minimal traditional city services. In this effort their two most effective weapons ordinarily are the mayor and the Board of Finance. The policies of the Notables are most easily achieved under a strong mayor if his policies coincide with theirs or under a weak mayor if they have the support of the Board of Finance. . . . New Haven mayors have continued to find it expedient to create confidence in their financial policies among businessmen by appointing them to the board" (pp. 81–2).
25. Dahl does discuss in general terms (pp. 79–84) changes in the level of tax rates and assessments in past years, but not actual decisions of the Board of Finance or their effects on the public school system.
26. *Ibid.,* p. 124.
27. "A rough test of a person's overt or covert influence," Dahl states in the first section of the book, "is the frequency with which he successfully initiates an important policy over the opposition of others, or vetoes policies initiated by others, or initiates a policy where no opposition appears" (*Ibid.,* p. 66).
28. *Ibid.,* p. 131.
29. Dahl is, of course, aware of the "law of anticipated reactions." In the case of the mayor's relationship with the CAC, Dahl notes that Lee was "particularly skillful in estimating what the CAC could be expected to support or reject (p. 137). However, Dahl was not interested in analyzing or appraising to what extent the CAC limited Lee's freedom of action. Because of his restricted concept of power, Dahl did not consider that the CAC might in this respect have exercised power. That the CAC did not initiate or veto actual

proposals by the mayor was to Dahl evidence enough that the CAC was virtually powerless; it might as plausibly be evidence that the CAC was (in itself or in what it represented) so powerful that Lee ventured nothing it would find worth quarreling with.

30. The fact that the initiator of decisions also refrains—because he anticipates adverse reactions—from initiating other proposals does not obviously lessen the power of the agent who limited his initiative powers. Dahl missed this point: "It is," he writes, "all the more improbable, then, that a secret cabal of Notables dominates the public life of New Haven through means so clandestine that not one of the fifty prominent citizens interviewed in the course of this study —citizens who had participated extensively in various decisions— hinted at the existence of such a cabal. . . " (p. 185).

    In conceiving of elite domination exclusively in the form of a conscious cabal exercising the power of decision-making and vetoing, he overlooks a more subtle form of domination; one in which those who actually dominate are not conscious of it themselves, simply because their position of dominance has never seriously been challenged.

31. Sayre and Kaufman, *op. cit.,* p. 640. For perceptive study of the "mobilization of bias" in a rural American community, see Arthur Vidich and Joseph Bensman, *Small Town in Mass Society* (Princeton, 1958).

II : Toward a New Diagnosis

4 : *Power To Do What?*

ANDREW HACKER

There has seldom been a more perplexed group of reviewers than those asked to comment upon *The Power Elite*. The book was "important," "provocative," even "brilliant." That it ought to be read and pondered was a universal recommendation. But in the final analysis what was most troublesome was Mills' perception of American society.

The America he described was quite different from that usually perceived by students of the social scene. He had a question: Who runs the country? And he had the answer: A power elite. But the reviewers remained skeptical, for to their minds neither question nor answer was spelled out sufficiently to be convincing. They wanted detailed illustrations showing just how the power elite uses its power. Nowhere, they complained, was there an inventory or even a sampling of the elite decisions that have shaped the course of American life.

From *The New Sociology,* edited by Irving L. Horowitz (New York: Oxford University Press, 1964), pp. 134–146. Copyright © 1964 by Oxford University Press, Inc.

"It is far from clear what kinds of decisions the decision-makers make," one reviewer commented.[1] Another wanted to know "what the power elite does and precisely how it does it."[2] A third found it "remarkable and indeed astounding" that Mills did not "examine an array of specific cases to test his major hypothesis."[3] The general perplexity was summarized by a critic who complained: "Curiously, except in a few instances, Mills fails to specify what the big decisions are."[4]

An attempt will therefore be made here to complete a piece of business that Mills left unfinished. But before this is done it is in order to comment on the limits of elite power in American society.

America has been and continues to be one of the world's most democratic nations. Here, far more so than elsewhere, the public is allowed to participate widely in the making of social and political policy. The public is not unaware of its power, and the ordinary American tends to be rather arrogant about his right and competence to participate. The average citizen, moreover, is not a deferential person, and he looks down on rather than up to those who in other times and places might be considered his "betters." This is why, from Alexander Hamilton and Alexis de Tocqueville to the present day, the specter of the "tyranny of the majority" has haunted America. The power of the public—Mills would call it the "mass"—is real, and its manifestations are all too familiar. In the realms of public education and popular culture, in civil liberties and civil rights, and often in local government—in all of these areas majority sentiment prevails. The people think they know what they want and are in no mood to be led to greener pastures. This is why we have driver-education courses in the high schools, lowbrow comedy on television, public loyalty investigations, and de facto racial segregation.[5] These conditions persist because they have the wholehearted backing of local and national majorities. Policy-makers know that in a democracy public sentiment must be accommodated.

It should be emphasized that these conditions are not the product of elite manipulation. If the majority flexes its muscles, it is usually a spontaneous show of strength and quite independent of the urgings of the mass media or the plans made in the higher circles. Indeed, the public throws up leaders of its own choosing on issues such as these. At one juncture it will be a *Joe Mc Carthy* Wisconsin senator, at another a Mississippi governor. *Huey Long* These personalities are outside the elite, and their power is a reflection of the power of the majority. Indeed, the elite has no real interest in or objection to democracy in the areas that have been mentioned here. The military establishment will cheerfully check the loyalty of its draftees; the large corporations are quite willing to sponsor televised trash; and the inner circle of the Executive Branch will move very slowly indeed in matters of desegregation. In short, the elite is content to let the public blow off steam on certain questions. This is acknowledged to be necessary, for democracy must have issues to squabble about. If attention is focused on fluoride in the water and progressivism in the schools, then eyes will be deflected from more important matters. For there are realms where the public cannot participate, must not participate, and ought not to want to participate.

To return to the original problem: Mills' failure to show "what kinds of decisions the decision-makers make," to "specify what the big decisions are." A reading of *The Power Elite* makes clear that the men who run America's large corporations stand at the center of the topmost circle. They, more than their military and governmental counterparts, have power that is both autonomous and unchecked. The military are still heavily controlled by the politicians, and the politicians must be responsive to the public.

The conventional view, of course, is that the businessman is far from a free agent. Any executive will wax eloquent on how he is hemmed in on all sides. He will point to a plethora of government agencies, all of which regulate his conduct. There is the Federal Trade Commission, the National Labor Relations Board, the Anti-trust Division of the Justice Department, and of course the Internal Revenue Service. And then there are labor unions, further limiting his freedom of action. He has customers and suppliers, telling him what they want and what he can get; and he has stockholders clamoring for dividends, capital gains, and efficient management. And of course there is the ubiquitous public that must be satisfied at all stages, lest bankruptcy be the consequence. The question, however, is not whether businessmen feel hamstrung, for they have protested their powerlessness since they were first told to buy safety-devices for their dangerous machines. The point is whether or not these limiting factors take on much significance when weighed against the areas of unrestricted action open to the corporate elite.

It should be noted at the outset that large corporations do not go bankrupt. They can be inefficient, as the steel companies have demonstrated, and still be profitable. Their relative share of the market can rise or fall, and their rank in the industry may change slightly over the years. But mergers and reorganizations keep the assets and production facilities intact. To be sure, the corporate elite must make its decisions with an eye on profitability. But in the highest circles the concern is with the expansion of the enterprise over a period of several decades, and profits are but a means to this end. The real issue is how autonomous these enterprises are and what are the consequences of their decisions for society as a whole. What, in short, can the corporate elite do with the power it is alleged to have?

First, in prices. Despite an occasional outburst from the White House, the corporate managers can administer prices as they see fit.[6] They are not required to submit proposed increases to any government agency for approval, and they may ask what the market will bear. Generally speaking, the market will pay what is asked.

On profits, stockholders expect only a certain modest dividend, and this is usually passed on to them without discussion.[7] Top management maintains a minimum level of earnings by its ability to fix prices. In addition it decides what proportion of the earnings will go to the stockholders and what proportion is to be retained by the company.

Wages are of course subject to collective bargaining. But this process simply maintains the status quo. For wage increases just about keep pace with the cost of living, and the share of a corporation's income going to wages remains about the same over the years. Management has even more freedom in setting salaries. Here it can determine who is to become wealthy and how great this wealth is to be. Decisions on executive compensation, in particular, go far toward determining aspirations for an entire society. The purchasing power bestowed on the men at and near the top makes for a style of life that becomes a goal for those lower in the pyramid.[8]

Enough has been said and written about organization men emphasizing that employee behavior is both scrutinized and shaped by those in the executive suites.[9] If it is asked why so many succumb to the pressure to conform, the answer is that most Americans want to succeed in their careers and are willing to pay the price of success. That such a high price is exacted by the corporate elite is itself instructive, for it has not been demonstrated that the bland and well-rounded personality results in more sales or higher production. Rather, this outlook is what management finds congenial to its own sensibilities. More significant, the habits inculcated in work-life inevitably spill over into private life—if such it can be called. The kinds of attitudes necessary for career-success are imparted to children and pervade marriage and other social relations.

The corporate elite decides what kinds of jobs are to be made available and how many of them there are to be. This is not simply management's traditional power to hire and fire. It is also the power to decide what kind of work individuals will do for a living. The decision to automate, for example, lessened the need for blue-collar workers and created permanent underemployment for many groups in society. The earlier decision to expand the number of white-collar jobs opened new opportunities to millions of Americans, thus elevating them to new stations in life and creating not only new benefits but also new anxieties. People fill jobs; jobs are not made for people. Corporate decisions to create certain types of employment cause people to alter their lives in such ways as to qualify for those positions. Those who cannot make the changes are consigned to the human discard-heap.

Corporate managements are free to decide where they will locate their plants and offices. The decision of many compa-

nies to have their headquarters in New York, for example, has
changed the face of that city. This power has also contributed,
probably more than anything else, to the suburban explosion,
for the burgeoning white-collar class must find a place to live.
A handful of executives decides which parts of the country are
to prosper and which are to stagnate. If over half the counties
in the United States lost population in the 1950–60 decade, this
is largely because the corporate elite was unwilling to locate
facilities in areas it considered unsuitable. On the other hand,
those regions it does favor experience a radical transformation.
New citizens move in and old values must adjust themselves
to new influences. Cities and towns, while welcoming branch
plants as sources of jobs and revenue, find that what were once
local decisions are now made from the outside and by outsiders.[10] Moreover, as corporations expand across the nation
they turn many of their white-collar employees into transients,
a rootless middle-class prepared to pick up stakes as management beckons it to new job opportunities. The nomadic life
has consequences for family and personality that are not without their disturbing qualities.

Quite obviously even the most respected corporation, with
the most persuasive advertising agency, cannot induce the
American public to buy a white elephant. But the example of
the Edsel—like President Kennedy's 1962 ultimatum on steel
prices—is an exception proving the rule. For if management is
sensitive to the kinds of products that consumers will be willing to purchase, it also has the power to persuade the public
that it ought to own such goods. Even more autonomy surrounds
decisions on methods and materials of production. What should
be noted is that the number and character of possessions have
a signal impact on the personality of the owner.[11] Materialism
is not uniquely American, nor is the high valuation placed on
material possessions entirely the result of management decisions. But the perpetuation of this system of values, with its
stress on tangible possession and labor-saving devices, is due
to the corporate elite's judgment about what sales are needed
if rates and turnover of production are to be kept at the optimum level.

Investment is the most important area of corporate decision-making, and it governs most of the decisions mentioned up to this point. Management alone decides when to invest—in new capital equipment, in new locations, in new processes, products, and personnel. It need not receive the approval of any governmental agency, and no such agency can compel a corporation to go ahead with an investment program if it feels like retrenching. While top executives will be attuned to the public's buying expectations, it can just as well shape those expectations by announcing a buoyant expansion program. The good will of investors need not be courted, since large corporations can use their retained earnings for investment purposes. And there is increasing reliance on the huge investing institutions—insurance companies, pension funds, banks, brokerage houses—for funds.[12] Representatives of these institutions sit on or are close to the boards of the large corporations and are really part of the corporate elite. Together they decide how and in what amounts capital will be invested over the decades to come. The power to make investment decisions is concentrated in a few hands, and it is the power to decide what kind of a nation America will be. Instead of government planning there is planning by an elite that is accountable to no outside agency. Its decisions set the order of priorities on national growth, technological innovation, and ultimately the values and behavior of human lives. Investment decisions are sweeping in their ramifications, and no one is unaffected by their consequences. Yet, this is an area where neither the public nor its government is able to participate. If the contours of the economy and society are being shaped in a hundred or so boardrooms, so far as the average citizen is concerned these decisions are in the lap of the gods.

Finally, it should be noted that the corporate elite is free to decide when the power at its disposal will not be used. It has already been noted that corporations have concluded that civil rights is not a concern of theirs, that they have made no voluntary effort to establish equal employment opportunities for all Americans. Ministers and professors may work for desegregation but executives, by far a more influential group, simply are not interested. While companies might, on their own initiative, endeavor to locate, train, and promote Negroes for positions of responsibility, such a suggestion would be looked upon as outlandish in any executive suite. Corporate management, by the same token, has decided that it bears no responsibility for upholding civil liberties, nor does it feel any obligation to stand behind employees who are attacked by self-appointed patriots. It might be proposed that corporations not only refuse to discharge employees who are unwilling to cooperate with legislative committees, but that they also make public their support for such dissenters. Needless to say, such a course of action does not occur to the corporate mind, even though such an exercise of influence would go far in the direction of defending freedoms of expression. Notwithstanding all the talk of a corporate conscience or a new dawn of corporate statesmanship, such rhetoric usually produces little more than a company contribution to the Boy Scouts or the Red Cross. On larger issues having political and moral overtones, the corporate elite remains quiescent, electing neither to lead the public when leadership is possible nor to defy the majority when that course is the only alternative.

These, then, are some of the decisions made by one segment of Mills' elite. These decisions add up to a substantial power, a power that is concentrated in a small circle of Americans who need not account for their behavior. The decisions of the corporate elite do not determine whether the nation is to have peace or war; but they do decide what will be the shape of the nation in the decades ahead. It should be clear by this time that the power of the corporate elite is not simply economic. On the contrary, its influence reaches far into society and has a deep impact on the character and personality of individual Americans. While additional forces are at work, the corporation is becoming our most characteristic institution and other agencies are taking secondary positions. As the corporation moves, so moves the nation. While predictions are difficult, it is possible to suggest that corporate tendencies will become accelerated in the years to come, with power growing more concentrated and individual citizens more dependent on large institutions for sus-

tenance and direction. Yet, even as this development takes
place, the power of the corporate elite will be invisible to the
unaided eye and the forms of political democracy will perpetuate the view that the public is master of its own destiny.

Mills never suggested that the corporate elite was a "conspiracy." The top managers of the largest companies do not
foregather at periodic intervals to make their key decisions in
concert. At the same time it is clear that they know what is on
one another's minds. Whether they come together casually at
their clubs or hunting lodges, or slightly more formally at the
Business Advisory Council or the Committee for Economic
Development or the Foreign Policy Association, they are definitely not isolated from each other. Informal conversation elicits
plans, hopes, and expectations. There is a community of interest
and sentiment among the elite, and this renders any thought of
a "conspiracy" both invalid and irrelevant. Moreover the critical
investment decisions bring together many members of the elite
—executives, bankers, brokers—and the agreement to expand
or retrench is clearly based on consultation and consensus. Such
decisions, in addition, are made with the knowledge of what
others are doing or plan to do. The lines of communication are
built into the system.

Nor is there any notion that the corporate elite is a "class,"
any more than the corporate world is "capitalist" in the traditional sense. The members of the elite come from a variety of
backgrounds, or at least from every stratum of the middle-
class.[13] Birth and breeding are of negligible importance, and
promotion to the highest corporate circles is based on talent
more than manners or connections. The conception of a "ruling
class" does not apply. Those in the elite group are simply the
men who sit in particular chairs at any particular time. The
chairs, moreover, have the power rather than their occupants.
And it is this point that deserves some elaboration.

The greater part of The Power Elite was a discussion of the
personal characteristics, backgrounds, and morals of the men
at the top. This emphasis on persons rather than positions grew
stronger as the book proceeded. Mills' closing paragraph deals

exclusively with the "men," the "they" who travel in the upper circles of power.

> The men of the higher circles are not representative men; their high position is not a result of moral virtue; their fabulous success is not firmly connected with meritorious ability. Those who sit in the seats of the high and the mighty are selected and formed by the means of power, the sources of wealth, the mechanics of celebrity, which prevail in their society. They are not men selected and formed by a civil service that is linked with the world of knowledge and sensibility. They are not men shaped by nationally responsible parties that debate openly and clearly the issues this nation now so unintelligently confronts. They are not men held in responsible check by a plurality of voluntary associations which connect debating publics with the pinnacles of decision. Commanders of power unequaled in human history, they have succeeded within the American system of organized irresponsibility.[14]

This, unfortunately, is a misplaced emphasis. It caused the book to be regarded as an attack on the *individuals* who preside over the corporate, military, and governmental bureaucracies. Mills, in so many words, accused these men of being not only pompous, vain, and ignorant, but also mediocre and immoral. This indictment has a great deal of truth in it. The men at the top are, as men, by no means an impressive group. Their character, however, is not at issue. For if the analysis is of power in contemporary American society, then the focus must be on the institutions rather than the individuals who staff them.

Mills gave some indication that this would be his line of approach in the opening pages of *The Power Elite.* There he pointed out that the elite are those with "access to the command of major institutions." Hope was held out that the institutions themselves would be analyzed in terms of their ability to make key decisions:

> The elite are simply those who have the most of what there is to have, which is generally held to include money, power, and prestige—as well as all the ways of life to which these lead. But the elite are not simply those who have the most, for they could not "have the most" were it not for their positions in the great institutions. For such institutions are the necessary bases of power,

of wealth, and of prestige. . . No one, accordingly, can be truly powerful unless he has access to the command of major institutions, for it is over these institutional means of power that the truly powerful are, in the first instance, powerful.[15]

There is little point in discussing who has the power unless one explores the sources of that power. This needs to be stressed because there is strong reason to believe that the institutional structure determines the behavior of the men who hold positions in it. Put another way, it does not really matter who the officeholders are as individuals; for anyone placed in such an office would have much the same outlook and display much the same behavior.

To be sure, it is a lot easier to talk of people than positions, of individuals rather than institutions. For one thing, only the most technically oriented reader can follow a discussion that omits personalities. Yet the really great social analysts—Marx, Weber, Veblen, Pareto—refused to be tempted in this direction. What is required, then, is an analysis of the great corporate institutions rather than the men who sit astride them.

Here are the names of a dozen of the institutions that direct the course of American society:

General Motors Corporation
Standard Oil Company of New Jersey
American Telephone and Telegraph Company
Atomic Energy Commission
Central Intelligence Agency (CIA)
Ford Foundation
National Education Association
Chase Manhattan Bank
Metropolitan Life Insurance Company
Columbia Broadcasting System
The New York Times
Merrill Lynch, Pierce, Fenner, and Smith

It is doubtful if even the well-informed citizen can name the president or chairman of half of these institutions. Nor should he feel any embarrassment about his ignorance. The man in one of the top chairs may have just arrived at his position last week, while the man in another may be just about to retire. Tenure is surprisingly short, and all incumbents are quite similar to those who have preceded and who will succeed them.

What is being said is that these institutions have lives and purposes of their own. No single person, not even the president or chairman, can be said to have made a critical corporate decision. If the man at the top sits at the controls, the car rides on rails he cannot move. The reason, of course, is that our corporate institutions are too large for a single individual to impress with his personality. Moreover the typical chief executive, sitting at the top for only a few years, spends much time in carrying out policies he did not himself inaugurate. His job is to organize his subordinates so that decisions will be carried out. He must, however, share the task of making those decisions, and it is hard to affix responsibility even at the top. The time has come when the institution in fact directs the man who in theory presides over it.[16]

The future holds in store a corporate America. The power that Mills attributed to the elite is a real power. The decisions the corporate elite is free to make are real decisions. Unfortunately the men at the top cannot in any meaningful way be held responsible for the actions the institutions take. Other men, in the same chairs, would behave no differently. At the same time we persist in thinking of great institutions as if they were small enterprises or voluntary associations. We assume either that they have no power or that their power is effectively nullified by countervailing forces. Corporate institutions are free to plan their future course of development, but they plan for their own purposes. The consequences are not simply profits but, more important, expansion of the corporate world into more and larger sectors of our national life. In defining their own roles and jurisdictions these institutions are oblivious to whether certain individuals are injured or neglected by the corporate thrust. At the same time they are above public control and take no responsibility for the social and psychological impact of their decisions. The situation, looked at from one vantage point, is highly rational and organized: corporate behavior is predictable and the corporate life is secure.

Viewed from a different direction a corporate America will

hang on the edge of anarchy. Despite their sophisticated rhetoric and civilized demeanor, the great institutions of the nation have the power to carry the public along a road it has not consented to travel and for which there are no discernible alternatives.

REFERENCES

1. Robert Bierstedt, *Political Science Quarterly*, 71 (December 1956), 607.
2. Alexander Heard, *Annals of the American Academy of Political and Social Science,* 311 (May 1957), 170.
3. Robert Dahl, *American Political Science Review,* 52 (June 1958), 466.
4. Daniel Bell, *American Journal of Sociology,* 64 (November 1958), 238. The "few instances," Bell points out, were all military decisions, such as dropping the atom bomb over Japan, intervening in Korea, and defending the offshore islands of Quemoy and Matsu. But these "examples" of autonomous elite decisions fail to underpin Mills' thesis. For they were, in reality, presidential decisions, and they were taken only after painstaking study of what the public reaction would be to them.
5. For an elaboration of this argument, see Andrew Hacker, "Common Men and Uncommon Men," *Nomos IV* (New York, 1962), pp. 308-33.
6. The steel industry is, of course, the outstanding example. See Gardiner C. Means, *Pricing Policy and the Public Interest* (New York, 1962).
7. The actual role of the presumed "owners" of American industry is laid bare in Joseph Livingston's *The American Stockholder* (Philadelphia, 1958).
8. In a *New Yorker* advertisement aimed at recruiting advertisers for its own columns, a newspaper widely circulated in executive circles proclaimed: "What the *Wall Street Journal* reader learns to favor, others everywhere will yearn to possess."
9. The better known are: William H. Whyte, Jr., *The Organization Man* (New York, 1956); Vance Packard, *The Pyramid Climbers* (New York, 1962); and Martin Gross, *The Brain Watchers* (New York, 1962).
10. The question of changing power relations in local communities is just beginning to be studied. For a brief analysis, see Ronald J. Pellegrin and Charles H. Coates, "Absentee-Owned Corporations and Community Power Structure," *American Journal of Sociology.* 61 (March 1956), 413-19. Mills himself did an important study in this area during World War II: "Small Business and Civic Welfare," Report of the Smaller War Plants Corporation to the Special Committee to Study Problems of American Small Business, Senate Document No. 135, 79th Congress, Second Session (Washington 1946).

11. The best work on new consumption patterns and what they mean has been done by David Riesman. See his essays in *Individualism Reconsidered* (Glencoe, 1954).

12. See A. A. Berle's two books, *The Twentieth Century Capitalist Revolution* (New York, 1954) and *Power Without Property* (New York, 1959).

13. For a study of the backgrounds of the presidents of America's 100 largest corporations, see Andrew Hacker "The Elected and the Anointed," *American Political Science Review,* 55 (September 1961), 539–49.

14. C. Wright Mills, *The Power Elite* (New York, 1956), p. 361.

15. *Ibid.,* p. 9.

16. John K. Galbraith has written: "Organization replaces individual authority; no individual is powerful enough to do much damage. Were it otherwise, the stock market would pay close attention to retirements, deaths, and replacements in the executive ranks of large corporations. In fact it ignores such details in tacit recognition that the organization is independent of any individual," *The Affluent Society* (Boston, 1958), p. 102. A former president of Du Pont, Crawford Grenewalt, says much the same thing: "The more effective an executive, the more his own identity and personality blend into the background of his organization." *The Uncommon Man* (New York, 1959), p. 72.

5 : The Public Philosophy: Interest-Group Liberalism

THEODORE LOWI

Until astonishingly recent times American national government played a marginal role in the life of the nation. Even as late as the eve of World War I, the State Department could support itself on consular fees. In most years revenues from tariffs supplied adequate financing, plus a surplus, from all other responsibilities. In 1800, there was less than one-half a federal bureaucrat per 1,000 citizens. On the eve of the Civil War there were only 1.5 federal bureaucrats per 1,000 citizens, and by 1900 that ratio had climbed to 2.7. This compares with 7 per 1,000 in 1940 and 13 per 1,000 in 1962—exclusive of military personnel.

The relatively small size of the public sphere was maintained in great part by the constitutional wall of separation between government and private life. The wall was occasionally scaled in both directions, but concern for the proper relation of private life and public order was always a serious and effective

From *American Political Science Review*, LXI (March 1967), 5–24.

issue. Americans always talked pragmatism, in government as in all other things; but doctrine always deeply penetrated public dialogue. Power, even in the United States, needed justification.

Throughout the decades between the end of the Civil War and the Great Depression, almost every debate over a public policy became involved in the larger debate over the nature and consequences of larger and smaller spheres of government. This period was just as much a "constitutional period" as that of 1789–1820. Each period is distinguished by its effort to define (or redefine) and employ a "public philosophy."

Lippmann's term is taken here to mean any set of principles and criteria above and beyond the reach of government and statesmen by which the decisions of government are guided and justified. This is not far removed from Lippmann's usage, except that he had in mind the abstract but quite specific public philosophy of bills of rights and natural law.[1] A country either possesses it or does not, loses it or regains it. We may end up agreeing that what Lippmann had in mind is the only public philosophy worthy of the name. But by altering the definition as above, we can use it analytically and critically in the mainstream of modern political science: A public philosophy is something that every stable polity possesses. It is the "political formula"—the "legal and moral basis, or principle, on which the power of the political class rests."[2] It is something that can and does change over generations. Some types of public philosophy may be better, in various ways, than others. And it is possible to discover what the prevailing public philosophy is and to assess its significance by straightforward interpretation of the policies of government and their impact, real or threatened, on society.

In the constitutional epoch immediately preceding our own, ending in 1937, the perennial issue underlying all debate on public policy—and therefore the key to public philosophy in that period—was the question of the nature of government itself and whether expansion or contraction best produced public good. Liberal and conservative regimes derived their principles and rationalizations of governing and policy formulation from their positions on the question. Expansion of government was demanded by liberals as the only means of combating the injustices of a brutal physical and social world that would not change as long as it was taken as natural. Favoring government expansion became the mark of the contemporary liberal. His underlying assumption was that the instruments of government provided the means for conscious induction of social change; without capacity for such change no experimentation with any new institutional forms or means of expanding rights would be possible. Opposition to such means, but not necessarily those forms or those rights, became the mark of the contemporary conservative.

There was unanimity on the criteria underlying the distinction between the adversaries. All agreed that a man's position was determined by his attitude toward government and his attitude toward deliberate social change or "planning." All agreed (and many persist in agreeing) that these two attitudes are consistent and reinforcing both as a guide for leaders in their choices among policies and as a criterion for followers in their choices among leaders. For example:

> Conservatism is committed to a discriminating defense of the social order against change and reform (liberalism). . . . By the Right, I mean generally those parties and movements that are skeptical of popular government, oppose the bright plans of the reformers and dogooders, and draw particular support from men with a sizeable stake in the established order. By the Left, I mean generally those parties and movements that demand wider popular participation in government, push actively for reform, and draw particular support from the disinherited, dislocated and disgruntled. As a general rule, to which there are historic exceptions, the Right is conservative or reactionary, the Left is liberal or radical.[3]

These two criteria arose out of a particular constitutional period, were appropriate to that period, and provided a mutually reinforcing basis for doctrine during the period. After 1937, the Constitution did not die from the Revolution, as many had predicted it would. But the basis for the doctrine of that period did die. Liberalism-conservatism as the source of the public philosophy no longer made any sense. Once the principle of positive government in a growing and indeterminable political sphere was established, criteria arising out of the very issue of *whether* such a principle should be established became extinguished. They were extinguished by the total victory of one side of the old dialogue over the other.

The old dialogue has passed into the graveyard of consensus. Yet is persists. Since it has no real, operable meaning any more, it is almost purely ritualistic. However, its persistence has had its real effects. The persistence of this state of affairs so far beyond its own day, has been responsible for two pathological conditions in the 1960's. The first is that the empty rhetoric has produced a crisis of public authority. Without a basis for meaningful adversary proceedings, there has been little, if any, conflict among political actors at the level where each is forced regularly into formulating general rules, applicable to individual acts of state and at one and the same time ethically plausible to the individual citizen. The tendency of individuals to accept governmental decisions because they are good has probably at no time in this century been less intense and less widely distributed in the United States. This is producing many problems of political cynicism and irresponsibility in everyday political processes; and these problems, in turn, have tended toward the second pathological condition, the emergence of an ersatz public philosophy that seeks to justify power and to end the crisis of public authority by parceling out public authority to private parties. That is, the emerging public philosophy seeks to solve the problem of public authority by defining it away. A most maladaptive "political formula," it will inevitably exacerbate rather than end the crisis, even though its short-run effect is one of consensus and stabilization.

THE OLD FORMULA VERSUS THE NEW TIMES

A brief look at a few hard cases will be sufficient to show how little can really be drawn from the old public philosophy to justify the key modern policies and practices in either the public or the private spheres. Figure 1 helps to show at a glance just how irrelevant the old criteria are. Diagramming and analyzing policies as "techniques of control" was used to good effect by Dahl and Lindblom.[4] In Figure 1 are arranged a few selected public policies and private policies or widely established practices. They are placed in two dimensions according to the two basic attributes of liberalism-conservatism. Above the line are public policies; below the line are private policies or examples of established business and group practices. This vertical dimension is a simple dichotomy.[5] Therefore, above the line is the "liberal" dimension, and below the line the "conservative" dimension. The horizontal dimension is a continuum. Each policy or practice is placed along the line from left to right roughly according to its real or probable impact upon the society. To the left is the liberal direction, where policies are placed if they are likely to affect a direct change in things. To the right is the conservative direction, where policies and practices are placed if they tend directly to maintain one or another status quo.

If the two criteria—attitude toward government and attitude toward change—were consistent and if together they described and justified programs, then liberal policies would be concentrated in the upper left corner, and conservative policies would be concentrated below the line to the right. Little study of the Diagram is necessary to discover that the inconsistencies between the two criteria are extreme. And little reflection is necessary to see that policy makers are being guided by some other principles, if principles do guide at all. The fact that private and public policies range across the extremes of maintenance and change suggests the simple but significant proposition that no institution with the capacity and resources for affecting the society works always in the same direction.[6] Yet a public philosophy based upon public-private and change-maintenance criteria requires unidirectional institutions. Obviously, the liberal-conservative dialogue made sense only up until, but not after, the establishment of positive government.[7]

Analysis of the real or potential impact of public policies shows how incomplete is the fit between the earlier public philosophy and the policies it is supposed to support and justify.

FIGURE 1. *Selected Public and Private Policies Arranged According to Probable Effect on Society*

Graduated income tax (potential)		Growth fiscal policies Graduated Income Tax (U.S.)	Counter-cyclical fiscal policies	Social Security programs based on insurance principles (U.S.)	Existing farm programs	Kennedy-Freeman farm proposals)
Social Security programs based on graduated income tax	Luxury taxes		Sales taxes			High tariffs Import quotas Utilities
	Real antitrust			Direct regulation (e.g. FCC, ICC, CAB, etc.)	Restraint of competition (NRA, fair trade, antiprice discrim.)	Group representation on boards
Civil rights package			Aids to small business			
Low tariffs	"Yardstick" regulation (TVA)			Antitrust by consent decree	Tax on colored margarine	Strict gold standard with no bank money
Competition in agriculture	Oligopoly with research competition	Oligopoly without competition (steel, cigarettes)	Trade associations	Monopoly		
New interest groups			Pools	Old interest groups (NAM, AFL-CIO, TWU, etc.)		
Competitive business		Brand names	Basing points			
Corporate philanthropy		Ethnic appeals of political campaigns	Price leadership			
			Fair trade policies			
Merit hiring and promotion			Union employment and automation policies			

Above the line: Public policies ("liberal").
Below the line: Private policies or practices ("conservative").
Toward the left side: Policies likely to produce change ("liberal").
Toward the right side: Policies likely to maintain existing practices ("conservative").

It shows that those who espouse social change in the abstract, especially government-engineered social change, are seldom peddling policies that would clearly effect any such change. Conversely, it shows that those who harangue on principle against government and change are frequently in real life pushing for strong doses of each. If these criteria do not really guide the leaders, they offer almost no plausible justification for the intelligent follower. A few examples in detail follow.

1. The income tax. All taxes discriminate. The political question arises over the kind of discrimination the society desires. The graduated or progressive income tax is capable of effecting drastic changes in the relations among classes and between man and his property. According to the two criteria in question, then, the steeply progressive income tax is "liberal" both because it is governmental and because it effects social change. Our own income tax structure can be called only mildly "liberal," if at all, because it is only mildly, if at all, progressive, allowing as it does full exemption on interest from public debt, fast write-offs, depletion allowances, host of "Louis B. Mayer Amendments," privileges on real estate transactions, and so on *ad nauseum*. It is generally understood that the effective ceiling on taxes is not 91% or 75% but a good deal less than 50%. And considering all taxes together, it seems fairly clear that they comprise a bastion against rather than a weapon for fluidity among classes and channels of opportunity. This is not an argument in favor of the one tax structure or the other, but rather one in favor of the proposition that no trace of a sign can be found of liberal-conservative principles underlying taxation, not even as a guide to compromise. During the legislative action in 1963–64, there was much discussion and debate on the impact of the tax cut on the rate of aggregate economic growth. But there was almost no consideration of the tax structure or the tax cut for its significance to the society. In fact, plans for large-scale tax reform were withdrawn altogether before the tax bill was ever formally proposed. As a consequence, taxation in the United States is a government policy to preserve the established economic relations among people and classes.

2. The social security system. This is, of course, a bundle of

policies, and accuracy would require classification of each. On balance, however, they are "liberal" only because they are governmental; they are conservative in their impact on social structure and opportunity. If they promote welfare, then, indeed, it is important to be able to say that a conservative policy *can* promote welfare. Above all else, old age insurance, unemployment compensation and the like are techniques of fiscal policy. They are, initially, important countercyclical devices, "automatic stabilizers," that work through the maintenance of demand throughout the business cycle and through the maintenance of existing economic relationships without dislocation. In this dimension, "liberals" are a good deal less willing to take chances than "conservatives."

At another dimension, social security in the United States is an even more interesting case of the gap between the old public philosophy and the real impact of established programs. For, social security programs are techniques of social as well as fiscal control, and as such they are clearly conservative. The American system of social security is based fairly strictly on an insurance principle, a principle of the spreading of risk through forced saving. Government's role is essentially paternalistic; speaking roughly, government raises the minimum wage by the amount of the employer's contribution, takes that plus about an equal amount from the employee's wages, and says, "This much of your income we'll not trust you to spend." This principle of contributory social security does not affect the class structure, the sum total of opportunity, or anything else; on the contrary, it tends to maintain existing patterns. It helps make people a little happier to be where they are doing what they are doing. The social security system is consistent with both criteria of liberalism only to the extent that it is based on a graduated income tax or to the extent that it supports those who did not contribute before entering the rolls. And that is a very small extent indeed.

The medicare program is significant as an addition to the scope and scale of social security, but in no important way does it change the social significance of social security. After President Kennedy proposed a medical care bill limited to the aged and based on "actuarial soundness," there was not even any need to debate the social significance of the bill. Actuarial soundness was a sufficient message that social security would remain altogether what it had been, except for the temporary addition of people who were already old and had made no contribution before entering the rolls. The only surprise in the medicare case was the difficulty of passage. But that was not due to a stalemate between liberalism and conservatism. It was due to a stalemate between the unorganized and apathetic elderly and the intensely felt and highly organized trade union interests of the American Medical Association. A program that originated with Bismarck was simply a while longer being needed in the United States.

3. The farm programs provide an equally good case of the irrelevance of policy to the old public philosophy. High price supports with crop controls, the center of farm policy for a generation, are supported by "liberals"; but they are "liberal" because and only because they are governmental. The entire establishment escaped death in 1949–50 only with urban-labor support, but that support proves nothing about liberalism.

What has been the purpose and what is the impact of such a program? Basically, the aim was to restore and to maintain a pre-1914 agriculture in face of extremely strong contrary financial, industrial and technological developments. The effect of the program has clearly been as intended, for far larger numbers of farmers and subsistence farms remain than are supportable in strictly economic terms. And the program perpetuates the established sizes of a farm and relationships among farmers by basing present quotas and controls upon past outputs, state by state, county by county, and farm by farm. The New Frontier and Great Society proposals must be ranked as even more "conservative," despite their governmental base, because they would have delegated to a few leading farmers or farm group leaders in each surplus commodity area the power to determine the quotas, thus allowing those most involved to decide *for themselves* just what there is about agriculture worth conserving. This is elevation of government-by-conflict-of-interest to a virtuous principle. Early in his presidency, Lyndon Johnson called the leaders of the major agriculture interest groups to formulate new policy solutions to agriculture. This was the beginning of the Johnson round. In music, a round is a form in which everything is repeated over and over again.

4. Business practices. The "conservative" side of the argument comes out no better upon examination. Competitive business enterprise is a highly dynamic force that usually makes change normal, innovation necessary, and influence by ordinary individuals over economic decisions possible. For these reasons many forms of competitive enterprise should be thought of as supported by real liberals despite the fact that government is only in a marginal way responsible for it. But, except for martyrs from Thurmond Arnold to Walter S. Adams who have sought vainly to use government to decentralize industry, the net impact of attitudes toward business from conservatives as well as liberals has been to restrain the system. One might say that the only difference between old-school liberals and conservatives is that the former would destroy the market through public means and the latter through private means. This is very largely due to the fact that, lacking any independent standards, all politicians depend upon those organized interests that already have access to government and to the media of communication. According to the second criterion of liberalism-conservatism, *all established interest groups are conservative.*[8] Government policy is one of many strategies organized interests feel free to pursue. In this respect it is useless to distinguish between NAM and AFL-CIO. Trade associations, for example, exist to "stabilize the market," in other words, to maintain existing relations among members despite any fluctuations in their respective sectors of the economy. They, in turn, are the primary determiners of private as well as public policies toward business and business competition. Holding companies, pools, market sharing, information sharing, interlocking directorships, price leadership, competition through advertising and not prices, and collusion in bidding are typical non-governmental policies, which become inevitable if they are not illegal. On the other hand, they are functionally in no way distinguishable from such governmental policies as basing points laws, fair trade laws, antiprice discrim-

ination laws, NRA codes, and so on. To the extent that liber-alism-conservatism is taken seriously as the source of public philosophy, liberals-conservatives become hemmed in by it, too rigid to withdraw their sentiments as new needs become old, vested interests. They are inevitably betrayed by the very groups that profited most by their support.

The enormous inconsistency between what public policy really is and what the old doctrine supposes it to be may turn out to be merely true but still inconsequential. This might be the case if it could be shown that American public men were the original pragmatists and were never in need of any doctrine other than the loose social code that binds us all. This possi-bility must be rejected. Stable countries, with their highly ra-tionalized political order, have great need of legitimizing rituals, perhaps more so than transitional societies where expectations are not so high. Moreover, the very persistence of the old cri-teria so far beyond their appropriate hour can be taken as an index to the need American elites have for doctrinal support.

The old public philosophy became outmoded because in our time it applies to the wrong class of objects. Statesmen simply no longer disagree about whether government should be in-volved; therefore they neither seek out the old criteria for guid-ance through their disagreements, nor do they really have need of the criteria to justify the mere governmental character of policies. But this does not mean that public men are not now being guided by some other, widely shared, criteria that do apply to the relevant class of objects. The good functionalist must insist upon being guided by the hypothesis that some political formula or public philosophy does exist. If it is obvi-ous that public men are no longer governed by the older public philosophy, then the next logical proposition is this: that there is some other public philosophy with which public policy be-haviors are consistent, but it may be one not clearly enough formulated to be well known yet beyond public men them-selves.

I contend that such criteria have emerged in a new and al-ready well-developed public philosophy through which public men are attempting to grapple with the pathologies created by the persistence of the old formula. I contend, further, that the new public philosophy is the source of important new political pathologies in America. I contend, finally, that the new public philosophy is pathological because it emerged not out of an evolution of the older but out of the total and complete silence of the older upon those objects with which any new public philosophy had to deal.

INTEREST-GROUP LIBERALISM

The weaknesses of the old liberalism-conservatism were not altogether clear before the 1960's. This tardiness is due simply to the intervention of two wars and then an eight-year period of relative quiescence in policy making and in the saliency of politics and government to the masses. Truman's Fair Deal agenda, already left over from the end of the New Deal, held fire for over a decade until it became a major part of the Democratic agenda of the 1960's and comprised a very large proportion of the successful record of the 89th Congress, the most actively legislating Congress since 1933. Even the historic *Brown v. Board of Education* decision failed to bring about noticeable expansion and intensification of political activity until the Little Rock debacle of 1957. With increasing pace thereafter, new pressures began to be placed upon political institutions, and another round of governmental activity was in the making. In many ways the period that began in 1957 with Little Rock and Sputnik was as much a constitutional revolution as that of the 1930's. In this decade—as measured by Federal budgets, personnel, the sheer proliferation of service and other agencies, or the expansion of public regulatory authority—there has clearly been a civil rights revolution, an educational revolution, and a scientific and technological revolution.

All of this activity proves that there is no end to government responsibility. It is not possible to automate all the stabilizers. The new activity in the 1960's also proves that the political apparatus of democracy can respond promptly once the constitutional barriers to democratic choice have been lowered. However, that is only the beginning of the story, because the almost total democratization of the Constitution and the contemporary expansion of the public sector has been accompanied by expansion, not by contraction, of a sense of illegitimacy about public objects. Here is a spectacular paradox. We witness governmental effort of gigantic proportion to solve problems forthwith and directly. Yet we witness expressions of personal alienation and disorientation increasing, certainly not subsiding, in frequency and intensity; and we witness further weakening of informal controls in the family, neighborhood and groups. We witness a vast expansion of effort to bring the ordinary citizen into closer rapport with the democratic process, including unprecedented efforts to confer upon the poor and ineducable the power to make official decisions involving their own fate. Yet at the very same time we witness crisis after crisis in the very institutions in which the new methods of decision-making seemed most appropriate.

It is as though each new program or program expansion were admission of prior governmental inadequacy or failure without necessarily being a contribution to order and well-being. The War on Poverty programs have become as often as not instruments of social protest. The Watts riots, the movements for police review boards in many cities, the sit-ins and marches even where no specifically evil laws are being enforced against a special race or group, the strikes and protests by civil servants, nurses, doctors, teachers, transport and defense workers, and others in vital occupations—all these and many others are evidence of increasing impatience with established ways of resolving social conflict and dividing up society's values. Verbal and organizational attacks on that vague being, the "power structure," even in cities with histories of strong reform movements and imaginative social programs, reflect increasing rejection of pluralistic patterns in favor of more direct prosecution of claims against society. Far from insignificant as a sign of the times is emergence of a third and a fourth national party movement, one on either extreme but alike in their opposition to centrist parties, electoral politics, and pre-election compromise. Many of these new patterns and problems may have been generated by racial issues, but it is clear that that was only a precipitant. The ironic fact is that the post-1937 political economy, either because of or in spite of government policies and two wars, had produced unprecedented prosperity, and as the national output increased arithmetically the rate of rising expectation must have gone up geometrically—in a modern expression of the Malthusian Law. Public authority was left to grapple with this alienating gap between expectation and reality.[9]

Prosperity might merely have produced a gigantic race among all to share in its benefits. The expansion of the public sector might have increased the legitimacy of government and other public objects through redistribution of opportunities to join the prosperity. Instead, the expansion of government that helped produce sustained prosperity also produced a crisis of public authority. Why? Because the old justification for that expansion had so little to say beyond the need for the expansion itself. The class of objects to which the new and appropriate public philosophy would have to apply should, it seems obvious, be the forms, structures and procedures of government control. There are vast technical, political and ethical questions involved in what are and what ought to be the consequences of the various ways in which power can be administered and employed. What constitutes "due process" in an age of positive government? What impact does one or another administrative process have upon society, upon the specific clientele whose compliance is sought, upon the sense of legitimacy among citizens, and upon the capacity of the next generation to respond, governmentally and otherwise, to the problems of its own time?

Out of the developing crisis in public authority has developed an ersatz political formula that does, for all its problems, offer the public man some guidance and some justification in his efforts to shape, form and provide for the administration of positive laws in the positive state. There are several possible names for this contemporary replacement of liberalism-conservatism. A strong possibility would be *corporatism*, but its history as a concept gives it several unwanted connotations, such as conservative Catholicism or Italian fascism, that keep it from being quite suitable. Another is *syndicalism*, but among many objections is the connotation of anarchy too far removed from American experience or intentions. However, the new American public philosophy is a variant of those two alien philosophies.

The most clinically accurate term to describe the American variant is *interest-group liberalism*. It may be called liberalism because it expects to use government in a positive and expansive role, it is motivated by the highest sentiments, and it possesses strong faith that what is good for government is good for the society. It is "interest-group liberalism" because it sees as both necessary and good that the policy agenda and the public interest be defined in terms of the organized interests in society. In brief sketch, the working model of the interest group liberal is a vulgarized version of the pluralist model of modern political science. It assumes: (1) Organized interests are homogeneous and easy to define, sometimes monolithic. Any "duly elected" spokesman for any interest is taken as speaking in close approximation for each and every member.[10] (2) Organized interests pretty much fill up and adequately represent most of the sectors of our lives, so that one organized group can be found effectively answering and checking some other organized group as it seeks to prosecute its claims against society.[11] And (3) the role of government is one of ensuring access particularly to the most effectively organized, and of ratifying the agreements and adjustments worked out among the competing leaders and their claims. This last assumption is supposed to be a statement of how our democracy works and how it ought to work. Taken together, these assumptions constitute the Adam Smith "hidden hand" model applied to groups. Ironically, it is embraced most strongly by the very people most likely to reject the Smith model applied in its original form to firms in the market.

These assumptions are the basis of the new public philosophy. The policy behaviors of old-school liberals and conservatives, of Republicans and Democrats, so inconsistent with liberalism-conservatism criteria, are fully consistent with the criteria drawn from interest-group liberalism: *The most important difference between liberals and conservatives, Republicans and Democrats*

—however they define themselves—*is to be found in the interest groups they identify with. Congressmen are guided in their votes, Presidents in their programs, and administrators in their discretion, by whatever organized interests they have taken for themselves as the most legitimate; and that is the measure of the legitimacy of demands.*

The assumptions of the model and the concluding behavioral proposition constitute, for better or worse, an important part of the working methodology of modern, empirical political science. However, quite another story with quite different consequences is how all of this became elevated from an hypothesis about political behavior to an ideology about how the democratic system ought to work and then became ultimately elevated to that ideology most widely shared among contemporary public men.

Interest-group Liberalism: An Intellectual History. The opening of the national government to positive action on a large scale was inevitably to have an impact upon political justification just as on political technique. However, the inventors of technique were less than inventive for justification of particular policies at particular times. Hansen, for instance, has observed that Keynes was no social reformer, nor had he any particular commitments to particular social ends.[12] Keynes helped discover the modern economic system and how to help it maintain itself, but his ideas and techniques could be used, and indeed have been used, to support many points of view. "Collective bargaining, trade unionism, minimum-wage laws, hours legislation, social security, a progressive tax system, slum clearance and housing, urban redevelopment and planning, education reform," Hansen observed of Keynes, "all these he accepted, but they were not among his preoccupations. In no sense could he be called the father of the welfare state."[13]

Nor was the doctrine of popular government and majority rule, which was so important in the victory of liberalism over conservatism, adequate guidance after the demise of liberalism-conservatism. If one reviews the New Deal period and thereafter he will see how little propensity Americans have had to use the majority rule justification. The reasons for this are fairly apparent. Justification of positive government programs on the basis of popular rule required above all a proclamation of the supremacy of Congress. The abdication of Congress in the 1930's in the passage of the fundamental New Deal legislation could never have been justified in the name of popular government. With all due respect to Congressmen, little discernible effort was made to do so. Statutory and investigatory infringements on civil liberties during World War II and during the Cold War, plus the popular support of McCarthyism, produced further reluctance to fall back on Congress and majority rule as the fount of public policy wisdom. Many who wished to use this basis anyway sought support in the plebiscitary character of the Presidency. However, "presidential liberals" have had to blind themselves to many complications in the true basis of presidential authority and to the true—the bureaucratic—expression of presidential will.[14]

The very practices that made convincing use of popular rule doctrine impossible—delegation of power to administrators, interest representation, outright delegation of power to trade associations and so on—were what made interest-group liberalism so attractive an alternative. And because the larger interest groups did claim large memberships, they could be taken virtually as popular rule in modern dress. Interest-group liberalism simply corresponded impressively well with the realities of power. Thus, it possessed a little of science and some of the trappings of popular rule. Political scientists, after all, were pioneers in insisting upon recognition of the group, as well as in helping to elevate the pressure-group system from power to virtue. Political scientists had for a long time argued that the group is the necessary variable in political analysis for breaking through the formalisms of government.[15] However, there was inevitably an element of approval in their methodological argument, if only to counteract the kind of recognition of the group that Steffens and other progressives and Muckrakers were more than willing to accord. In 1929, Pendleton Herring concluded his inquiry with the argument that:

[The national associations] represent a healthy democratic development. They rose in answer to certain needs. . . . They are part of our representative system. . . . These groups must be welcomed for what they are, and certain precautionary regulations worked out. The groups must be understood and their proper place in government allotted, if not by actual legislation, then by general public realization of their significance.[16]

Following World War II, one easily notes among political scientists the widespread acceptance of the methodology and, more importantly here, the normative position. Among political scientists the best expression of interest-group liberalism was probably that of Wilfred Binkley and Malcolm Moos. The fact that it was so prominent in their American government basic textbook suggests that it tended to reflect conventional wisdom among political scientists even in 1948. Binkley and Moos argued that the "basic concept for understanding the dynamics of government is the multi-group nature of modern society or the modern state."[17] Political reality could be grasped scientifically as a "parallelogram of forces" among groups, and the public interest is "determined and established" through the free competition of interest groups: "The necessary composing and compromising of their differences is the practical test of what constitutes the public interest."[18]

The fact that a doctrine has some support in the realities of power certainly helps to explain its appeal as a doctrine.[19] But there were also several strongly positive reasons for the emergence of this particular doctrine. The first, and once perhaps the only, is that it has helped flank the constitutional problems of federalism. Manifestations of the corporate state were once limited primarily to the Extension Service of the Department of Agriculture, with self-administration by the land grant colleges and the local farmers and commerce associations. Self-administration by organized groups was an attractive technique precisely because it could be justified as so decentralized and permissive as to be hardly federal at all.[20] Here began the ethical and conceptual mingling of the notion of organized private groups with the notions of "local government" and "self-government." Ultimately direct interest group participation in government became synonymous with self-government, first for reasons of strategy, then by belief that the two were indeed synonymous. As a propaganda strategy it eased acceptance in the courts, then among the locals who still believed the farmer was and should be independent. Success as strategy increased usage; usage helped elevate strategy to doctrine. The users began to believe in their own symbols.

A second positive appeal of interest-group liberalism is strongly related to the first. Interest-group liberalism helps solve a problem for the democratic politician in the modern state where the stakes are so high. This is the problem of enhanced conflict and how to avoid it. The politician's contribution to society is his skill in resolving conflict. However, direct confrontations are sought only by the zealous ideologues and "outsiders." The typical American politician displaces and defers and delegates conflict where possible; he squarely faces conflict only when he must. Interest-group liberalism offers a justification for keeping major combatants apart. It provides a theoretical basis for giving to each according to his claim, the price for which is a reduction of concern for what others are claiming. In other words, it transforms logrolling from necessary evil to greater good. This is the basis for the "consensus" so often claimed these days. It is also the basis for President Kennedy's faith that in our day ideology has given over to administration. It is inconceivable that so sophisticated a person as he could believe, for example, that his setting of guidelines for wage and price increases was a purely administrative act. Here, in fact, is a policy that will never be "administered" in the ordinary sense of the word. The guidelines provide a basis for direct and regular policy-making between the President (or his agent) and the spokesmen for industry and the spokesmen for labor. This is a new phase of government relations with management and labor, and it is another step consistent with the interest-group liberal criterion of direct access.

The third positive appeal of interest-group liberalism is that it is a direct, even if pathological, response to the crisis of public authority. The practice of dealing only with organized claims in formulating policy, and of dealing exclusively through organized claims in implementing programs helps create the sense that power need not be power at all, nor control control. If sovereignty is parceled out among the groups, then who's out anything? As Max Ways of *Fortune* put it, government power, group power and individual power may go up simultaneously. *If* the groups to be controlled control the controls, *then* "to administer does not always mean to rule."[21] The inequality of power, ultimately the involvement of coercion in government decisions, is always a gnawing problem in a democratic culture. Rousseau's General Will stopped at the boundary of a Swiss canton. The myth of the group and the group will is becoming the answer to Rousseau in the big democracy.

President Eisenhower talked regularly about the desirability of business-government "partnerships," despite the misgivings in his farewell address about the "military-industrial complex." However, explicit and systematic expression of interest-group liberalism is much more the contribution of the Democrats. There is little reason to believe that one party believes more ardently than the other; but the best evidence can be found among the more articulate Democrats, especially in the words of two of the leading Democratic intellectuals, Professors John Kenneth Galbraith and Arthur Schlesinger, Jr.[22] To Professor Galbraith: "Private economic power is held in check by the countervailing power of those who are subject to it. The first begets the second."[23] Concentrated economic power stimulates other business interests (in contrast to the Smithian consumer), which organize against it. This results in a natural tendency toward equilibrium. But Galbraith is not really writing a theoretical alternative to Adam Smith; he is writing a program of government action. For he admits to the limited existence of effective countervailing power and proposes that where it is absent or too weak, government policy should seek out and support or, where necessary, create the organizations capable of countervailing. Government thereby pursues the public interest and makes itself superfluous at the same time. This is a sure-fire, nearly scientific, guide to interest-group liberalism. Professor Schlesinger's views are summarized for us in the campaign tract he wrote in 1960. To Schlesinger, the essential difference between the Democratic and Republican parties is that the Democratic party is a truly multi-interest party in the grand tradition extending back to Federalist No. 10. In power, it offers multi-interest administration and therefore ought to be preferred over the Republican Party and:

> What is the essence of a multi-interest administration? It is surely that the leading interests in society are all represented in the interior processes of policy formation—which can be done only if members or advocates of these interests are included in key positions of government. . . .[24]

This theme Schlesinger repeated in his more serious and more recent work, *A Thousand Days*. Following his account of the 1962 confrontation of President Kennedy with the steel industry and the later decision to cut taxes and cast off for expansionary rather than stabilizing fiscal policy, Schlesinger concludes:

> The ideological debates of the past began to give way to a new agreement on the practicalities of managing a modern economy. There thus developed in the Kennedy years a national accord on economic policy—a new consensus which gave hope of harnessing government, business and labor in rational partnership for a steadily expanding American economy."[25]

Interest-group Liberalism and Public Policies in the 1960's. A significant point in the entire argument is that the Republicans would disagree with Schlesinger on the *facts* but not on the *basis* of his distinction. The Republican rejoinder would be, in effect, "Democratic Administrations are *not* more multi-interest than Republican." And, in my opinion, this would be almost the whole truth. This principle has been explicitly applied in the formulation of a large number of policies, especially since the return of the Democrats to power in 1961. That is, policy makers have in numerous new programs added elements of official group representation and have officially applied "participatory democracy" to the implementation as well as the formulation of law as part of the justification of their action. There are additional policies where evidence of the application of interest-group liberalism is clear even though not as consciously intended or as much a part of the record of self-praise.

President Kennedy provides an especially good starting point because his positions were clear and because justification was especially important to him. No attention need be paid to the elements of liberalism-conservatism in his program[26] but only to the consistency of his requests with interest-group liberalism. John Kennedy was bred to a politics of well-organized and autonomous units of power. Locally they were more likely ethnic, religious and neighborhood organizations, but they had to be reckoned with as powerful interest groups. The national party he set out to win in 1956 was also a congeries of autonomous factions and blocs; and it has been said that he succeeded by recreating the "New Deal coalition." But there is a vast difference between pluralism inside political parties and legitimized pluralism built into government programs. The one does not necessarily follow from the other, unless leaders believe it is desirable. President Kennedy's proposals and rhetoric mark his belief in that desirability. Many of his most important proposals mark his very real contribution to the corporatizing of the government-group nexus in the United States.

The agriculture problem, high and early on the New Frontier agenda, was to be solved somewhat differently from all earlier attempts, and that difference is much to the point. At local levels, federal agriculture programs had always been corporative, with committees of local farm dignitaries applying the state and national standards to local conditions.[27] President Kennedy proposed simply to bring this pattern to the center and to have the farmers, represented by group leaders, *set* the standards as well as apply them. Essentially, this was NRA applied to agriculture.

There was no attempt to reinstitute an industrial NRA pattern, but there were, just the same, moves toward recognition of the organized side of industry in the "interior processes" of government. First, as earlier observed, by direct presidential act guidelines for profits and wages were set up. Notice was thereby served that henceforth "industrial policy" would be made by direct bargaining between President and each and every leader of an industrial sector. Quite separately, but along parallel industrial lines, this meant the same sort of bargaining between President and union leaders. It is beside the point to argue whether Kennedy or Johnson has been more lenient in applying the guidelines to the unions. It is even beside the point to argue whether this new technique of control means more government involvement and direction than alternative techniques. The point is that the pattern of control and the manner of its impact are basically corporativistic. "Partnership" is the measure of success.

Many other relations of government to industry have tended toward the same pattern in the 1960's, whether they come this way full-blown from President or emerge from Congress this way only at the end. COMSAT is a combination out of 1930's Italy and 1950's France. Like the Italian practice of "permanent receivership," COMSAT is a combine of kept private companies, sharing in stock and risk with the government. Like the many French public and mixed corporations, there is direct "interest representation" on the Board. The "public" stamp is placed on it by adding to the interest-laden Board three presidentially appointed members; but one of these is a representative of Big Labor and one a representative of Big Industry. By the end of 1966, there was already talk among the carriers (the communications industries) of forming a combine within the combine to regularize and stabilize losses suffered by any of them as a result of obsolescence and competition.

The Trade Expansion Act of 1962, for another example, was the first American tariff based upon broad categories of goods rather than single items. From the beginning, categorization of goods paralleled the lines of jurisdiction of the leading trade associations and organized farm commodities groups.[28] The semi-official role of trade associations was expected to increase and expand through those parts of the new law providing relief through subsidy for injuries proven to have been sustained by tariff cuts.

There were, of course, many Kennedy proposals that are economy-wide in intention, but even some of these have one peculiarity or another that distinguishes them less from the interest-group policies than first appearances suggest. The investment tax credit, for example, was industry-wide, but it involved a reduction rather than an enlargement of the governmental sphere. Appalachia involved a bold regional concept overwhelmingly broader than any organized groups; however, the strong veto power given the state governors allows for, and was expected to allow for, maximum return of group representation through the back door. Appalachia is more clearly a case of interest-group liberalism if we include, as we should, state and local government agencies as groups to be directly represented in implementation of policies. This becomes an important characteristic of "creative federalism." In Appalachia the governors in the region commit Federal funds to development plans formulated by state agencies, local agencies, and private groups.

During the Johnson Administration the doctrines and policies of interest-group liberalism have been elevated to new highs of usage and rationalization. It is coming of age by being provided with new and appropriate halo words. The most important is "creative federalism," about which President Johnson and his Great Society team have spoken frequently and enthusiastically. This and related terms—such as partnership, maximum feasible participation, and, above all, consensus—seem to be very sincerely felt by present government leaders. The sentiments are coming to be shared widely among non-government leaders and are at the bottom of the extraordinary business support Johnson received during his most active period of legislative creativity. Probably the most accurate and sympathetic analysis of creative federalism and the role it is playing in the Great Society has been provided by *Fortune Magazine*. As *Fortune* and many other observers would agree, creative federalism is not federalism. Federalism divides sovereignty between duly constituted levels of government. "Creative federalism" is a parceling of powers between the central government and *all* structures of power, governments and non-governments. In fact, little distinction is made between what is government and what is not. It is, according to the enthusiastic definition of *Fortune* writer Max Ways, "a relation, cooperative and competitive, between a limited central power and other powers that are essentially independent of it." The difference between federalism and "creative federalism" is no mere academic distinction. Creative federalism involves a "new way of organizing federal programs . . . [in which simultaneously] the power of states and local governments will increase; the power of private organizations, including businesses, will increase; the power of individuals will increase."[29]

In line with the new rationale, President Johnson and his Administration have expanded the degree to which private organizations and local authorities become endowed with national sovereignty. Corporativistic programs inherited from the New Deal have been strengthened in the degree to which they can share in the new, explicit rationale. This has been particularly noticeable in the power and natural resources field, where policies are now quite explicitly left to the determination of those participants who know the "local situation" best. It is quite at the center of Great Society expansions of existing programs. When still Assistant Secretary for Education, Francis Keppel described federal education policy this way: "To speak of 'federal aid' [to education] simply confuses the issue. It is more appropriate to speak of federal support to special purposes . . . an investment made by a partner who has clearly in mind the investments of other partners—local, state and private."[30]

The most significant contribution of the Great Society to the growing ratio such corporativistic programs bear to the sum total of federal activity is the War on Poverty, particularly the community action program. To the old progressive the elimination of poverty was a passionate dream, to the socialist a philosophic and historic necessity. To the interest-group liberal, poverty is becoming just another status around which power centers ought to organize. If one hasn't organized, then organize it. In so organizing it, poverty is not eliminated, but inconsistency in the manner of government's relation to society is reduced. Organizing the poor, something that once was done only in the Threepenny Opera, helps legitimize the interest-group liberal's preference for dealing only with organized claims. The "Peachum factor" in public affairs is best personified in Sargent Shriver. In getting the War on Poverty under way Shriver was misunderstood in many matters, particularly on any insistence that the poor be represented in some mathematically exact way. But one aspect of the doctrine was clear all the time. This was (and is) that certain types of groups should always be involved some way. As he listed them they are: "governmental groups," philanthropic, religious, business, and labor groups, and "the poor."[31] The significance lies primarily in the equality of the listing. "Governmental groups" are simply one more type of participant.

Interest-group liberalism thus seems closer to being the established, operative ideology of the American elite than any other body of doctrine. The United States is far from 100 per cent a corporate state; but each administration, beginning with the New Deal revolution, has helped reduce the gap. And it is equally significant that few if any programs organized on the basis of direct interest representation or group self-administration have ever been eliminated. To the undoubted power of organized interests has now been added the belief in their virtue. There would always be delegation of sovereignty to interest groups in some proportion of the total body of governmental activities. The new context of justification simply means far more direct delegation than the realities of power, unsupported by legitimacy, would call for.

In sum, modern liberals are ambivalent about government. Government is obviously the most efficacious way of achieving good purposes in our age. But it is efficacious because it is involuntary; as one of the founders of modern social science put it, modern government possesses a monopoly of legal coercion in a society. To live with their ambivalence, modern policy makers have fallen into believing that public policy involves merely the identification of the problems toward which government ought to be aimed. It pretends, through "pluralism," "countervailing power," "creative federalism," "partnership," and "participatory democracy," that the unsentimental business of coercion is not involved and that the unsentimental decisions of how to employ coercion need not really be made at all. Stated in the extreme, the policies of interest-group liberalism are end-oriented. Few standards of implementation, if any, accompany delegations of power. The requirement of standards has been replaced by the requirement of participation. The requirement of law has been replaced by the requirement of contingency.

THE COSTS OF INTEREST-GROUP LIBERALISM

For all the political advantages interest-group liberals have in their ideology, there are high costs involved. Unfortunately, these costs are not strongly apparent at the time of the creation of a group-based program. As Wallace Sayre once observed, the gains of a change tend to be immediate, the costs tend to be cumulative. However, it takes no long-run patience or the spinning of fine webs to capture and assess the consequences of group-based policy solutions. Three major consequences are suggested and assessed here: (1) the atrophy of institutions of popular control; (2) the maintenance of old and creation of new structures of privilege; and (3) conservatism, in several senses of the word.

1. In his *The Public Philosophy*, Lippmann was rightfully concerned over the "derangement of power" whereby modern democracies tend first toward unchecked elective leadership and then toward drainage of public authority from elective leaders down into their constituencies. However, Lippmann erred if he thought of constituencies only as voting constituencies. Drainage has tended toward "support group constituencies," and with special consequence. Parceling out policy-making power to the most interested parties destroys political responsibility. A program split off with a special imperium to govern itself is not merely an administrative unit. It is a structure of power with impressive capacities to resist central political control.

Besides making conflict-of-interest a principle of government rather than a criminal act, participatory programs shut out the public. To be more precise, programs of this sort tend to cut out all that part of the mass that is not specifically organized around values strongly salient to the goals of the program. They shut out the public, first, at the most creative phase of policy making—the phase where the problem is first defined. Once problems are defined, alliances form accordingly and the out-

come is both a policy and a reflection of superior power. If the
definition is laid out by groups along lines of established group
organization, there is always great difficulty for an amorphous
public to be organized in any other terms. The public is shut
out, secondly, at the phase of accountability. In programs in
which group self-administration is legitimate, the administrators
are accountable primarily to the groups, only secondarily to
President or Congress as institutions. In brief, to the extent
that organized interests legitimately control a program there is
functional rather than substantive accountability. This means
questions of equity, balance and equilibrium to the exclusion
of questions of overall social policy and questions of whether
or not the program should be maintained or discontinued. It
also means accountability to experts first and amateurs last;
and an expert is a man trained and skilled in the mysteries and
technologies of the program. These propositions are best illustrated by at least ten separate, self-governing systems (representing over 10 billion dollars per year in spending and loaning)
in agriculture alone.[32] There are many other, although perhaps
less dramatic, illustrations.

Finally, the public is shut out by tendencies toward conspiracy to shut the public out. One of the assumptions underlying direct group representation is that on the boards and in
the staff and among the recognized outside consultants there
will be regular countervailing and checks and balances. In
Schattschneider's terms, this would be expected to expand the
"scope of conflict." But there is nothing inevitable about that,
and the safer assumption might well be the converse. One
meaningful illustration, precisely because it is an absurd extreme, is found in the French system of interest representation.
Maurice Bye reports that as the communist-controlled union,
the CGT, intensified its participation in post-war government
it was able to influence representatives of interests other than
the employees. In a desperate effort to insure the separation
and countervailing of interests on the boards, the government
issued the decree that "each member of the board must be
independent of the interests he is not representing."[33] After a
1964 review of the politics of agriculture and of five major

efforts of their post-war administrations to bring the ten separate self-governing agriculture systems under a minimum of central control, I was led to the following conclusion:

> These systems . . . have become practically insulated from the three central sources of democratic political responsibility. Thus, within the Executive branch, they are autonomous. Secretaries of Agriculture have tried and failed to consolidate or even to coordinate related programs. Within Congress, they are sufficiently powerful to be able to exercise an effective veto or create a stalemate. And they are almost totally removed from the view, not to mention the control, of the general public. (Throughout the 1950's, Victor Anfuso of Brooklyn was the only member of the House Agriculture Committee from a non-farm constituency.)[34]

This, I suggest, is a tendency in all similarly organized programs.

2. Programs following the principles of interest-group liberalism create privilege, and it is a type of privilege particularly hard to bear or combat because it is touched with the symbolism of the state. The large national interest groups that walk the terrains of national politics are already fairly tight structures of power. We need no more research to support Michels' iron tendency toward oligarchy in "private governments." Pluralists ease our problem of abiding the existence of organized interests by characterizing oligarchy as simply a negative name for organization: In combat people want and need to be organized and led. Another, somewhat less assuaging, assertion of pluralism is that the member approves the goals of the group or is free to leave it for another, or can turn his attention to one of his "overlapping memberships" in other groups. But however true these may be in pluralistic *politics*, everything changes when some of the groups are co-opted by the state in pluralistic *government*. The American Farm Bureau Federation is no "voluntary association" insofar as it is a legitimate functionary in Extension work. NAHB, NAREB, NAACP or NAM are no ordinary lobbies after they become part of the "interior processes of policy formation."

The more clear and legitimized the representation of a group or its leaders in policy formation, the less voluntary is membership in that group and the more necessary is loyalty to its leadership for people who share the interests in question. And, the more clear the official practice of recognizing only organized interests, the more hierarchy is introduced into the society. It is a well-recognized and widely appreciated function of formal groups in modern societies to provide much of the necessary every-day social control. However, when the very thought processes behind public policy are geared toward those groups they are bound to take on much of the involuntary character of *public* control. The classic example outside agriculture is probably the Rivers and Harbors Congress, a private agency whose decisions in the screening of public works projects have almost the effect of law. And, as David Truman observes, arrangements where "one homogeneous group is directly or indirectly charged with the administration of a function . . . [in a] kind of situation that characterizes the occupational licensing boards and similar 'independent' agencies . . . have become increasingly familiar in regulatory situations in all levels of government."[35]

Even when the purpose of the program is the uplifting of the underprivileged, the administrative arrangement favored by interest-group liberalism tends toward creation of new privilege instead. Urban redevelopment programs based upon federal support of private plans do not necessarily, but do all too easily, become means by which the building industry regularizes itself. An FHA run essentially by the standards of the NAREB became a major escape route for the middle class to leave the city for suburbia rather than a means of providing housing for all. Urban redevelopment, operating for nearly two decades on a principle of local government and local developer specification of federal policy, has been used in the South (and elsewhere) as an effective instrument for Negro removal. Organizing councils for the poverty program have become first and foremost means of elevating individual spokesmen for the poor and of determining which churches and neighborhood organizations shall be duly recognized channels of legitimate demand. Encouragement of organization among Negroes and the White and non-White poor is important. Early recognition of a few among many emerging leaders and organizations as legitimate administrators or policy-makers takes a serious risk of destroying the process itself (more on this directly below).

3. Government by and through interest groups is in impact conservative in almost every sense of that term. Part of its conservatism can be seen in another look at the two foregoing objections: Weakening of popular government and support of privilege are, in other words, two aspects of conservatism. It is beside the point to argue that these consequences are not intended. A third dimension of conservatism, stressed here separately, is the simple conservatism of resistance to change. David Truman, who has not been a strong critic of self-government by interest groups, has, all the same, identified a general tendency of established agency-group relationships to be "highly resistant to disturbance." He continues:

New and expanded functions are easily accommodated, provided they develop and operate through existing channels of influence and do not tend to alter the relative importance of those influences. Disturbing changes are those that modify either the content or the relative strength of the component forces operating through an administrative agency. In the face of such changes, or the threat of them, the "old line" agency is highly inflexible.[36]

If this is already a tendency in a pluralistic system, then agency-group relationships must be all the more inflexible to the extent that the relationship is official and legitimate.

The war-on-poverty pattern, even in its early stages, provides a rich testing ground. I observed above that early official cooption of poverty leaders creates privilege before, and perhaps instead of, alleviating poverty. Another side of this war is the war the established welfare groups are waging against the emergence of the newly organizing social forces. Many reports are already remarking upon the opposition established welfare and church groups are putting up against the new groups. Such opposition led to abandonment of Syracuse's organize-the-poor project and the retreat of Sargent Shriver's Office of Economic Opportunity to "umbrella groups" spon-

sored by City Hall.[37] Old and established groups doing good
works might naturally look fearfully upon the emergence of
competing, perhaps hostile, groups. That is well and good—
until their difference is one of "who shall be the government?"
Conservatism then becomes necessary as a matter of survival.

The tendency toward the extreme conservatism of sharing
legitimate power with private organizations is possibly stronger
in programs more strictly economic. Adams and Gray reviewed
figures on assignment of FM radio broadcasting licenses and
found that as of 1955, 90 per cent of the FM stations were
merely "little auxiliaries" of large AM networks. They also
note that the same pattern was beginning to repeat itself in
FCC licensing of UHF television channels.[38] The mythology
may explain this as a case of "interest group power," but that
begs the question. Whatever power was held by the networks
was based largely on the commitment the FCC implied in the
original grants of licenses. Having granted exclusive privileges
to private groups in the public domain (in this case the original assignment of frequencies) without laying down practical
conditions for perpetual public retention of the domain itself,
the FCC had actually given over sovereignty. The companies
acquired property rights and legally vested interests in the grant
that interfere enormously with later efforts to affect the grant.
Thus, any FCC attempt to expand the communications business
through FM would deeply affect the positions and "property"
of the established AM companies and networks. Issuing FM
licenses to new organizations would have required an open
assault on property as well as the established market relations.
Leaving aside all other judgments of the practice, it is clearly
conservative.[39] Granting of licenses and other privileges uncon-
ditionally, and limiting sovereignty by allowing the marketing
of properties to be influenced by the possession of the privilege,
are practices also to be found in oil, in water power, in the
newer sources of power, in transportation, in the "parity" programs of agriculture.

Wherever such practices are found there will also be found
strong resistance to change. Already the pattern is repeating
itself in form and consequences in the policies regarding our

newest resource, outer space. As earlier observed, the private members of COMSAT very early in the life of the new corporation made arrangements to protect themselves against the impact of new developments on old facilities. In addition to that, and more significantly here, the constituents of COMSAT have moved to exclude all other possible entrants and alternative ways of organizing the economics of space communication. In response to Ford Foundation's proposal for a separate satellite system for educational television, COMSAT officially moved to cut off any chance of a rival by (1) opposing Ford vigorously, (2) interpreting the statute and charter to be a grant of trust for the entire public interest in the field, (3) seeking a ruling to that effect from the FCC, (4) showing that stockholders in COMSAT and in the carrier members of COMSAT, such as A.T.&T., would be dealt an unfair blow, and (5) producing an alternative plan whereby the Ford system would be created within COMSAT, being underwritten by all the major carriers and "users" (i.e., the telephone and telegraph companies and the commercial networks).[40]

There are social and psychological mechanisms as well as economic and vested interests working against change. As programs are split off and allowed to establish self-governing relations with clientele groups, professional norms usually spring up, governing the proper ways of doing things. These rules-of-the-game heavily weight access and power in favor of the established interests, just as American parliamentary rules-of-the-game have always tended to make Congress a haven for classes in retreat. For example, as public health moved from a regulatory to a welfare concept, local health agencies put up impressive resistance against efforts to reorganize city and county health departments accordingly. Herbert Kaufman chronicles the vain forty-year reorganization effort in New York City.[41] An important psychological mechanism working against change is one that can be found in criticisms of the electoral devices of proportional and occupational representation. PR tends to rigidify whatever social cleavages first provide the basis for PR, because PR encourages social interests to organize, then perpetuates them by allowing them to become "constituencies."

This is all the more true as interests actually become not merely groups but parties represented by name and bloc in parliament.[42] Even in less formalized situations, legitimizing a group gives it the advantages of exposure and usage as well as direct power, access and privilege.

INTEREST-GROUP LIBERALISM
AND HOW TO SURVIVE IT

Quite possibly all of these developments are part of some irresistible historical process. In that case policy-makers would never really have had any alternative when they created group-based programs. And in that case the ideology of interest-group liberalism simply reflects and rationalizes the realities of power. However, the best test of a deterministic hypothesis is whether real-world efforts to deny it fail. Thus, a consideration of remedies is worthwhile.

We might begin where Truman ended his extremely influential work on pluralistic America. After reviewing several possible "palliatives" Truman concludes essentially that the pluralistic political system is not doomed at all but, to the contrary, is self-corrective:

> To the extent that the kind of dynamic stability that permits gradual adaptation is a function of elements within the system itself, the key factors will not be new. The group process will proceed in the usual fashion. Whether it eventuates in disaster will depend in the future as in the past basically upon the effects of overlapping membership, particularly the vitality of membership in those potential groups based upon interests held widely throughout the society. The memberships are the means both of stability and of peaceful change. In the future as in the past, they will provide the answer to the ancient question: *quis custodiet ipsos custodes?* Guardianship will emerge out of the affiliations of the guardians.[43]

But it is self-corrective only if there is overlapping and confrontation among groups, and too many examples above suggest that (1) there is a strong tendency, supported by a great deal of conscious effort, to keep confrontation to a minimum and that (2) "membership in potential groups" is confined to values about the "rules-of-the-game" about which there is strong consensus in general but, due to their generality, extreme permissiveness in particular, short-run situations. Thus, it cannot be assumed that the conditions necessary for the self-corrective system necessarily exist. It is wrong to assume that social pluralism (which is an undeniable fact about America) produced *political* pluralism.

However, the important question is not whether Truman and others are wrong but whether the conditions necessary for their self-corrective system can be deliberately contrived. The effort here is to propose some such contrivances. Two introductory observations should be made about them. First, it is assumed that positive government is here to stay and expand. Thus, proposals for return to a principle of lesser government and for policies in the lower left-hand corner of the Diagram, while logical and perhaps desirable, are not acceptable. Second, it is assumed that *real* political pluralism is a desirable form of democracy and that it is a desirable democratic antidote to the "incorporated pluralism" which has been the object of criticism throughout this essay.

1. The first part of the remedy is attractive precisely because it is so obvious. This is to discredit interest-group liberalism as official ideology. Essentially, this is the effort of this paper. Unless we are locked in a predetermined secular trend, a change of ideology can affect the pattern of power just as the pattern of power can affect ideology. Certainly the egalitarian ideology has affected the distribution of power in every country where it has had any currency at all. A change of ideology could keep to a minimum the number of programs that merely incorporate the forces responsible for passage. Some other ideology would provide a basis for resisting many of the most outrageous claims for patronage and privilege made by organized interests.

2. The second part of the remedy is institutional and also suggests the direction a new ideology ought to take. This is to push direct group access back one giant step in the political process, somehow to insulate administrative agencies from full

group participation. This means restoration of the Federalist No. 10 ideology in which "factions" are necessary evils that require regulation, not accommodation. Madison defined faction as "a number of citizens, whether amounting to a majority or minority of the whole, who are united and actuated by some common impulse of passion, or of interest, *adverse to the right of other citizens, or to the permanent and aggregate interests of the community.*" As a manifestation of the ideology prevalent today, it is worth noting that Truman quotes Madison's definition but ends his quote just before the parts I emphasized above.[44] That part of Madison's definition should be returned to full faith and credit, and the only way to do that and to be sure that it and the true self-regulatory character of pluralism can be institutionalized is *to keep group interests in constant confrontation with one another in Congress.* Once an agency is "depoliticized" or "made independent" by handing it over to its organized clientele, the number of "factions" is reduced from a competitive to an oligopolistic situation; competition lasts only until the remaining few groups learn each other's goals and each adjusts to the others. Lippmann is concerned for a "derangement of power" in which *governing* has been drained away from the executive to the assembly and to the electorate, and neither is qualified to govern. The American pattern would suggest another kind of derangement altogether, a derangement brought about by Congress's direct extension of its own principles of representation over into the executive.

Pushing group representation and "participatory democracy" back into Congress and away from the executive requires several relatively traditional steps. The first would be revival of a constitutional doctrine that is still valid but widely disregarded. This is the rule that the delegation of legislative power to administrative agencies must be accompanied by clear standards of implementation.[45] This involves revival of the rule of law to replace the rule of bargaining as a principle of administration. It does not involve reduction of the public sphere. It *is* likely to make more difficult the framing and passage of some programs; but one wonders why any program should be acceptable if its partisans cannot clearly state purpose and means. Revival of the rule of law would also tend to dispel much of the cynicism with which the most active citizen views public authority.

Another way to restore competition to groups and ultimately push them back to Congress is to foster a truly independent executive. Development of a real Senior Civil Service is vital to this in the way it would tend to develop a profession of public administration, as distinct from a profession of a particular technology and a career within a specific agency. The makings of a Senior Civil Service lie already within the grasp of the Civil Service Commission if it has the wit to perceive its opportunity in its Career Executive Roster and its Office of Career Development and its Executive Seminar Center. The independent Senior Civil Servant, who could be designed for weakness in agency loyalty, combined with the imposition of clearer standards and rules governing administrative discretion, together would almost necessarily centralize and formalize, without denying, group access to agencies. In turn this would almost necessarily throw more groups together, increase their competition, expand the scope of that competition, and ultimately require open, public settlement of their differences. This would throw groups back more frequently into Congress and would also increase presidential opportunity to control the bureaucracies. The legitimacy of these institutions would be further confirmed.

3. A third part of the remedy has to do with programs themselves, although the recommendation overlaps No. 2 in that it has much to do with institutional roles. This is to set a Jeffersonian absolute limit of from five to ten years on every enabling act. As the end approaches, established relations between agency and clientele are likely to be shaken by exposure and opposition. This is as important as the need for regular evaluation of the existence of the program itself and of whether it should be abolished, expanded or merged with some other program. There is a myth that programs are evaluated at least once a year through the normal appropriations process and that specialized appropriations and authorizations subcommittees review agency requests with a fine tooth comb. However, yearly evaluation, especially the appropriations process, gets at only

the incremental and marginal aspects of most programs, rarely at the substance. Here is an example of the earlier distinction between functional and substantive accountability. The very cost-consciousness and detail that makes yearly review functionally rational is the basis of its weakness as a substantively rational process.

This proposal, like the proposal for a return to a rule of law, injects an element of inefficiency into the system. But our affluence is hardly worth the trouble if we cannot spend some of it on maintaining due process, pluralism and other system values. It also injects instability, but it is the very sort of instability that is supposed to make the pluralistic system work. It is amazing and distressing how many 1930's left-wing liberals have become 1960's interest-group liberals out of a concern for instability.

4. The fourth and final part of a reform program bears some resemblance to an old-line constitutional argument. Restoration of the *Schechter* and *Panama* requirement would tend to do more than strengthen the rule of law, enhance real political competition, and dispel political cynicism. It might also provide a basis for establishing some practical and functional limitations on the scope of federal power. That is to say, if an applicable and understandable set of general rules must accompany every federal program, then, except in some clear emergency, federal power could not extend to those objects for which no general rules are either practicable or desirable. Where regional or local variation is to be encouraged, State Government is really the proper unit. Argument for restoration of State Government is not based on mere antiquarian admiration of federalism or fear of national domination. It is an immensely practical argument. State Governments have been systematically weakened by Home Rule, by federal absorption of tax base, and by federal-local relations. Yet the cities, even with federal help, have proven unable to cope because the problems have outgrown their boundaries. The State possesses all the powers of its cities plus the territorial containment of most of the new metropolitan realities. The State may be the only governmental unit capable of coping with contemporary problems. Uncondi-

tional rebates of federal revenues to the States and obedience
to a rule of law may leave the way open for expansion of federal activities in which there is reasonable chance of success
without loss of federal control and without loss of legitimacy.

No individual interest group can be expected to take fullest
account of the consequences of its own claims. This is what
Presidents and Congresses are for, and this is what will continue to be delegated away as long as the ideology of interest-
group liberalism allows. In effect this means that restoring
pluralism as an effective principle of democratic politics requires destroying it as a principle of government. If this is to
be accomplished, reform must begin with the replacement of
interest-group liberalism with some contemporary version of the
rule of law. The program of reform must include at least: debate that centers upon the actual consequences of public policies and of their forms of implementation; a legislative process
that regularly treats enabling legislation rather than revision;
political brokers that have to deal in substantive as well as
functional issues; and adaptation of public controls to local
needs through choice of appropriate level of government rather
than through delegation of the choice to the most interested
parties.

REFERENCES

1. See especially Clinton Rossiter and James Lare (eds.), *The Essential Lippmann* (New York,Vintage, 1965), pp. 171 ff.
2. Gaetano Mosca, *The Ruling Class* (New York, McGraw-Hill, 1939),
p. 70.
3. Clinton Rossiter, *Conservatism in America* (New York, Knopf,
1955), pp. 12 and 15.
4. Robert A. Dahl and Charles E. Lindblom, *Politics, Economics and
Welfare* (New York, Harper, 1953), Chapter 1.
5. The distance above or below the line is not meant to convey additional information about the degree of public involvement. However, as Dahl and Lindblom's analysis suggests, that is a desirable
and practicable consideration.
6. Placement along the continuum is gross and informal. However, it
is clear that no basis for placing these policies according to impact
could reduce their spread. And, differences of opinion as to the
placement of specific policies (should antitrust go in the middle or

over on the left?) would lead to the very kind of policy analysis political scientists need to get involved in.

7. Some, especially "liberals," might object, arguing that the true basis of the distinction is public vs. private but that it involves much more than merely change vs. maintenance. Equality and welfare as well as change are the attributes of public policies. Adding dimensions to the one diagram would overly complicate it, but some response to the objection can be made: (1) A strong element of the equality dimension is already present in the sense that those policies on the left do present change and "change toward equality." However, (2) note the fact that, at least to this observer, "equality" is present among public but also among private policies and practices. Furthermore, (3) many public policies aim at the reduction of equalizing (as well as change) forces in the private sphere. Those in the upper right area of the Diagram serve as examples. Thus, "equality" is not a basis for distinguishing positions any more than "change," with or without consideration of the equality aspects of change. I will not attempt to defend the absence of the "welfare" dimension except to say that no definition of welfare could possibly show that it is strictly within the province of the public or the private sphere. Any diagram based on *any* definition of "welfare" would show policies above and below the line and to the left and the right.

8. They are so placed in Figure 1. Interest groups are not policies strictly speaking. However, individuals and corporations belong to and support trade associations and other groups as a matter of policy; and each such group formulates relatively clear policies supported by the members. Placing "old interest groups" in the lower part of Figure 1 and to the right is meant to convey two hypotheses: (1) that the existence of the group is itself conservative, and (2) that it is highly probable that the policies formulated by such old groups will be conservative.

9. The preceding two paragraphs were taken, with revision, from the Introductory Essay of my *Private Life and Public Order* (New York, W. W. Norton, 1967).

10. For an excellent inquiry into this assumption and into the realities of the internal life of the interests, see Grant McConnell, "The Spirit of Private Government," *American Political Science Review*, 52 (1963), 754–770; see also Clark Kerr, *Unions and Union Leaders of Their Own Choosing* (Santa Barbara, Fund for the Republic, 1957); and S. M. Lipset *et al.*, *Union Democracy* (New York, 1962). See also Arthur S. Miller, *Private Governments and the Constitution* (Santa Barbara, Fund for the Republic, 1959).

11. It is assumed that "countervailing power" usually crops up somehow. Where it does not, government ought to help create it. See John K. Galbraith, *American Capitalism* (Boston, Houghton Mifflin, 1952).

12. Alvin H. Hansen, *The American Economy* (New York, McGraw-Hill, 1957) pp. 152ff.

13. *Ibid.*, pp. 158–59. Keynes said ". . . the Class War will find me on the side of the educated bourgeoisie": quoted in *ibid.*, p. 158.

14. No citations are necessary to emphasize the fact that presidential delegation and subdelegation to administrators is just as extensive as congressional. As to the popular basis of presidential authority, see Robert A. Dahl, *A Preface to Democratic Theory* (Chicago, University of Chicago Press, 1956); and Willmoore Kendall, "The Two

Majorities," *Midwest Journal of Political Science,* 4 (1960), pp. 317–345.

15. For pioneer expressions, see Arthur F. Bentley, *The Process of Government* (Chicago, University of Chicago Press, 1908); and E. Pendleton Herring, *Group Representation Before Congress* (Baltimore, Johns Hopkins Press, 1929). More recent arguments of the same methodological sort are found in David Truman, *The Governmental Process* (New York, Knopf, 1951); and Earl Latham, *The Group Basis of Politics* (Ithaca, Cornell University Press, 1952).

16. *Op. cit.,* p. 268.

17. *A Grammar of American Politics* (New York, Knopf, 1950), p. 7.

18. *Ibid.,* pp. 8–9. In order to preserve value-free science, many pluralists ("group theorists") denied public interest altogether, arguing instead that there is a "totally inclusive interest" and that it is served by letting groups interact without knowing what it is. Cf. Truman, *op. cit.,* pp. 50–51.

19. For discussions of the extent to which group theory is a satisfactory statement of reality, see my "American Business, Public Policy, Case-Studies and Political Theory," *World Politics,* 16 (1964), pp. 677–715, and the excellent essays cited therein.

20: For more on the expansion and justification of these practices in agriculture see my "How the Farmers Get What They Want," *Reporter,* May 21, 1964, pp. 35ff.

21. " 'Creative Federalism' and the Great Society," *Fortune,* January, 1966, p. 122.

22. A third major intellectual of the Kennedy Administration was Professor Richard E. Neustadt. That he is a political scientist makes all the more interesting his stress upon the necessary independence of the Presidency rather than the desirability of presidential partnerships and countervailing power. See his *Presidential Power* (New York, Wiley, 1960).

23. Galbraith, *op. cit.,* p. 118.

24. Arthur Schlesinger, Jr., *Kennedy or Nixon—Does It Make Any Difference?* (New York, Macmillan, 1960), p. 43.

25. Arthur M. Schlesinger, Jr., *A Thousand Days,* as reprinted in *Chicago Sun-Times, January* 23, 1966, Section 2, p. 3.

26. By proper application of the old-school criteria, Kennedy was on balance conservative. Most of his programs belong to the right of center (on the Diagram, horizontal axis), and he did an amazing number of things that showed a preference for private sector activity (on the Diagram, vertical axis). Examples include his "actuarially sound" medicare, his investment tax credit and tax cut proposals, his preference for expansion of housing through investment incentives his reluctance to ask for new civil rights legislation, his appreciation for governmental contracting and other executive powers to deal with civil rights, his opposition to "Powell Amendments" and parochial school aid in federal education legislation, his concerted effort to make agriculture controls work, his support for very permissive depressed areas legislation that would bail out needy businesses and industries while reducing needs or pressures of entrepreneurs to move to some other section of the country.

27. See for example, "'How the Farmers Get What They Want," *op. cit.*

28. See Raymond Bauer *et al., American Business and Public Policy* (New York, Atherton, 1963), pp. 73ff.

29. *Op. cit.,* p. 122.

30. Quoted in *Congressional Quarterly,* Weekly Report, April 22, 1966, p. 833.

31. Jules Witcover and Erwin Knoll, "Politics and the Poor: Shriver's Second Thoughts," *Reporter,* December 30, 1965, p. 24.

32. "How The Farmers Get What They Want," *op. cit.*

33. Mario Einaudi *et al., Nationalization in France and Italy* (Ithaca, Cornell University Press, 1955), pp. 100–101, emphasis added.

34. "How The Farmers Get What They Want," *op. cit.,* p. 36.

35. *Op. cit.,* p. 462. For a profound appreciation of the public power of private authorities in occupational licensing, see York Willbern, "Professionalization in State and Local Government: Too Little or Too Much?" *Public Administration Review,* Winter, 1954. See also Arthur S. Miller, *op. cit.*

36. *Op. cit.,* pp. 467–468.

37. Witcover and Knoll, *op. cit.*

38. Walter S. Adams and Horace Gray, *Monopoly in America* (New York, Macmillan, 1955), pp. 48–50.

39. Cf. *ibid.,* pp. 44–46, and their discussion, from a different point of view, of the "abridgement of sovereignty by grants of privilege," See also Merle Fainsod *et al., Government and the American Economy* (New York, Norton, 1959), pp. 400–404. They observe the same thing happening in television and for the same reasons.

40. See accounts in *New York Times,* August 2 and August 29, 1966, and *Times Magazine,* August 12, 1966, p. 38.

41. Herbert Kaufman, "The New York City Health Centers," Interuniversity Case Program. Wallace Sayre and Herbert Kaufman in *Governing New York City* (New York, Russell Sage, 1960), Chapter XIX, generalize on this pattern. They refer to "islands of functional power" as the formal power structure of the city. Each island enjoys considerable autonomy, each is a system of administrators and their "satellite groups," each resists interactions with other islands. The big city is possibly in an advanced stage of what in this paper is observed as an important tendency at the national level. Because of the tragic stalemate in the cities, these pronounced city patterns might serve as a better warning than my illustrations drawn from national practices. See also Herbert Kaufman, *Politics and Policies in State and Local Governments* (Englewood Cliffs, Prentice-Hall, 1963), Chapter V.

42. Cf. Carl Friedrich, *Constitutional Government and Democracy* (Boston, Ginn and Co, 1950), pp. 291–294. See also a classic critique of occupational representation by Paul H. Douglas, "Occupational versus Proportional Representation," *American Journal of Sociology,* September, 1923; and David Truman, *op. cit.,* pp. 525–526.

43. *Op. cit.,* p. 535.

44. *Op. cit.,* p. 4.

45. This rule is made more interesting for the argument here because it was given new currency in the *Schechter Poultry* and *Panama Refining* cases, both of which involved the most extreme instance of delegation of sovereignty to groups, the NRA. For a recent expression, see Judge Henry J. Friendly's *The Federal Administrative Agencies* (Cambridge, Harvard University Press, 1962), pp. 5 ff.

6 Is There a Military-Industrial Complex which Prevents Peace?: Consensus and Countervailing Power in Pluralistic Systems

MARC PILISUK

THOMAS HAYDEN

The term "military-industrial complex" is very much in the literature. If its most sinister depictions are correct, then the peace researcher who works with the hope that his research may actually improve chances for world peace is wasting his time. A research finding, like a bit of knowledge, is always double-edged in what it portends for application. The project which tells us the surest steps to peace, tells us with equal certainty the steps which must be bypassed if peace is shunned. If there exists an omnipotent elite, committed to militarism, then there is simply no basis for hope that voices for peace have gotten, or can get, an influential channel into inner policy circles. If, on the other hand, the pluralist thesis can be said to apply in full even to basic policy directions of preparedness for war or for peace, then some influential decision makers must be eagerly awaiting the research findings on paths to

From the *Journal of Social Issues*, XXI:3 (1965), 67–68, 75–99. A longer version of this article appears in R. Perrucci and M. Pilisuk, *The Triple Revolution: Social Problems in Depth* (Boston: Little, Brown, 1968).

peace with intentions to press for their immediate application.

Because we agree with neither of the above positions, because we believe that most research workers in this area tend either to ignore or to over-rate the potential consequences of their work to peace, and because we feel that consideration of the conditions which dictate major directions of policy is essential for an evaluation of any contribution to peace research, we are bringing the concept of the "military-industrial complex" to both the microscope and the scalpel. The implications of this inquiry point to a research approach which does have relevance to the decision process and to the most central agencies of social change, and resistance to change, within American society. . . .

THE THESIS OF ELITE CONTROL

Mills is by far the most formidable exponent of the theory of a power elite. In his view, the period in America since World War II has been dominated by the ascendance of corporation and military elites to positions of institutional power. These "commanding heights" allow them to exercise control over the trends of the business cycle and international relations. The Cold War set the conditions which legitimize this ascendance, and the decline and incorporation of significant left-liberal movements, such as the CIO, symbolize the end of opposition forces. The power elite monopolizes sovereignty, in that political initiative and control stem mainly from the top hierarchical levels of position and influence. Through the communications system the elite facilitates the growth of a politically indifferent mass society below the powerful institutions. This, according to the Mills argument, would explain why an observer finds widespread apathy. Only a small minority believes in actual participation in the larger decisions which affect their existence and only the ritual forms of "popular democracy" are practiced by the vast majority. Mills' argument addresses itself to the terms of three basic issues, i.e., scope of decision power, awareness of common interest, and the definition of power exerted.

By *scope*, we are referring to the sphere of society over which an elite is presumed to exercise power. Mills argues that the scope of this elite is general, embracing all the decisions which in any way could be called vital (slump and boom, peace and war, etc.). He does not argue that *each* decision is directly determined, but rather that the political alternatives from which the "Deciders" choose are shaped and limited by the elite through its possession of all the large-scale institutions. By this kind of argument, Mills avoids the need to demonstrate how his elite is at work during each decision. He speaks instead in terms of institutions and resources. But the problem is that his basic evidence is of a rather negative kind. No major decisions have been made for 20 years contrary to the policies of anti-communism and corporate or military aggrandizement; *therefore* a power elite must be prevailing. Mills might have improved his claims about the scope of elite decisions by analyzing a series of actual decisions in terms of the premises which were *not* debated. This could point to the mechanisms (implicit or explicit) which led to the exclusion of these premises from debate. By this and other means he might have found more satisfying evidence of the common, though perhaps tacit, presuppositions of seemingly disparate institutions. He then might have developed a framework analyzing "scope" on different levels. The scope of the Joint Chiefs of Staff, for instance, could be seen as limited, while at the same time the Joint Chiefs could be placed in a larger elite context having larger scope. Whether this could be shown awaits research of this kind. Until it is done, however, Mills theory of scope remains open to attack, but conversely, is not subject to refutation.

Mills' theory also eludes the traditional requirements for inferring monolithic structure, i.e., consciousness of elite status, and coordination. The modern tradition of viewing elites in this way began with Mosca's *The Ruling Class* in a period when family units and inheritance systems were the basic means of conferring power. Mills departs from this influential tradition precisely because of his emphasis on institutions as the basic elements. If the military, political, and economic *institutional orders* involve a high coincidence of interest, then the groups composing the institutional orders need not be monolithic, conscious, and coordinated, yet still they can exercise elite power.[1] This means specifically that a military-industrial complex could exist as an expression of a certain fixed ideology (reflecting common institutional needs), yet be "composed" of an endless shuffle of specific groups. For instance, 82 companies have dropped out of the list of 100 top defense contractors, and only 36 "durables" have remained on the list in the years since 1940. In terms of industry, the percentage of contracts going to the automobile industry dropped from 25 per cent in World War II to 4 per cent in the missile age. At the same time, the aircraft companies went from 34 to 54 per cent of all contracts, and the electronics industry from 9 to 28 per cent (Peck and Scherer, 1962). Mills' most central argument is that this ebb-and-flow is not necessarily evidence for the pluralists. His stress is on the unities which underlie the procession of competition and change. The decision to change the technology of warfare was one which enabled one group to "overcome" another in an overall system to which both are fundamentally committed. Moreover, the decision issued from the laboratories and planning boards of the defense establishment and only superficially involved any role for public opinion. The case studies of weapons development by Peck and Scherer, in which politics is described as a marginal ritual, would certainly buttress Mills' point of view.

Making this institution analysis enables Mills to make interesting comments on his human actors. The integration of institutions means that hundreds of individuals become familiar with several roles: general, politician, lobbyist, defense contractor. These men are the power elite, but they need not know it. They conspire, but conspiracy is not absolutely essential to their maintenance. They mix together easily, but can remain in power even if they are mostly anonymous to each other. They make decisions, big and small, sometimes with the knowledge of others and sometimes not, which ultimately control all the significant action and resources of society.

Where this approach tends to fall short is in its unclarity about how discontinuities arise. Is the military-industrial complex a feature of American society which can disappear and still leave the general social structure intact? Horst Brand has suggested a tension between financial companies and the defense industries because of the relatively few investment markets created by defense (1962). Others are beginning to challenge the traditional view that defense spending stimulates high demand and employment. Their claim is that the concentration of contracts in a few states, the monopolization of defense and space industry by the largest 75 or 100 corporations, the low multiplier effect of the new weapons, the declining numbers of blue-collar workers required, and other factors, make the defense economy more of a drag than a stimulant (Melman *et al.*, 1963; Etzioni, 1964). Mills died before these trends became the subject of debate, but he might have pioneered in discussion of them if his analytic categories had differentiated more finely between various industries and interest groups in his power elite. His emphasis was almost entirely on the "need" for a "permanent war economy" just when that need was being questioned even among his elite.

However, this failure does not necessarily undermine the rest of Mills' analysis. His institutional analysis is still the best means of identifying a complex without calling it monolithic, conscious and coordinated. Had he differentiated more exactly he might have been able to describe various degrees of commitment to an arms race, a rightist ideology constricting the arena of meaningful debate, and other characteristics of a complex. This task remains to be done, and will be discussed at a later point.

Where Mills' theory is most awkward is in his assertions that the elite can, and does, make its decisions against the will of others and regardless of external conditions. This way of looking at power is inherited by Mills, and much of modern sociology, directly from Max Weber. What is attributed to the elite is a rather fantastic quality: literal omnipotence. Conversely, any group that is *not* able to realize its will even against the resistance of others is only "influential" but not an elite. Mills attempts to defend this viewpoint but, in essence, modifies it. He says he is describing a tendency, not a finalized state of affairs. This is a helpful device in explaining cracks in the monolith—for instance, the inability of the elite to establish a full corporate state against the will of small businessmen. However, it does not change the ultimate argument—that the power elite cannot become more than a tendency, cannot realize its actual self, unless it takes on the quality of omnipotence.

When power is defined as this kind of dominance, it is easily open to critical dispute. The conception of power depicts a vital and complex social system as essentially static, as having within it a set of stable governing components, with precharted interests which infiltrate and control every outpost of decision-authority. Thereby, internal accommodation is made necessary and significant change, aside from growth, becomes impossible. This conception goes beyond the idea of social or economic determinism. In fact, it defines a "closed social system." A "closed system" may be a dramatic image, but it is a forced one as well. Its defender sees events such as the rise of the labor movement essentially as a means of rationalizing modern capitalism. But true or false as this may be, did not the labor movement also constitute a "collective will" which the elite could not resist? An accommodation was reached, probably more on the side of capital than labor, but the very term "accommodation" implies the existence of more than one independent will. On a world scale, this becomes even more obvious. Certainly the rise of communism has not been through the will of capitalists, and Mills would be the first to agree. Nor does the elite fully control technological development; surely the process of invention has some independent, even if minor, place in the process of social change.

Mills' definition of power as dominance ironically serves the pluralist argument, rather than countering it. When power is defined so extremely, it becomes rather easy to claim that such power is curbed in the contemporary United States. The pluralists can say that Mills has conjured up a bogeyman to explain his own failure to realize his will. This is indeed what has been done in review after review of Mills' writings. A leading pluralist thinker, Edward Shils, says that Mills was too much influenced by Trotsky and Kafka:

Power, although concentrated, is not so concentrated, so powerful, or so permeative as Professor Mills seems to believe. . . .
There have been years in Western history, e.g. in Germany during the last years of the Weimar Republic and under the Nazis,
when reality approximated this picture more closely. . . . But as
a picture of Western societies, and not just as an ideal type of
extreme possibilities which might be realized if so much else that
is vital were lacking, it will not do (Shils, 1961).

But is Mills' definition the only suitable one here? If it is,
then the pluralists have won the debate. But if there is a way
to designate an irresponsible elite without giving it omnipotence, then the debate may be recast at least.

This fundamental question is not answered in the other major books which affirm the existence of a military-industrial
complex. Cook's *The Warfare State* and Perlo's *Militarism and
Industry* are good examples of this literature which is theoretically inferior to Mills' perplexing account.

Cook's volume has been pilloried severely by deniers of the
military-industrial complex. At least it has the merit of creating
discussion by being one of the few dissenting books distributed
widely on a commercial basis. It suffers, however, from many
of the same unclarities typical of the deniers. Its title assumes
a "warfare state" while its evidence, although rich, is only a
compilation of incidents, pronouncements, and trends, lacking
any framework for weighing and measuring. From his writing
several hypotheses can be extracted about the "face of the
Warfare State," all of them suggestive but none of them con-
clusive: (1) the Department of Defense owns more property
than any other organization in the world;[2] (2) between 60 and
70 per cent of the national budget is consistently allocated to
defense or defense related expenditures; (3) the Military and
Big Business join in an inevitable meeting of minds over bil-
lions of dollars in contracts the one has to order and the other
to fulfill; (4) the 100 top corporations monopolize three-fourths
of the contracts, 85 per cent of them being awarded without
competition; (5) as much as one-third of all production and
service indirectly depends on defense; (6) business and other
conservative groups, even though outside of the Defense estab-

lishment, benefit from the warfare emphasis because it keeps subordinate the welfare-state which is anathema to them (pages 20–24, 162–202).

Cook's work, much more than Mills', is open to the counterargument that no monolithic semi-conspiratorial elite exists. Even his definitions of vested interests are crude and presumed. Moreover, he suffers far more than Mills from a failure to differentiate between groups. For instance, there is nothing in his book (written in 1962) which would explain the economic drag of defense spending, which Cook perceptively observed in a *Nation* article, "The Coming Politics of Disarmament" in 1963. One year he wrote that Big Business was being fattened off war contracts, but the next year the "prolonged arms race has started, at last, to commit a form of economic hara-kiri." "Hara-kiri" does not happen spontaneously; it is a culmination of long-developing abnormalities. That Cook could not diagnose them before they became common in congressional testimony illustrates the lack of refinement in his 1962 analysis. Cook's failure lies in visualizing a monolith, which obscures the strains which promote new trends and configurations.

It is in this attention to strains that Perlo's book is useful. He draws interesting connections between the largest industrial corporations and the defense economy, finding that defense accounts for 12 per cent of the profits of the 25 largest firms. He adds the factor of foreign investment as one which creates a further propensity in favor of a large defense system, and he calculates that military business and foreign investments combined total 40 per cent of the aggregate profits among the top 25. He draws deeper connections between companies and the major financial groups controlling their assets.

This kind of analysis begins to reveal important disunities within the business community. For instance, it can be seen that the Rockefellers are increasing their direct military investments while maintaining their largest foreign holdings in extremely volatile Middle Eastern and Latin American companies. The Morgans are involved in domestic industries of a rather easy-to-convert type, and their main foreign holdings are in the "safer" European countries, although they too have "unsafe" mining interests in Latin America and Africa. The First National City Bank, while having large holdings in Latin American sugar and fruit, has a more technical relation to its associated firms than the stock-owner relation. The Mellons have sizeable oil holdings in Kuwait, but on the whole are less involved in defense than the other groups. The DuPonts, traditionally the major munitions makers, are "diversified" into the booming aerospace and plutonium industries, but their overseas holdings are heavily in Europe. Certain other groups with financial holdings, such as Young and Eaton interests in Cleveland, have almost no profit stake in defense or foreign investments. On the other hand, some of the new wealth in Los Angeles is deeply committed to the aerospace industry.

Perlo makes several differentiations of this sort, including the use of foreign-policy statements by leading industrial groups. But he does not have a way to predict under what conditions a given company would actively support economic shifts away from the arms race. These and other gaps, however, are not nearly as grave as his lack of analysis of other components of the military-industrial complex.[3] There is no attempt to include politicians, military groups, and other forces in a "map" of the military-industrial complex which Perlo believes exists. This may be partly because of the book's intent, which is to document profiteering by arms contractors, but for whatever reason, the book is not theoretically edifying about the question we are posing. Nor does it refute the pluralist case. In fact, it contains just the kind of evidence that pluralist arguments currently emply to demonstrate the absence of a monolith.

Revising the Criteria for Inferring Power

After finding fault with so many books and divergent viewpoints, the most obvious conclusion is that current social theory is currently deficient in its explanation of power. We concur with one of Mills' severest critics, Daniel Bell, who at least agrees with Mills that most current analysis concentrates on the "intermediate sectors," e.g., parties, interest groups, formal structures, without attempting to view the underlying system of "renewable power independent of any momentary group of actors" (Bell, 1964). However, we have indicated that the only formidable analysis of the underlying system of renewable power, that of Mills, has profound shortcomings because of its definition of power. Therefore, before we can offer an answer of our own to the question, "Is there a military-industrial complex which blocks peace?", it is imperative to return to the question of power itself in American society.

We have agreed essentially with the pluralist claim that ruling-group models do not "fit" the American structure. We have classified Mills' model as that of a ruling-group because of his Weberian definition of power, but we have noted also that Mills successfully went beyond two traps common to elite theories, *viz.*, that the elite is total in the scope of its decisions, and that the elite is a coordinated monolith.

But we perhaps have not stressed sufficiently that the alternative case for pluralism is inadequate in its claim to describe the historical dynamics of American society. The point of our dissent from pluralism is over the doctrine of "countervailing power." This is the modern version of Adam Smith's economics and of the Madisonian or Federalism theory of checks-and-balances, adapted to the new circumstances of large-scale organization. Its evidence is composed of self-serving incidents and a faith in semi-mystical resources. For instance, in the sphere of political economy, it is argued that oligopoly contains automatic checking mechanisms against undue corporate growth, and that additionally, the factors of "public opinion" and "corporate conscience" are built-in limiting forces.[4] We believe that evidence in the field, however, suggests that oligopoly is a means of stabilizing an industrial sphere either through tacit agreements to follow price leadership or rigged agreements in the case of custom-made goods; that "public opinion" tends much more to be manipulated and apathetic than independently critical; that "corporate conscience" is less suitable as a description than Reagan's term, "corporate arrogance."

To take the more immediate example of the military sphere, the pluralist claim is that the military is subordinate to broader, civilian interests. The first problem with the statement is the ambiguity of "civilian." Is it clear that military men are more "militaristic" than civilian men? To say so would be to deny the increasing trend of "white-collar militarism." The top strategists in the Department of Defense, the Central Intelligence Agency, and the key advisory positions often are Ph.D.'s. In fact, "civilians" including McGeorge Bundy, Robert Kennedy, James Rostow, and Robert McNamara are mainly responsible for the development of the only remaining "heroic" form of combat: counter-insurgency operations in the jungles of the underdeveloped countries. If "militarism"[5] has permeated this deeply into the "civilian" sphere, then the distinction between the terms becomes largely nominal. Meisel's description is imaginative and alluring:

> What we still honor with the name of peace is only the domestic aspect of a world-wide industrial mobilization let up at intervals by the explosions of a shooting war. . . . The industrial revolution in its class-struggle aspect is becoming externalized, projected upon the industrial field, that it is being relegated, so to speak, from barricade to barracks. . . . The armies, navies, and air forces of our time [are] the embodiment of the industrial revolution in its aggressive form (Meisel, 1962, pp. 157–158).

While the more traditional military men have not taken kindly to the takeover of military planning by civilian professors, the takeover has, nonetheless, gone far. More than 300 universities and non-profit research institutions supply civilian personnel to, and seek contracts from, the Department of Defense. Approximately half of these institutions were created specifically to do specialized strategic research. Probably the most influential of the lot of these civilian centers is the Rand Corporation.

Consistent with its Air Force origins, Rand's civilian army of almost 1,000 professional researchers and supporting personnel derives most of its support from Air Force Project Rand Studies. Rand charges the Air Force 6 per cent of the estimated cost of the contracts which the Air Force farms out to private industry as a result of work done at Rand. This brings the Air Force contribution to Rand to over 80 per cent, where it has been for the past few years. When a large Ford Foundation Grant permitted Rand's reorganization in May of 1948, the organization was granted virtual autonomy from the Air Force and from Douglas Aviation which were its original parents. Such autonomy seemed necessary both to draw independent intellectuals into the establishment and to promote the image of objectivity in its research. The charter establishes a non-profit corporation to "further and promote scientific, educational and charitable purposes, all for the public welfare and security of the United States of America." The actual measure of Rand autonomy should not be taken solely from its dependence upon Air Force money. In actual practice, Rand scholars have differed with the Air Force and on issues quite important to the Air Force. The turns of the cold war strategies from massive retaliation through finite deterrence and limited war, through counter-force, and on into controlled response had never, until 1961 and 1962, involved major reductions in any type of weaponry other than the post Korean War automotive cutbacks. Automotives were, however, a largely civilian market industry. The first place where the strategic innovations served not only to rationalize existing weaponry (in the more specialized defense industry) or to call for accelerated development in additional areas, but also to call for "cost effectiveness" or cutting back in a favored weapon area, came at the expense of the Air Force. In short order the Skybolt and the RS 70 met their demise. For a time, Harvard economist Charles Hitch (first with Rand, then Defense Department comptroller) and perhaps the entire battalion of systems analysts at Rand were personally unpopular with Air Force brass. The Air Force was particularly incensed over the inclination and ability of Rand personnel to consult directly with the Defense Department and bypass the Air Force. Rand, incidentally, maintains a permanent Washington office which facilitates such confrontation. This is not exactly what Air Force spokesmen intend when they see Rand serving the function of giving "prestige type support for favored Air Force proposals to the Department of Defense and the Congress" (Friedman, 1963). The controversy shows that there is obviously no monolithic influence in defense policy. It shows also that civilian and military factions are involved and that, in this instance, even the combined influential interests of traditional Air Force leaders and industrial aircraft contractors could not hold sway over the civilian analysts. The case also illustrates the weakness of the pluralist argument. The controversy, involving sums of money exceeding the total requested for President Johnson's war on poverty, did not threaten to starve either the Air Force or the aircraft industries. Indeed, it was a controversy among family members all sharing the same source of income and the same assumptions regarding the need for maximal military strength in the cold war. While Rand scientists played the role of civilian efficiency experts in this particular controversy, Rand experts have clearly played the role of military expansionists in civilian clothing at other times. Albert Wohlstetter and Herbert Dinerstein, Rand experts on military strategy and Soviet policy, deserve major credits for the creation of the mythical "missile gap" and for the equally unreal–pre-emptive war strategy for the Soviet Union during the period from Sputnik, in October of 1957, until the issue of inadequate military preparedness helped bring the New Frontier to Washington. Among the possible consequences of the U.S. missile buildup to overcome the mythical gap may well have been the Soviet resumption of nuclear tests in defiance of the moratorium, an act which completed a rung of the spiralling arms race which in turn nourishes all factions, civilian and military, who are engaged in military preparedness. We do not wish to labor the point that Rand experts have, at times, allowed the assumptions of their own ideology to form the basis of their rational analyses of Soviet capability and intentions. The point we wish to stress here is merely that the apparent flourishing of such civilian agencies as Rand (it earned over 20 million dollars in 1962 with all the earnings going into expansion and has already spawned the nonprofit Systems Development Corporation with annual earnings exceeding 50 million dollars) is no reflection of countervailing power. The doctrine of controlled response under which the RS 70 fell was one which served the general aspirations of each of the separate services; of the Polaris and Minuteman stabile deterrent factions, of the brushfire or limited war proponents, guerrilla war and paramilitary operations advocates, and of the counterforce adherents. It is a doctrine of versatility intended to leave the widest range of military options for retaliation and escalation in U.S. hands. It can hardly be claimed as victory against military thought. The fighting may have been intense but the area of consensus between military and civilian factions was great.

The process of "civilianizing" the military is not restricted to the level of attitudes but extends to the arena of social interaction. Traditionally, the military has been a semi-caste quite apart from the mainstream of American life. But that changed with World War II; as Mills points out:

> Unless the military sat in on corporate decisions, they would not be sure that their programs would be carried out; and unless the corporation chieftains knew something of the war plans, they could not plan war production . . . the very organization of the economics of war made for the coincidence of interest and the political mingling among economic and military chiefs (Mills, 1959, p. 212).

One relatively early statement (January 1944), by Charles E. Wilson shows that the intermeshing of military and industrial leaders was, at least on the part of some, a self-conscious and policy-oriented enterprise. Wilson proposed a permanent war economy led by the Commander in Chief and the War Department, in cooperation with an industrial partner whose response and cooperation must be free from such political accusations as the "merchants of death" label. The program would not be a creature of emergency but rather an interminable measure to eliminate emergencies. "The role of Congress," Wilson added, "is limited to voting the funds" (Swomley, 1959). Now, twenty years later we can report a personal interview with a midwestern Congressman, a fourteen-year veteran, suggesting some truth to Wilson's projection.

It is not possible for a Congressman to know, according to veteran Congressman George Meader, whether defense cutbacks are feasible. The whole area is very complicated and technical and Congress has very few military experts in its membership or on its research staffs. When budget time comes about, the Department of Defense sends literally hundreds of experts to report before committee hearings. We have to take the word of the people who know. This paraphrased statement regarding the rubber stamping of more than 60 per cent of the national budget was made by a congressman who claims a perfect record in opposition to the growth of governmental bureaucracy and to federal spending. If we were to examine the dozen or so congressional "experts" to whom Congressman Meader makes reference we find among them a number of high ranking reserve officers and a number representing districts or states economically dependent upon either military bases, or defense contracts, or both.

The same kind of planning requirements for modern war forced an overlapping of politicians with military and businessmen. There, too, the very nature of world war, and especially cold war, integrated military, political, and economic concepts of strategy, making the military officer much more than a cog. A variety of recent studies demonstrates the outcome of these developments. The 1959 hearings and survey by the House Armed Services Subcommittee disclosed that over 1400 retired officers with the rank of major or higher (including 261 of general or flag rank) were in the employ of the top 100 defense contractors (Hébert Subcommittee of the House Armed Services Committee, 1959). Coffin listed 74 Senators and Representatives with continuing status in the armed forces (Coffin, 1964). By 1957, 200 active (not reserve) generals or admirals were on assignment to "nonmilitary" departments of the government or to international or interservice agencies. An added 1300 colonels or naval officers of comparable rank and 6000 lower grade officers were similarly assigned (Swomley, 1959). Janowitz studied an historical sample of over 700 generals and admirals, administered questionnaires to about 600 current Pentagon staff officers, and interviewed 113 career officers. He found an "elite in transition" toward civilian and managerial habits: (1) the basis of authority and discipline is changing from authoritarian domination to greater reliance on manipulation, persuasion, and group consensus; (2) the skill differential between civilians and soldiers is narrowing because of the need for technical specialties in the military; (3) officers are being recruited from a broader status and class base, reflecting the demand for more specialists; (4) the source of prestige recognition is shifting from military circles to the public at large; (5) this growth makes the officer define himself more and more as a political, rather than a technical, person with concerns about national security concepts and affairs (Janowitz, 1960, pp. 3–16, 442–452). These trends clearly demonstrate that the traditional American separation of military and civilian is outmoded. The new, blurred reality has not been successfully defined.

The main point here is that the pluralist argument relies on "countervailing forces" which are more mythical than real. The Wise and Ross book shows indisputably that at least during certain instances the Executive is not countervailing the CIA. Moreover, who is countervailing the "military-civilian" Executive centered in the Pentagon and the White House? What Knorr sees as a "peacefare state" countervailing the "warfare state" is merely its white-collar brother. The symbolic figure of the Arms Control and Disarmament Agency demonstrates this reality vividly. One side of the ACDA figure is a diplomat with tie and attaché case; the other side is a warrior dedicated to the pursuit of stabilizing control measures which might assure national advantages in a never ending cold war.

ACDA's narrow conception of its own role is as much a function of its internal quest for respectability as it is a matter of the prerogatives given it by a reluctant Congress. It has sought respectability not only in its apparent choice of essentially technical questions for study but also in its manner of study. One favored study technique is to collapse large socially significant questions into several questions answerable by short-term studies and suited for study by the grossly oversimplified techniques of policy appraisal employed by those same operations research corporations which serve, and live upon, defense contracts. These organizations have traditionally produced quick answers embedded in rationalistic models which ring with scientism and jargon. *Strategy and Conscience*, a powerfully written book by Anatol Rapoport, documents the manner in which the rationalist models employed in such strategic studies frequently conceal (often unknowingly) gross assumptions of the nature of the cold war. The point here is that if these are the same assumptions which necessitate a high level of military preparedness, then it matters little whether the studies are commissioned by civilian or military authorities.

CONSENSUS

All that countervailing power refers to is the relationship between groups who fundamentally accept "the American system" but who compete for advantages within it. The corporate executive wants higher profits, the laborer a higher wage. The President wants the final word on military strategies, the Chairman of the Joint Chiefs does not trust him with it. Boeing wants the contract, but General Dynamics is closer at the time to the Navy Secretary and the President, and so on: what is prevented by countervailing forces is the dominance of society by a group or clique or a party. But this process suggests a profoundly important point: that *the constant pattern in American society is the rise and fall of temporarily irresponsible groups*. By temporary we mean that, outside of the largest industrial conglomerates,[6] the groups which wield significant power to influence policy decisions are not guaranteed stability. By irresponsible we mean that there are many activities within their scope which are essentially unaccountable in the democratic process. These groups are too uneven to be described with the shorthand term "class." Their personnel have many different characteristics (compare IBM executives and the Southern Dixiecrats), and their needs as groups are different enough to cause endless fights, as, for example, small vs. big business. No one group or coalition of several groups can tyrannize the rest, as is demonstrated, for example, in the changing status of the major financial groups, particularly the fast-rising Bank of America which has been built from the financial needs of the previously neglected small consumer.

However, it is clear that these groups exist within consensus relationships of a more general and durable kind than their conflict relationships. This is true, first of all, of their social characteristics. Tables 1, 2, and 3 combine data from Suzanne Keller's compilation of military, economic, political and diplomatic elite survey materials in *Beyond the Ruling Class* (1963) and from an exhaustive study of American elites contained in Warner, *et al., The American Federal Executive* (1963). Data on elites vary slightly from study to study because of varying operational definitions of the elite population. However, the data selected here are fairly representative and refer exclusively to studies with major data collected within the decade of the fifties.

The relevant continuities represented in these data suggest an educated elite with an emphasis upon Protestant and business-oriented origins. Moreover, the data suggest inbreeding with business orientation in backgrounds likely to have been at least maintained, if not augmented, through marriage. The consistencies suggest orientations not unlike those which are to be

TABLE 1: *Social Characteristics of American Elites*

	Nativity (% Foreign Born)	Rural-Urban (% Urban Born[a])	Religion (% Protestant)	Education (% College Grads)
Military	2	30–40[c]	90	73–98[c]
Economic	6	65	85	61
Political	2	48	81	91
Diplomatic	4	66	81	81
U.S. Adult Males	7[b]	42[d]	65	7[b]

[a] Towns of 2,500 or more.
[b] Thirty years of age and older.
[c] Taking the services separately.
[d] 1910 U.S. Population.

The majority of foreign-born and second-generation comes from Northwestern Europe. The proportion of foreign-born from these areas is significantly lower for the general male population.

The difference between "political" and "diplomatic" and "economic" indicated that Congress, in the 1950's was more conservative—especially in its small business and non-integrationist attitudes—than the federal executive or the corporation leaders. The sharp difference between "military" and the rest lumps military policymakers with lower level personnel, thus underemphasizing the new trend cited by Janowitz.

found in examination of editorial content of major business newspapers and weeklies and in more directly sampled assessments of elite opinions.[7]

The second evidence of consensus relationships, besides attitude and background data indicating a pro-business sympathy, would come from an examination of the *practice* of decision making. By analysis of such actual behavior we can understand which consensus attitudes are reflected in decision-making. Here, in retrospect, it is possible to discover the values and assumptions which are defended recurrently. This is at least a rough means of finding the boundaries of consensus relations. Often these boundaries are invisible because of the very infrequency with which they are tested. What are visible most of the time are the parameters of conflict relationships among different groups. These conflict relationships constitute the ingredients of experience which give individuals or groups their uniqueness and varieties, while the consensus relations constitute the common underpinnings of behavior. The tendency in social science has been to study decision-making in order to study group differences; we need to study decision-making also to understand group commonalities.

Were such studies done, our hypothesis would be that certain "core beliefs" are continuously unquestioned. One of these, undoubtedly, would be that efficacy is preferable to principle

TABLE 2: *Father's Occupation (in per cent)*

	Civilian Federal Executives	Military Executives	Business Leaders	Total U.S. Male Pop., 1930
Unskilled Laborer	4	2	5	33
Skilled Laborer	17	12	10	15
White-Collar (clerk or sales)	9	9	8	12
Foreman	5	5	3	2
Business Owner	15	19	26	7
Business Executive	15	15	23	3
Professional	19	18	14	4
Farm Owner or Manager	14	9	8	16
Farm Tenant or Worker	1	1	1	6
Other	1	1	2	2

in foreign affairs. In practice, this means that violence is preferable to non-violence as a means of defense. A second is that private property is preferable to collective property. A third assumption is that the particular form of constitutional government which is practiced within the United States is preferable to any other system of government. We refer to the preferred mode as limited parliamentary democracy, a system in which institutionalized forms of direct representation are carefully retained but with fundamental limitations placed upon the prerogatives of governing. Specifically included among the areas of limitation are many matters encroaching upon corporation property and state hegemony. While adherence to this form of government is conceivably the strongest of the domestic "core values," at least among business elites, it is probably the least strongly held of the three on the international scene. American relations with, and assistance for, authoritarian and semi-feudal regimes occurs exactly in those areas where the recipient regime is evaluated primarily upon the first two assumptions and given rather extensive leeway on the last one.

The implications of these "core beliefs" for the social system are immense, for they justify the maintenance of our largest institutional structures: the military, the corporate economy, and a system of partisan politics which protects the concept of limited democracy. These institutions, in turn, may be seen as current agencies of the more basic social structure. We use the term "social structure" as Robert S. Lynd does, as the stratifi-

TABLE 3: *Business and Executive Origins of Elites and Their Wives* (*in per cent*)

Occupation	Political Executives F	Political Executives SF	Foreign-service Executives F	Foreign-service Executives SF	Military Executives F	Military Executives SF	Civilian Federal Executives F	Civilian Federal Executives SF	Business Leaders F	Business Leaders SF
Minor executive	10	10	11	11	15	12	11	11	11	7
Major executive	6	5	9	9	5	7	4	4	15	8
Business owner	21	25	19	24	19	22	20	23	26	28
Professional	24	19	25	23	18	19	19	16	14	15
Military executive					9	11				

F = Father.
SF = Spouse's father.

cation of people identified according to kinship, sex, age, division of labor, race, religion, or other factors which differentiate them in terms of role, status, access to resources, and power. According to Lynd:

> This structure establishes durable relations that hold groups of people together for certain purposes and separate them for others. Such social structures may persist over many generations. Its continuance depends upon its ability to cope with historical changes that involve absorption of new groupings and relations of men without fundamental change in the structure of the society of a kind that involves major transfer of power (Lynd, 1959).

The "renewable basis of power" in America at the present time underlies those institutional orders linked in consensus relationships: military defense of private property and parliamentary democracy. These institutional orders are not permanently secure, by definition. Their maintenance involves a continuous coping with new conditions, such as technological innovation, and with the inherent instabilities of a social structure which arbitrarily classifies persons by role, status, access to resources, and power. The myriad groups composing these orders are even less secure because of their weak ability to command "coping resources"; e.g., the service branches are less stable than the institution of the military, particular companies are less stable than the institutions of corporate property, political parties are less stable than the institution of parliamentary government.

In the United States there is no ruling group. Nor is there any easily discernible ruling institutional order, so meshed have the separate sources of elite power become. But there is a social structure which is organized to create and protect power centers with only partial accountability. In this definition of power we are avoiding the Weber-Mills meaning of *omnipotence* and the contrary pluralist definition of power as consistently *diffuse*. We are describing the current system as one of overall "minimal accountability" and "minimal consent." We mean that the role of democratic review, based on genuine popular consent, is made marginal and reactive. Elite groups are minimally accountable to publics and have a substantial, though by no means maximum, freedom to shape popular attitudes. The reverse of our system would be one in which democratic participation would be the orienting demand around which the social structure is organized.

Some will counter this case by saying that we are measuring "reality" against an "ideal," a technique which permits the conclusion that the social structure is undemocratic according to its distance from our utopian values. This is a convenient apology for the present system, of course. We think it possible, at least in theory, to develop measures of the undemocratic in democratic conditions, and place given social structures along a continuum. These measures, in rough form, might include such variables as economic security, education, legal guarantees, access to information, and participatory control over systems of economy, government, and jurisprudence.

The reasons for our concern with democratic process in an article questioning the power of a purported military-industrial complex are twofold. First, just as scientific method both legitimizes and promotes change in the world of knowledge, democratic method legitimizes and promotes change in the world of social institutions. Every society, regardless of how democratic, protects its core institutions in a web of widely shared values. But if the core institutions should be dictated by the requisites of military preparedness, then restrictions on the democratic process—i.e., restrictions in either mass opinion exchange (as by voluntary or imposed news management) or in decision-making bodies (as by selection of participants in a manner guaranteeing exclusion of certain positions)—such restrictions would be critical obstacles to peace.

Second, certain elements of democratic process are inimical to features of militarily oriented society, and the absence of these elements offers one type of evidence for a military-industrial complex even in the absence of a ruling elite. Secretary of Defense Robert McNamara made the point amply clear in his testimony in 1961 before the Senate Armed Services Committee:

Why should we tell Russia that the Zeus development may not be satisfactory? What we ought to be saying is that we have the most perfect anti-ICBM system that the human mind will ever devise. Instead the public domain is already full of statements that the Zeus may not be satisfactory, that it has deficiencies. I think it is absurd to release that level of information (Military Procurement Authorization Fiscal Year 1962).

Under subsequent questioning McNamara attempted to clarify his statement, that he only wished to delude Russian, not American, citizens about U.S. might. Just how this might be done was not explained.

A long established tradition exists for "executive privilege" which permits the President to refuse to release information when, in his opinion, it would be damaging to the national interest. Under modern conditions responsibility for handling information of a strategic nature is shared among military, industrial, and executive agencies. The discretion regarding when to withhold what information must also be shared. Moreover, the existence of a perpetual danger makes the justification "in this time of national crisis" suitable to every occasion in which secrecy must be justified. McNamara's statement cited above referred not to a crisis in Cuba or Viet Nam but rather to the perpetual state of cold war crisis. And since the decision about what is to be released, and when, is subject to just such management, the media became dependent upon the agencies for timely leaks and major stories. This not only adds an aura of omniscience to the agencies, but gives these same agencies the power to reward "good" journalists and punish the critical ones.

The issues involved in the question of news management involve more than the elements of control available to the President, the State Department, the Department of Defense, the Central Intelligence Agency, the Atomic Energy Commission, or any of the major prime contractors of defense contracts. Outright control of news flow is probably less pervasive than voluntary acquiescence to the objectives of these prominent institutions of our society. Nobody has to tell the wire services when to release a story on the bearded dictator of our hemisphere or the purported brutality of Ho Chi Minh. A frequent model, the personified devil image of an enemy, has become a press tradition. In addition to a sizeable quantity of radio and television programming and spot time purchased directly by the Pentagon, an amount of service valued at $6 million by *Variety* is donated annually by the networks and by public relations agencies for various military shows (Swomley, 1959). Again, the pluralistic shell of an independent press or broadcasting media is left hollow by the absence of a countervailing social force of any significant power.

The absence of a countervailing force for peace cannot, we have claimed, be demonstrated by an absence of conflicting interests among powerful sectors of American society. Indeed, such conflicts are ever-present examples of American pluralism. Demonstrating the absence of a discussion of the shared premises among the most potent sectors of society would go far in highlighting the area of forced or acquiescent consensus. But even the absence of debate could not complete the case unless we can show how the accepted premises are inconsistent with requisites of a viable peace-time social system. It is to this question, of the compatibility of the unquestioned assumption of American society with conditions of peace, that we now turn. The "core beliefs" which we listed as unchallenged by any potent locus of institutionalized power are:

a. Efficacy is preferable to principle in foreign affairs (thus military means are chosen over non-violent means);
b. Private property is preferable to public property; and
c. Limited parliamentary democracy is preferable to any other system of government.

What characteristics of a continuing world system devoid of military conflict fly in the face of these assumptions?

We identify three conditions for enduring peace which clash with one or more of the core beliefs. These are: (1) the requirements for programming an orderly transition and the subsequent maintenance of a non-defense economy within a highly automated and relatively affluent society; (2) the conditions for peaceful settlement of internal disputes within underdeveloped countries and between alien nations and commercial interests; and (3) the conditions under which disparities in living standards between have and have-not nations can be handled with minimum violence.

If one pools available projections regarding the offset programs, especially regional and local offset programs, necessary to maintain economic well-being in the face of disarmament in this country, the programs will highlight two important features. One is the lag time in industrial conversion. The second is the need for coordination in the timing and spacing of programs. One cannot reinvest in new home building in an area which has just been deserted by its major industry and left a ghost town. The short-term and long-term offset values of new hospitals and educational facilities will differ in the building and the utilization stages, and regional offset programs have demonstrable interregional effects (Reiner, 1964). Plans requiring worker mobility on a large scale will require a central bank for storing job information and a smooth system for its dissemination. Such coordination will require a degree of centralization of controls beyond the realm which our assumption regarding primacy of private property would permit.

Gross intransigence can be expected on this issue. Shortly after Sperry Rand on Long Island was forced to make major cutbacks of its professional and engineering staff to adapt to the termination of certain defense contracts, the union approached Sperry's management with the prospect of collaborating in efforts to commence contingency plans for diversification. The response, by Carl A. Frische, President of Sperry Gyroscope, a division of Sperry Rand, remains a classic. There must be no "government-controlled mechanisms under the hood of the economy." He suggested, with regard to such planning, that "we let Russia continue with that." (*Long Island Sunday Press,* February 23, 1964.) Sperry is an old-timer in defense production. Its board of directors averages several years older than the more avant garde board of directors of, say, General Dynamics. But the prospect of contingency planning will be no more warmly welcomed in the newer aeroframe industry (which is only 60 per cent convertible to needs of a peace-time society) (McDonagh and Zimmerman, 1964). Private planning, by an individual firm for its own future does occur, but, without coordinated plans, the time forecast for market conditions remains smaller than the lag time for major retooling. A lag time of from six to ten years would not be atypical before plans by a somewhat overspecialized defense contractor could result in retooling for production in a peace-time market. In the meantime, technological innovations, governmental fiscal or regulatory policies, shifts in consumer preferences, or the decisions by other firms to enter that same market could well make the market vanish. Moreover, the example of defense firms which have attempted even the smaller step toward diversification presents a picture which has not been entirely promising (Fearon and Hook, 1964). Indeed, one of several reasons for the failures in this endeavor has been that marketing skills necessary to compete in a private enterprise economy have been lost by those industrial giants who have been managing with a sales force of one or two retired generals to deal with the firm's only customer. Even if the path of successful conversion by some firms were to serve as the model for all individual attempts, the collective result would be poor. To avoid a financially disastrous glutting of limited markets some coordinated planning will be needed.

The intransigence regarding public or collaborative planning occurs against a backdrop of a soon-to-be increasing army of unemployed youth and aged, as well as regional armies of unemployed victims of automation. Whether one thinks of work in traditional job market terms or as anything worthwhile that a person can do with his life, work (and some means of livelihood) will have to be found for these people. There is much work to be done in community services, education, public health, and recreation, but this is people work, not product work. The lack of a countervailing force prevents the major reallocation of human and economic resources from the sector defined as preferable by the most potent institutions of society. One point must be stressed. We are not saying that limited planning to cushion the impact of arms reduction is impossible. Indeed, it is going on and with the apparent blessing of the Department of Defense (Barber, 1963). We are saying that the type of accommodation needed by a cutback of $9 billion in R & D and $16 billion in military procurement requires a type of preparation not consistent with the unchallenged assumptions.

Even the existence of facilities for coordinated planning does not, to be sure, guarantee the success of such planning. Bureaucratic institutions, designed as they may be for coordination and control, do set up internal resistance to the very coordination they seek to achieve. The mechanisms for handling these bureaucratic intransigencies usually rely upon such techniques as bringing participants into the process of formulating the decisions which will affect their own behavior. We can conceive of no system of coordinated conversion planning which could function without full and motivated cooperation from the major corporations, the larger unions, and representatives of smaller business and industry. Unfortunately, it is just as difficult to conceive of a system which would assure this necessary level of participation and cooperation. This same argument cuts deeper still when we speak of the millions of separate individuals in the "other America" whose lives would be increasingly "administered" with the type of centralized planning needed to offset a defense economy. The job assignment which requires moving, the vocational retraining program, the development of housing projects to meet minimal standards, educational enrichment programs, all of the programs which are conceived by middle-class white America for racially mixed low income groups, face the same difficulty in execution of plans. Without direct participation in the formulation of the programs, the target populations are less likely to participate in the programs and more likely to continue feelings of alienation from the social system which looks upon them as an unfortunate problem rather than as contributing members. Considering the need for active participation in real decisions, every step of coordinated planning carries with it the responsibility for an equal step in the direction of participatory democracy. This means that the voice of the unemployed urban worker may have to be heard, not only on city council meetings which discuss policy on the control of rats in his dwelling, but also on decisions about where a particular major corporation will be relocated and where the major resource allocations of the country will be invested. That such decision participation would run counter to the consensus on the items of limited parliamentary democracy and private property is exactly the point we wish to make.

Just as the theoretical offset plans can be traced to the sources of power with which they conflict, so too can the theoretical plans for international governing and peace-keeping operations be shown to conflict with the unquestioned beliefs. U.S. consent to international jurisdiction in the settlement of claims deriving from the nationalization of American overseas holdings or the removal of U.S. military installations is almost inconceivable. Moreover, the mode of American relations to less-developed countries is so much a part of the operations of those American institutions which base their existence upon interminable conflict with Communism that the contingency in which the U.S. might have to face the question of international jurisdiction in these areas seems unreal. Offers to mediate, with Cuba by Mexico, with North Viet Nam by France, are bluntly rejected. Acceptance of such offers would have called into question not one but all three of the assumptions in the core system. International jurisdictional authority could institutionalize a means to call the beliefs into question. It is for this reason (but perhaps most directly because of our preference for forceful means) that American preoccupation in those negotiations regarding the extension of international control which have taken place deal almost exclusively with controls in the area of weaponry and police operations and not at all in the areas of political or social justice.[8]

The acceptance of complete international authority even in the area of weaponry poses certain inconsistencies with the preferred "core beliefs." Non-violent settlement of Asian-African area conflicts would be slow and ineffective in protecting American interests. The elimination, however, of military preparedness, both for projected crises and for their potential escalation, requires a faith in alternate means of resolution. The phasing of the American plan for general and complete disarmament is one which says in effect: prove that the alternatives are as efficient as our arms in protection of our interests and then we disarm. In the short term, however, the effectiveness of force always looks greater.

The state of world peace contains certain conditions imposed by the fact that people now compare themselves with persons who have more of the benefits of industrialization than they themselves. Such comparative reference groups serve to increase the demand for rapid change. While modern communications heighten the pressures imposed by such comparisons, the actual disparities revealed in comparison speak for violence. Population growth rates, often as high as 3 per cent, promise population doubling within a single generation in countries least able to provide for their members. The absolute number of illiterates as well as the absolute number of persons starving is greater now than ever before in history. Foreign aid barely offsets the disparity between declining prices paid for the prime commodities exported by underdeveloped countries and rising prices paid for the finished products imported into these countries (Horowitz, 1962). All schemes for tight centralized planning employed by these countries to accrue and disperse scarce capital by rational means are blocked by the unchallenged assumptions on private property and limited parliamentary democracy. A recent restatement of the principle came in the report of General Lucius Clay's committee on foreign aid. The report stated that the U.S. should not assist foreign governments "in projects establishing government owned industrial and commercial enterprises which compete with existing private endeavors." When Congressman Broomfield's amendment on foreign aid resulted in cancellation of a U.S. promise to India to build a steel mill in Bokaro, Broomfield stated the case succinctly: "The main issue is private enterprise vs. state socialism." (*The Atlantic*, September, 1964, p. 6.) Moreover, preference for forceful solutions assures that the capital now invested in preparedness will not be allocated in a gross way to the needs of underdeveloped countries. Instead, the manifest crises periodically erupting in violence justify further the need for reliance upon military preparedness.

We agree fully with an analysis by Lowi (1964) distinguishing types of decisions for which elite-like forces seem to appear and hold control (redistributive) and other types in which pluralist powers battle for their respective interests (distributive). In the latter type the pie is large and the fights are over who gets how much. Factional strife within and among military industrial and political forces in our country are largely of this nature. In redistributive decisions, the factions coalesce, for the pie itself is threatened. We have been arguing that the transition to peace is a process of redistributive decision.

Is there, then, a military-industrial complex which prevents peace? The answer is inextricably imbedded in the mainstream of American institutions and mores. Our concept is not that American society contains a ruling military-industrial complex. Our concept is more nearly that American society *is* a military-industrial complex. It can accommodate a wide range of factional interests from those concerned with the production or utilization of a particular weapon to those enraptured with the mystique of optimal global strategies. It can accommodate those with rabid desires to advance toward the brink and into limitless intensification of the arms race. It can even accommodate those who wish either to prevent war or to limit the destructiveness of war through the gradual achievement of arms control and disarmament agreements. What it cannot accommodate is the type of radical departures needed to produce enduring peace.

The requirements of a social system geared to peace, as well as the requirements for making a transition to such a social system, share a pattern of resource distribution which is different from the one the world now has. Moreover, these requirements for peace are, in significant measure, inconsistent with constraints set by the more enduring convergencies among power structures in the United States. The same is true whether one speaks of allocation of material or of intellectual resources. Both are geared to the protection of the premises rather than to avenues of change. We are not saying that war is inevitable or that the changes cannot be made. We are saying that the American political, military, and industrial system operates with certain built-in stabilizers which resist a change in the system. If there is to be peace, as opposed to detente or temporary absence of war, marked changes will be needed. Whether this society can or will accommodate to such changes is a question which is fundamentally different from the questions posed by most studies conventionally grouped under the rubric of peace research. One difference which marks the question of capacity to accommodate is in the theoretical conception or model of the cold war which is assumed. And a second distinction lies in the manner in which the end product of the research may be suited to meet the social forces (as apart from the intellectual arguments) which promote long-term changes in policy.

NOTES

1. See James H. Meisel, *The Myth of the Ruling Class,* for the best available discussion of this innovation in theorizing about elites.
2. Swomley (1964) accounts for Department of Defense holdings equivalent in size to eight states of the U.S.A. Kenneth Boulding, including personnel as well as property criteria, calls the Department of Defense the world's third largest socialist state. (Personal discussion, 1963).
3. In an earlier book, *The Empire of High Finance* (1957), he documented the close relations of the major financial groups and the political executive. He did not, however, carry this analysis to congressmen and senators, nor did he offer sufficient comparative evidence to demonstrate a long-term pattern.
4. For this argument, see A. A. Berle, *The Twentieth Century Capitalist Revolution,* and J. K. Galbraith, *American Capitalism.* For sound criticisms, but without sound alternatives, see Mills' and Perlo's books. Also see Michael Reagan, *The Managed Economy* (1963), and Berland Nossiter, *The Mythmakers* (1964), for other refutations of the countervailing power thesis.
5. We are defining the term as "primary reliance on coercive means, particularly violence or the threat of violence, to deal with social problems."
6. The term used in recent hearings by Senator Philip A. Hart refers to industrial organizations like Textron, which have holdings in every major sector of American industry.
7. For some interesting work bearing upon the attitudes of business and military elites see (Angell, 1964; Bauer et al., 1963; Eells and Walton, 1961; and Singer, 1964).
8. An objective account of the major negotiations related to disarmament which have taken place may be found in Frye (1963).

REFERENCES

Angell, Robert C. A study of social values: content analysis of elite media. *The Journal of Conflict Resolution, VIII,* 1964, 4, 329–85.

Barber, Arthur. Some industrial aspects of arms control. *The Journal of Conflict Resolution, VII,* 1963, 3, 491–95.

Bauer, Raymond A., I. Pool, and L. Dexter, *American Business and Public Policy.* New York: Atherton, 1963.

Bell, Daniel. *The End of Ideology.* New York: The Free Press, 1959.

Berle, Adolph A. *The Twentieth Century Capitalist Revolution.* New York: Harcourt, 1954.

Brand, Horst. Disarmament and American capitalism. *Dissent,* Summer, 1962, 236–251.

Coffin, Tristran. *The Passion of the Hawks.* New York: Macmillan, 1964.

Cook, Fred J. *The Warfare State.* New York: Macmillan, 1962.

Eells, Richard, and C. Walton. *Conceptual Foundations of Business.* Homewood, Illinois: Irwin, 1961.

Etzioni, Amitai. *The Hard Way to Peace.* New York: Collier, 1962.

———. *The Moon-Doggle.* Garden City, N.Y.: Doubleday, 1964.

Fearon, H. E., and R. C. Hook, Jr. The shift from military to industrial markets. *Business Topics,* Winter, 1964, 45–52.

Friedman, S. The RAND Corporation and our Policy Makers, *Atlantic Monthly,* September, 1963, 61–58.

Frye, W. R. Characteristics of recent arms-control proposals and agreements. In Brennan, D. G. (Ed.), *Arms Control, Disarmament, and National Security.* New York: Braziller, 1963.

Galbraith, J. K. *American Capitalism.* Boston: Houghton Mifflin, 1956.

———. Poverty among nations. *The Atlantic Monthly,* October, 1962, 47–53.

Horowitz, David. *World Economic Disparities: The Haves and the Have-nots.* Center for Study of Democratic Institutions: Santa Barbara, 1962.

Janowitz, Morris. *The Professional Soldier.* New York: The Free Press, 1960.

Keller, Suzanne. *Beyond the Ruling Class.* New York: Random House, 1963.

Knorr, Klaus. Warfare and peacefare states and the acts of transition. *The Journal of Conflict Resolution, VII,* 1963, 4, 754–62.

Long Island Sunday Press, February 23, 1964.

Lowi, Theodore J. American business, public policy, case-studies, and political theory, *World Politics,* July, 1964, 676–715.

Lynd, Robert S., and Helen Merrill. *Middletown.* New York: Harcourt, 1959.

McDonagh, James J., and Steven M. Zimmerman. A program for civilian diversifications of the airplane industry. In *Convertibility of Space and Defense Resources to Civilian Needs.* Subcommittee on Employment and Manpower. U.S. Senate, 88th Congress. Washington: U.S. Government Printing Office, 1964.

Meisel, James H. *The Fall of the Republic.* Ann Arbor: University of Michigan Press, 1962.

————. *The Myth of the Ruling Class*. Ann Arbor: University of Michigan Press, 1958.

Melman, Seymour (Ed.). *A Strategy for American Security,* New York: Lee Offset Inc., 1963.

————. *The Peace Race*. New York: Braziller, 1962.

Military Procurement Authorization Fiscal Year 1962. Hearings before the Committee on Armed Services, U.S. Senate, 87th Congress, 1st Session, U.S. Govt. Printing Office, 1961.

Mills, C. Wright. *The Causes of World War III*. New York: Simon & Schuster, 1958.

————. *The Power Elite*. New York: Oxford, 1959.

Nossiter, Berland. *The Mythmakers: An Essay on Power and Wealth,* Boston: Houghton Mifflin, 1964.

Peck, M. J. and F. M. Scherer. *The Weapons Acquisition Process*. Boston: Harvard, 1962.

Perlo, Victor. *Militarism and Industry*. New York: International Publishers, 1963.

Rapoport, Anatol. *Strategy and Conscience*. New York: Harper, 1964.

Raymond, Jack. *Power at the Pentagon*. New York: Harper, 1964.

Reagan, Michael. *The Managed Economy*. New York: Oxford, 1963.

Reiner, Thomas. Spatial criteria to offset military cutbacks. Paper presented at the University of Chicago Peace Research Conference, November 18, 1964.

Report on the world today. *The Atlantic,* September, 1964, 4–8.

Shils, Edward. Professor Mills on the calling of sociology. *World Politics, XIII,* 1961, 4.

Singer, J. David. A study of foreign policy attitudes. *The Journal of Conflict Resolution, VIII,* 1964, 4, 424–85.

Swomley, J. M., Jr. The growing power of the military. *The Progressive,* January, 1959.

————. *The Military Establishment*. Boston: Beacon Press, 1964.

Warner, W. Lloyd, P. P. Van Riper, N. H. Martin, and O. F. Collins. *The American Federal Executive*. New Haven: Yale University Press, 1963.

III : Standards and Strategies of Change

7 : *The Public Interest*

BRIAN BARRY

I

A Tribunal of Enquiry claims that the public interest requires journalists to disclose their sources of information; the Restrictive Practices Court invalidates an agreement among certain manufacturers as contrary to the Restrictive Practices Act and therefore contrary to the public interest; the National Incomes Commission says that a proposed rise for the workers in an industry would be against the public interest. These examples could be multiplied endlessly. Each day's newspaper brings fresh ones. In arguments about concrete issues (as opposed to general rhetoric in favour of political parties or entire societies) "the public interest" is more popular than "justice," "fairness," "equality," or "freedom."

Why is this? Roughly, there are two possible answers. One is

From *Proceedings of the Aristotelian Society*, Supp. 38 (1964), 1–18. Reprinted by courtesy of the Editor of the Aristotelian Society, Copyright 1964 The Aristotelian Society.

that "the public interest" points to a fairly clearly definable range of considerations in support of a policy, and if it is a very popular concept at the moment all this shows is that (for better or worse) these considerations are highly valued by many people at the moment. This is my own view. The other answer is that politicians and civil servants find it a handy smoke-screen to cover their decisions, which are actually designed to conciliate the most effectively deployed interest.

These sceptics often buttress their arguments by pointing out that most theoretical writing about "the public interest" is vague and confused. This theme is copiously illustrated by Frank J. Sorauf in his article "The Public Interest Reconsidered,"[1] and by Glendon Schubert in his book *The Public Interest*.[2] But it is a familiar idea that people who are perfectly well able to *use* a concept may nevertheless talk rubbish *about* it, so even if many of the writings about the concept are confused it does not follow that the concept itself is. A more cogent line of argument is to construct a definition of "the public interest" and then show that, so defined, nothing (or not much) satisfies it. From this, it can be deduced that most uses of the phrase in political discussion must be either fraudulent or vacuous. Like Sorauf and Schubert, the best-known expositors of the view are Americans—one may mention A. F. Bentley's *The Process of Government*[3] and D. B. Truman's *The Governmental Process*.[4] But the most succinct and recent treatment is to be found in Chapters 3 and 4 of *The Nature of Politics* by J. D. B. Miller,[5] and it is to a criticism of these chapters that I now turn.

II

Miller defines "interest" as follows: "we can say that an interest exists when we see some body of persons showing a *common concern* about particular matters" (p. 39). On the basis of this he later puts forward two propositions. First, one is not "justified in going beyond people's own inclinations in order to tell them that their true interest lies somewhere else" (p. 41).

It "seems absurd" to suppose that an interest can exist if those whose interest it is are not aware of it (p. 40). And secondly, a "common concern . . . must be present if we are to say that a general interest exists." "A common concern will sometimes be found in the society at large, and sometimes not. More often it will not be there" (p. 54).

Apart from the last point, which is a statement of fact and one I shall not query here, these propositions follow analytically from the original definition of "interest," though Miller does not see this clearly. Everything hinges on that slippery word "concern" which plays such a crucial part in the definition. One can be concerned *at* (a state of affairs) or concerned *about* (an issue) or concerned *with* (an organization or activity) or, finally, concerned *by* (an action, policy, rule, etc.). The noun, as in "so-and-so's concerns" can correspond to any of the first three constructions, and it seems plain enough that in these three kinds of use nobody can be concerned without knowing it. In the fourth use, where "concerned by" is roughly equivalent to "affected by," this is not so: someone might well be affected by an economic policy of which he had never heard. But the noun "concern" does not have a sense corresponding to this, nor does Miller stretch it to cover it. Naturally, if "interest" is understood in terms of actual striving, no sense can be given to the idea of someone's having an interest but not pursuing it. Similarly, if "interest" is defined as "concern" it hardly needs several pages of huffing and puffing against rival conceptions (pp. 52–54) to establish that "common or general interest" must be equivalent to "common or general concern."

Since, then, Miller's conclusions follow analytically from his definition of "interest," with the addition of a factual premise which I am not here disputing, I must, if I am to reject his conclusions, reject his definition. Miller can, of course, define "interest" any way he likes; but if he chooses a completely idiosyncratic definition he can hardly claim to have proved much if it turns out that most of the things that people have traditionally said about interests then become false or meaningless. He clearly believes himself to be taking part in a debate with previous writers and it is because of this that he is open to criticism.

Let us start from the other end. Let us begin by considering the things we normally want to say about interests, the distinctions which we normally want to draw by using the concept, and then see whether it is not possible to construct a definition of "interest" which will make sense of these ordinary speech habits.

The first part of Miller's definition, which makes interests *shared* concerns, conflicts with our normal wish to draw a distinction between someone's private or personal interests on the one hand and the interests which he shares with various groups of people on the other hand. Simply to rule out the former by fiat as Miller does seems to have nothing to recommend it. It might perhaps be argued in defence of the limitation that only interests shared among a number of people are politically important, but it can surely be validly replied that this is neither a necessary nor a sufficient condition.

The second part of the definition equates a man's interests with his concerns. This conflicts with a great many things we ordinarily want to say about interests. We want to say that people can mistake their interests, and that while some conflicts are conflicts of interests, others (e.g., "conflicts of principle") are not. We distinguish between "disinterested" concern and "interested" concern in a particular matter; we find it convenient to distinguish "interest groups" (e.g., The National Farmers' Union) from "cause" or "promotional" groups (e.g., The Abortion Law Reform Association). "They cooperate because they have a common interest" is ordinarily taken as a genuine explanation, rather than a pseudo-explanation of the "*vis dormitiva*" type, as it would be if cooperation were identified with (or regarded as a direct manifestation of) a common interest. We allow that one can recognize something as being in one's interest without pursuing it. Finally, we do not regard it as a contradiction in terms to say, "I realize that so-and-so would be in my interests but nevertheless I am against it." These points are all inconsistent with Miller's definition, and in addition the last of them is inconsistent with any attempt such as that of S. I. Benn to define a man's interests as "something he thought he could *reasonably* ask for."[6]

Can a definition be found which will make sense of all these uses of "interest"? I suggest this: a policy, law, or institution is in someone's interest if it increases his opportunities to get what he wants—whatever that may be. Notice that this is a definition of "*in* so-and-so's interests." Other uses of "interest" all seem to me either irrelevant or reducible to sentences with this construction. Thus, the only unforced sense that one can give to "What are your interests?," which Benn imagines being put seriously to a farmer, is that it is an enquiry into his favourite intellectual preoccupations or perhaps into his leisure activities—applications of "interest" whose irrelevance Benn himself affirms. Otherwise, it has no normal application, though a "plain man" with an analytical turn of mind (such as John Locke) might reply:

> Civil interest I call life, liberty, health and indolency of body; and the possession of outward things, such as money, houses, furniture and the like (*Letter Concerning Toleration*).

This might be regarded as a specification of the kinds of ways in which a policy, law, or institution must impinge on someone before it can be said to be "in his interests." Unpacked into more logically transparent (if more long-winded) terms it might read: "A policy, law, or institution may be said to be in someone's interests if it satisfies the following conditions. . . ."

The main point about my proposed definition, however, is that it is always a *policy* that is said to be "in so-and-so's interest"—not the actual manner in which he is impinged upon. (From now on I shall use "policy" to cover "policy, law, or institution.") There are straightforward criteria specifying the way in which someone has to be affected by a policy before that policy can be truly described as being "in his interests"; but whether or not a given policy will bring about such results may quite often be an open question.

It is this feature of "interest" which explains how people can "mistake their interests"—item number one on the list of "things we want to say about interests." The stock argument against this possibility is that if you assert it you must commit yourself to the view that "some people know what's good for other people better than they do themselves." But this can now be seen to rest on a gross equivocation. The presumably illiberal, and therefore damaging, view to be saddled with would be the view that policies which impinge on people in ways which they dislike may nevertheless be said to be "in their interests." But this is not entailed by the statement that people may "mistake their interests." All that one has to believe is that they may think a policy will impinge upon them in a way which will increase their opportunities to get what they want when in fact it will do the opposite. Whether his opportunities are increased or narrowed by being unemployed is something each man may judge for himself; but it is surely only sensible to recognize that most people's opinions about the most effective economic policies for securing given ends are likely to be worthless. In his Fireside Chat on June 28, 1934, President Roosevelt said:

> The simplest way for each of you to judge recovery lies in the plain facts of your own individual situation. Are you better off than you were last year? Are your debts less burdensome? Is your bank account more secure? Are your working conditions better? Is your faith in your own individual future more firmly grounded?

It is quite consistent to say that people can "judge recovery for themselves" without respecting their opinions about the efficacy of deficit financing.

The other "things we normally want to say" also fit the proposed definition. People may want policies other than those calculated to increase their opportunities—hence the possibility of "disinterested action" and "promotional groups." Similarly, a man may definitely not want a policy which will increase his opportunities (perhaps because he thinks that the policy is unfair and that others should get the increase instead). Hence the possibility of someone's not wanting something that he acknowledges would be in his interests. Finally, nothing is more common than for someone to agree that a policy would increase his opportunities if adopted, and to want it to be adopted, but at the same time to say that the addition of his own efforts to the campaign to secure its adoption would have such a small probability of making the decisive difference between success and failure for the campaign that it is simply not worth making the effort; and of course if everyone is in the habit of reasoning like this a policy which is in the interests of a great many people, but not greatly in the interests of any of them, may well fail to receive any organized support at all.

No doubt there is room for amplification of my definition of what it is for a policy to be in someone's interest. In particular the phrase "opportunities to get what he wants" needs closer analysis, and account should be taken of the expression "so-and-so's *best* interests" which tends to be used where it is thought that the person in question would make such an unwise use of increased opportunities that he would be better off without them (e.g., a heavy drinker winning a first dividend on the football pools). However, I doubt whether refinements in the definition of "interest" would alter the correctness or incorrectness of what I have to say about "the public interest," so I turn now to that expression.

III

If "interest" is defined in such a way that "this policy is in *A*'s interest" is equivalent to "*A* is trying to get this policy adopted," the fact that there is conflict over the adoption of nearly all policies in a state is decisive evidence against there being a "public interest" in any but a few cases. But on the definition of "interest" I have proposed this would no longer be so. A policy might be truly describable as "in the public interest" even though some people opposed it. This could come about in a way already mentioned: those who oppose the policy might have "mistaken their interests." In other words, they may think the policy in question is not in their interests when it really is. Most opposition in the U.S.A. to unbalanced budgets can be explained in this way, for example. Disagreements about defence and disarmament policy are also largely disagreements about the most effective means to fairly obvious common goals such as national survival and (if possible) independence.

There are two other possibilities. One is that the group opposing the measure is doing so in order to further a different measure which is outside the range of relevant comparisons. The other possibility is that the opposing group have a special interest in the matter which counteracts their interest as members of the public. I do not accept these two descriptions to be clear; I shall devote the remainder of the paper to trying to make them so, taking up the former in this section and IV, and the latter in V.

Comparison enters into any evaluation in terms of interests. To say that a policy would be in someone's interests is implicitly to compare it with some other policy—often simply the continuance of the *status quo*. So if you say that a number of people have a common interest in something you must have in mind some alternative to it which you believe would be worse for all of them. The selection of alternatives for comparison thus assumes a position of crucial importance. Any policy can be made "preferable" by arbitrarily contrasting it with one sufficiently unpleasant. Unemployment and stagnation look rosy compared with nuclear war; common interests in the most unlikely proposals can be manufactured by putting forward as the alternative a simultaneous attack by our so-called independent deterrent on Russia and the U.S.A. All this need do is remind one that one thing may be "in somebody's interest" *compared with something else* but still undesirable compared with other possibilities. The problem remains: is there (in most matters) any one course of action which is better for everyone than any other? Fairly obviously, the answer is: No. Any ordinary proposal would be less in my interest than a poll tax of a pound a head, the proceeds to be given to me. And this can be repeated for everybody else, taking each person one at a time. This, however, seems as thin a reason for denying the possibility of common interests as the parallel manoeuvre in reverse was for asserting their ubiquity. In both cases the comparison is really irrelevant. But what are the criteria for relevance? The simplest answer (which will later have to have complications added) is that the only proposals to be taken into account when estimating "common interests" should be proposals which treat everyone affected in exactly the same way. Take the traditional example of a law prohibiting assault (including murder). If no limitation is imposed upon the range of alternatives it is easy to show that there is no "common interest" among all the members of a society in having such a law directed equally at everyone. For one could always propose that instead the society should be divided into two classes, the members of the first class being allowed to assault the members of the second class with impunity but not vice versa, as with Spartans and Helots; or each member of the first group might be put in this position only *vis-à-vis* particular members of the second group. (Examples of this can be drawn from slave-holding, patriarchal, or racially discriminatory systems such as the ante-bellum South, ancient Rome, and Nazi Germany respectively.) It could perhaps be argued that the "beneficiaries" under such an unequal system become brutalized and are therefore in some sense "worse off" than they would be under a regime of equality. But the whole point of "interest"—and its great claim in the eyes of liberals—is that the concept is indifferent to moral character and looks only at opportunities.

Yet even the most sceptical writers often admit that a law prohibiting assault by anyone against anyone is a genuine example of something which is "in the public interest" or "in everyone's interest." This becomes perfectly true when the alternatives are restricted to those which affect all equally, for then the most obvious possibilities are (a) that nobody should assault anybody else and (b) that anybody should be allowed to assault anybody else. And of these two it is hardly necessary to call on the authority of Hobbes to establish that, given the natural equality of strength and vulnerability which prevents anyone from having reasonable hopes of gaining from the latter set-up, the former is "everyone's interest."

IV

A convenient way of examining some of the ramifications of this theory is to work over some of the things Rousseau says in the *Social Contract* [7] about the "General Will." Judging from critiques in which Rousseau figures as a charlatan whose philosophical emptiness is disguised by his superficial rhetoric, it is hard to see why we should waste time reading him, except perhaps on account of his supposedly malign influence on Robespierre. I doubt the fairness of this estimate, and I am also inclined to deprecate the tendency (often though not always combined with the other) to look on Rousseau through Hegelian spectacles. We need to dismantle the implausible psychological and metaphysical theories (e.g., "compulsory rational freedom" and "group mind") which have been foisted on Rousseau by taking certain phrases and sentences (e.g., "forced to be free" and "moral person") out of context. As a small contribution to this process of demythologizing Rousseau I want to suggest here that what he says about "the general will" forms a coherent and ingenious unity if it is understood as a treatment of the theme of common interests.

Rousseau's starting point, which he frequently makes use of, is that any group will have a will that is general in relation to its constituent members, but particular with respect to groups in which it in turn is included. Translating this into talk about interests it means that any policy which is equally favourable to all the members of a given group will be less favourable to member A than the policy most favourable to A, less favourable to member B than the policy most favourable to B, and so on; but it will be more favourable to each of the members of the group than any policy which has to be equally beneficial to an even larger number of people. Suppose, for example, that a fixed sum—say a million pounds—is available for wage increases in a certain industry. If each kind of employee had a separate trade union one might expect as many incompatible claims as there were unions, each seeking to appropriate most of the increase for its own members. If for example there were a hundred unions with a thousand members apiece each employee might have a thousand pounds (a thousandth of the total) claimed on his behalf, and the total claims would add up to a hundred million pounds. At the other extreme if there were only one union, there would be no point in its putting in a claim totalling more than a million pounds (we assume for convenience that the union accepts the unalterability of this amount) and if it made an equal claim on behalf of each of its members this would come to only ten pounds a head. Intermediate numbers of unions would produce intermediate results.

Rousseau's distinction between the "will of all" and the "general will" now fits in neatly. The "will of all" is simply shorthand for "the policy most in A's interests, taking A in isolation; the policy most in B's interests, taking B in isolation; and so on." (These will of course normally be different policies for $A, B,$ and the rest.) The "general will" is a *single* policy which is equally in the interests of all the members of the group. It will usually be different from any of the policies mentioned before, and less beneficial to anyone than the policy most beneficial to himself alone.

We can throw light on some of the other things Rousseau says in the one-page chapter II.iii of the *Social Contract* by returning to the trade union example. Suppose now that the leaders of the hundred trade unions are told that the money will be forthcoming only if a majority of them can reach agreement on a way of dividing it up. A possible method would be for each leader to write down his preferred solution on a slip of paper, and for these to be compared, the process continuing until a requisite number of papers have the same proposal written on them. If each started by writing down his maximum demand there would be as many proposals as leaders—the total result would be the "will of all." This is obviously a dead end, and if no discussion is allowed among the leaders, there is a good chance that they would all propose, as a second best, an equal division of the money. (There is some experimental evidence for this, presented in Chapter 3 of Thomas Schelling's *The Strategy of Conflict*.[8]) Such a solution would be in accordance with the "general will" and represents a sort of highest common factor of agreement. As Rousseau puts it, it arises when the pluses and minuses of the conflicting first choices are cancelled out.

If instead of these arrangements communication is allowed, and even more if the groups are fewer and some leaders control large block votes, it becomes less likely that an equal solution will be everyone's second choice. It will be possible for some leaders to agree together to support a proposal which is less favourable to any of their members than each leader's first choice was to his own members, but still more favourable than any solution equally beneficial to all the participants. Thus, as Rousseau says, a "less general will" prevails.

In II.iii. Rousseau suggests that this should be prevented by not allowing groups to form or, if they do form, by seeing that they are many and small. In the less optimistic mood of IV.i., when he returns to the question, he places less faith in mechanical methods and more in widespread civic virtue. He now says that the real answer is for everyone to ask himself "the right question," i.e., "What measures will benefit me in common with everyone else, rather than me at the expense of everyone else?" (I have never seen attention drawn to the fact that this famous doctrine is something of an afterthought whose first and only occurrence in the *Social Contract* is toward the end.) However, this is a difference only about the most effective means of getting a majority to vote for what is in the common interest of all. The essential point remains the same: that only where all are equally affected by the policy adopted can an equitable solution be expected.

> The undertakings which bind us to the social body are obligatory only because they are mutual; and their nature is such that in fulfilling them we cannot work for others without working for ourselves. . . . What makes the will general is less the number of voters than the common interest uniting them; for, under this system, each necessarily submits to the conditions he imposes on others: and this admirable agreement between interest and justice gives to the common deliberations an equitable character which at once vanishes when any particular question is discussed, in the absence of a common interest to unite and identify the ruling of the judge with that of the party. (II.iv.)

Provided this condition is met, nobody will deliberately vote for a burdensome law because it will be burdensome to him too: this is why no *specific* limitations on "the general will" are needed. Disagreements can then be due only to conflicts of opinion—not to conflicts of interest. Among the various policies which would affect everyone in the same way, each person has to decide which would benefit himself most—and, since everyone else is similarly circumstanced, he is automatically deciding at the same time which would benefit everyone else most. Thus, to go back to our example of a law prohibiting assault: disagreement will arise, if at all, because some think they (in common with everyone else) would make a net gain of opportunities from the absence of any law against assault, while others think the opposite. This is, in principle, a dispute with a right and wrong answer; and everyone benefits from the right answer's being reached rather than the wrong one. Rousseau claims that a majority is more likely to be right than any given voter, so that someone in the minority will in fact gain from the majority's decision carrying the day. This has often been regarded as sophistical or paradoxical, but it is quite reasonable once one allows Rousseau his definition of the situation as one in which everyone is cooperating to find a mutually beneficial answer, for so long as everyone is taken as having an equal, better than even chance of giving the right answer, the majority view will (in the long run) be right more often than that of any given voter. (Of course, the same thing applies in reverse: if each one has on average a *less* than even chance of being right, the majority will be *wrong* more often than any given voter.) The formula for this was discovered by Condorcet and has been presented by Duncan Black on page 164 of his *Theory of Committees and Elections*.[9] To illustrate its power, here is an example: if we have a voting body of a thousand, each member of which is right on average 51 per cent of the time, what is the probability in any particular instance that a 51 per cent majority has the right answer? The answer, rather surprisingly perhaps, is: better than two to one (69 per cent). Moreover, if the required majority is kept at 51 per cent and the number of voters raised to ten thousand, or if the number of voters stays at one thousand the required majority is raised to 60 per cent, the probability that the majority (5,100 to 4,900 in the first case or 600 to 400 in the second) has the right answer rises virtually to unity (99.97 per cent). None of this, of course, shows that "Rousseau was right" but it does suggest that he was no simpleton.

To sum up, Rousseau calls for the citizen's deliberations to comprise two elements: (a) the decision to forgo (either as un-attainable or as immoral) policies which would be in one's own personal interest alone, or in the common interest of a group smaller than the whole, and (b) the attempt to calculate which, of the various lines of policy that would affect oneself equally with all others, is best for him (and, since others are like him, for others). This kind of two-step deliberation is obviously reminiscent of the method recommended in Mr. Hare's *Freedom and Reason,*[10] with the crucial difference that whereas Mr. Hare will settle for a willingness to be affected by the policy in certain hypothetical circumstances, Rousseau insists that my being affected by the policy must actually be in prospect. There is no need to construct a special planet to test my good faith—my bluff is called every time. By the same token, the theory I have attributed to Rousseau requires far more stringent conditions to be met before something can be said to be in the common in-terest of all than the vague requirement of "equal consideration" put forward by Benn and Peters in their *Social Principles and the Democratic State.*[11]

V

Even if Rousseau can be shown to be consistent it does not follow that the doctrine of the *Social Contract* has wide applica-tion. Rousseau himself set out a number of requirements that have to be met before it applies at all: political virtue (rein-forced by a civil religion), smallness of state, and rough eco-nomic equality among the citizens. And even then, as he points out plainly, it is only a few questions which allow solutions that touch all in the same way. If only some are affected by a matter the "general will" cannot operate. It is no longer a case of each man legislating for himself *along with others,* but merely one of some men legislating *for* others. It is fairly obvious that Rousseau's requirements are not met in a great modern nation state—a conclusion that would not have worried him. But since I am trying to show that "the public interest" is applicable in just such a state it does have to worry me. It is here that I must introduce my remaining explanation of the way in which something can be "in the public interest" while still arousing opposition from some.

Think again of the examples with which I began this paper. The thing that is claimed to be "in the public interest" is not *prima facie* in the interests of the journalist whose sources may dry up, the workers whose rise is condemned, or the business-men whose restrictive practices are outlawed. But do first appearances mislead? After all, the journalist along with the rest gains from national security, and workers or industrialists gain along with the rest from lower prices. To avoid a flat con-tradiction we need more refined tools; and they exist in ordinary speech. Instead of simply saying that some measure is "in his interests" a man will often specify some role or capacity in which it is favourable to him: "as a parent," "as a businessman," "as a house owner," and so on. One of the capacities in which everyone finds himself is that of "a member of the public." Some issues allow a policy to be produced which will affect everyone in his capacity as a "member of the public" and no-body in any other capacity. This is the pure "Rousseau" situa-tion. Then there are other issues which lack this simplicity but still do not raise any problems because those who are affected in a capacity other than that of "member of the public" are either affected in that capacity in the same direction as they are in their other capacity of "member of the public" or at least are not affected so strongly in the contrary direction as to tip the overall balance of their interest (what I shall call their "net interest") that way. Although this is not quite what I have called the "Rousseau" situation, the "Rousseau formula still works. Indeed, Rousseau sometimes seems explicitly to accept this kind of situation as satisfactory, as when he says (III.xv.)

that in a well-ordered state "the aggregate of the common happiness furnishes a greater proportion of that of each individual."

Finally, we have the familiar case where for some people a special interest outweighs their share in the public interest. The journalist may think, for example, that compulsory disclosure of sources would indeed be in the public interest but at the same time conclude that his own special interest as a journalist in getting information from people who want to stay anonymous is more important to him than the marginal gain in security that is at stake. In such cases as this Rousseau's formula will not work, for although everyone still has a common interest in the adoption of a certain policy *qua* "member of the public," some have a net interest in opposing it.

To adopt the policy which is "in the public interest" in such a case is still different from deliberately passing over an available policy which would treat everyone equally, for in the present case there *is* no such policy available. Even so, it involves favouring some at the expense of others, which makes it reasonable to ask whether it is justifiable to recommend it. Various lines of justification are possible. Bentham seems to have assumed that in most matters there was a public interest on one side (e.g., in cheap and speedy legal procedures) and on the other side the "sinister" interest of those who stood to gain on balance from abuses (e.g., "Judge & Co.") and to have believed (what is surely not unreasonable) that a utilitarian calculation would generally give the verdict to the policy favouring "the public." On a different tack, it might be argued that it is inequitable for anyone to benefit from "special privileges" at the expense of the rest of the community. But unfortunately neither of these is as clear as it looks because a hidden process of evaluation has already gone on to decide at what point an interest becomes "sinister" and how well placed someone must be to be "privileged." The cheapest and speediest dispensation of law could be obtained by conscripting the legal profession and making them work twelve hours a day for subsistence rations; but this would no doubt be ruled out by a utilitarian as imposing "hardship" and by the believer in distributive justice as not giving a "just reward" for the work done. Thus, by the time one has fixed the level of rewards beyond which one is going to say that "privilege" and "sinister interest" lie it is virtually analytic that one has defined a "good" solution (whether the criteria be utilitarian or those of distributive justice).

It is clearer to say that in these "non-Rousseauan" situations the public interest has to be balanced against the special interests involved and cannot therefore be followed exclusively. But "the public interest" remains of prime importance *in politics,* even when it runs against the net interest of some, because interests which are shared by few can be promoted by them whereas interests shared by many have to be furthered by the state if they are to be furthered at all. Only the state has the universality and the coercive power necessary to prevent people from doing what they want to do when it harms the public and to raise money to provide benefits for the public which cannot, or cannot conveniently, be sold on the market: and these are the two main ways in which "the public interest" is promoted. This line of thought brings us into touch with the long tradition that finds in the advancement of the interests common to all one of the main tasks of the state. The peculiarity of the last two centuries or so has lain in the widespread view that the other traditional candidates—the promotion of True Religion or the enforcement of the Laws of Nature and God—should be eliminated. This naturally increases the relative importance of "the public interest."

A contributory factor to this tendency is the still continuing process of social and economic change which one writer has dubbed the "organizational revolution." These developments have in many ways made for a more humane society than the smaller-scale, more loosely articulated, nineteenth-century pattern of organization could provide. But they have had the incidental result of making obsolete a good deal of our inherited conceptual equipment. Among the victims of this technological unemployment are "public opinion" and "the will of the people." On most of the bills, statutory instruments, and questions of administrative policy which comes before Parliament there is little corresponding to the nineteenth-century construct of "public opinion": the bulk of the electorate holding well-informed, principled, serious views. Even when an issue is sufficiently defined and publicized for there to be a widespread body of "opinion" about it these opinions are likely to be based on such a small proportion of the relevant data that any government which conceived its job as one of automatically implementing the majority opinion would be inviting disaster.

This does not entail that voting with universal suffrage is not a better way of choosing political leaders than any alternative; but if "public opinion" is a horse that won't run this means that "public interest" has to run all the harder to make up, since as we have seen it has the advantage of operating where those affected by the policy in question have not even heard of it and would not understand it if they did. Consider for example the arrangements which enable the staffs of organizations whose members are affected by impending or existing legislation to consult with their opposite numbers in governing departments about its drafting and administration. This system of "functional representation," which now has almost constitutional status, would not get far if each side tried to argue from the *opinions* of its clients (the organization members and "the public" respectively) on the matter; but their *interests* do provide a basis for discussion, a basis which leaves room for the uncomfortable fact that in a large organization (whether it be a trade union, a limited company, or a state) information and expertise are just as likely to be concentrated in a few hands as is the formal power to make decisions.

VI

At the beginning of this paper I suggested that the popularity of "the public interest" as a political justification could be attributed either to its vacuity or to its being used to adduce in support of policies definite considerations of a kind which are as a matter of fact valued highly by many people. If my analysis of "the public interest" is correct, it may be expected

to flourish in a society where the state is expected to produce
affluence and maintain civil liberties but not virtue or religious
conformity, a society which has no distinction between different
grades of citizen, and a society with large complex organizations
exhibiting a high degree of rank and file apathy. I do not think
it is necessary to look any further for an explanation of the
concept's present popularity.

REFERENCES

1. Sorauf, Frank J. "Public Interest Reconsidered," *Journal of Politics,*
   XIX (November 1957), 616–639.
2. Schubert, Glendon A. *The Public Interest: A Critique of the Theory
   of a Political Concept* (New York: The Free Press, 1961).
3. Bentley, Arthur. *The Process of Government,* ed. by Peter F. Ode-
   gard (Cambridge: Belknap Press of Harvard University Press, 1967).
4. Truman, David Bicknell. *The Governmental Process* (New York:
   Knopf, 1951).
5. Miller, John D. B. *The Nature of Politics* (London: Duckworth,
   1962).
6. Benn, Stanley I. "Interests in Politics," *Proceedings of the Aristotelian
   Society* (London: Harrison and Sons, 1960), pp. 127–140.
7. Rousseau, Jean Jacques. *The Social Contract and Discourses* trans.
   by G. D. H. Cole (New York: Dutton Press, 1950).
8. Schelling, Thomas C. *The Strategy of Conflict* (Cambridge: Harvard University Press, 1960).
9. Black, Duncan. *The Theory of Committees and Elections* (Cambridge: Cambridge University Press, 1958).
10. Hare, Richard M. *Freedom and Reason* (Oxford: Clarendon Press,
    1963).
11. Benn, Stanley, and R. S. Peters, *Social Principles and The Demo-
    cratic State* (London: Allen and Unwin, 1959).

8: Human Nature and Participatory Democracy

ARNOLD S. KAUFMAN

Some theorists have argued that because man's nature is what it is a democracy of participation is undesirable. Others have held that man's nature, together with certain sociological truths, makes a democracy of participation, or even of majority rule, impossible. I will examine the way in which various conceptions of human nature are related to participatory democracy; for the actual relevance of conceptions of human nature to participatory democracy is not usually shown clearly. Consequently, fundamental problems of democratic theory are not formulated precisely enough. My aim is to weaken the hold that certain sceptical dogmas have on the minds of those who might otherwise be inclined to take more seriously the task of increasing the participatory element in modern industrial societies.

Pessimistic conceptions of man on the basis of which social

From *Responsibility*, Nomos III, Carl J. Friedrich, editor. New York: The Liberal Arts Press, 1960, pp. 266–289.

philosophies are reared fall into two classes. There are those who, while arguing that human weaknesses are statistically inevitable, nevertheless believe that any particular person's weaknesses are largely remediable. Then there are those who believe that, for the most part, human weaknesses are not remediable.

Walter Lippmann has provided us with a good example of the first type of theory. His book, *The Public Philosophy*,[1] consists of diagnosis and remedy. In the diagnostic portion Lippmann describes the decline of Western democracies, ultimately attributing the deterioration that has taken place during the last half century to men's acquisitiveness, their lack of basic self-discipline and of intellectual attainment. Though he does not oppose political democracy (he thinks that unless responsive government exists there is bound to be disorder, and in modern industrial societies adequate responsiveness can only be achieved through political democracy, that is, a relatively free opposition and relatively free elections), he maintains that a democracy will only function well if these defects of human character are considerably remedied. Thus, Lippmann pleads for renewal of what he calls "the traditions of civility"; of those traits of character and those beliefs which among other things incline men to choose the best possible representatives. Only if the electorate chooses well, and then permits those elected to govern, will the decline of Western liberal democracy be halted.

What institutional remedies does Lippmann propose for the ills he so eloquently diagnoses? His only practical suggestion is that educational practices be transformed. Otherwise he suggests only that through moral suasion men may be led to discover for themselves the general guides to conduct which should govern their lives. This discovery will be achieved by being "coolly and lucidly rational."

Lippmann's remedies are inadequate. Traditionally, liberal theorists have required that educational institutions carry an intolerable share of the burden of the civilizing process. In fact, performance of an educational task the size of that required is bound to reflect the defects of the surrounding community. Education cannot escape being corrupted by what is evil in its social context. The alternative, education for an elite, is not just nor can it serve the function Lippmann would require of it.

The very framework of commitment within which Lippmann poses the issues rules out the one condition which, more than any other institutional arrangement, is capable of producing widespread distribution of those traits of character and capabilities desired—direct participation. He wills the end, but not the means. For he is caught up in a conflict of his own construction. On the one hand he believes that men ought to acquire certain traits of character, on the other he is too pessimistic about human capabilities to consider empowering the mass in a way which is indispensable to the development of those traits. In practice, Lippmann's position reduces to a variant of the view that human weaknesses are not ultimately remediable. Collectively society should not act; individually they cannot act effectively.

The view that institutional remedies for defects of human character are impossible has taken two forms: psychological and religious. But the religious position entails psychological claims. For, suppose man has all the defects attributed to him by, say, Reinhold Niebuhr; then whether or not this is due to God's intention, the pernicious attributes must exist psychologically. So we must first ask the psychological question, "Do men have certain ineradicable traits which are bad?" and seek the empirical answer.[2]

It should be noted that the question is not "Are men constitutionally wicked?" The argument which links the undesirability of participatory democracy to man's essential nature presupposes only that men cannot be trusted. It does not follow that they ought to be blamed (or punished) for the harmful things they do.

Among contemporary psychologists, psychoanalytic theorists alone have addressed themselves to the problem which interests us. They base their conclusions on a mass of clinical data. The difficulty is that they do not speak with one voice.

This is partly due to Freud's uncertainty. He was very tentative in his conclusions about man's constitutional destructiveness. He originally held that all our thoughts and activities are governed by what he called "the pleasure principle," by which he meant the tendency to diminish unpleasurable tension by lowering that tension. Pleasure is due to an economic reaction of the organism to stress. Thus, dreams are wish-fulfilling because the organism reduces unpleasurable tension by expending in dream-phantasies the energy which induces the tension. But, Freud pointed out, certain phenomena do not seem to be explainable on this basis; in particular, various tendencies to repeat painful experience. Thus children often repeat a painful pattern of separation from parents, soldiers who suffer war trauma relive in dreams the experience which causes their great pain, and persons who have married unhappily, in certain circumstances, repeat the pattern on other occasions. In all these instances the repetition seems to serve no economic purpose; it is not governed by the pleasure principle. The pain inflicted on oneself seems to be pointlessly masochistic.

Freud tried to deal with the problem these clinical findings generated in a monograph entitled *Beyond the Pleasure Principle*. There he suggests the existence of an instinct which lies, so to speak, beyond the pleasure principle. This he called "the death instinct." This is not the place to describe the argument in detail. Suffice it to say that, proceeding with great ingenuity, Freud makes a very convincing case for the supposition that masochistic repetition reflects a tendency to return to an original state of quiescence, or death. But if masochism can be partly explained on this basis, so can certain forms of sadism which are simply the projection on to others of qualities hated and punished in oneself. Thus Freud very tentatively concludes that men are by nature potentially destructive. Only repression and other defenses prevent them from giving their instinctual destructiveness completely free reign.

I emphasize the tentativeness of Freud's conclusion because he himself insists on it. In a passage near the end of his monograph he writes:

It is true that my assertion of the regressive character of instincts (the death instinct) . . . rests upon observed material—namely on the facts of the compulsion to repeat. It may be, however, that I have overestimated their significance. . . . Unfortunately, people are seldom impartial where ultimate things, the great problems of science and life, are concerned. *Each of us is governed in such cases by deep-rooted internal prejudices, into whose hands our speculation unwittingly plays.* Since we have such good grounds for being distrustful, our attitude towards the results of our own deliberations cannot well be other than one of cool benevolence.[3]

Freud himself must thus have anticipated the fact that his followers would differ about his quite fundamental conclusion. There are those who agree with Freud's postulating of a death instinct, pushing the implication even further than he did himself. Thus Melanie Klein writes,

I consider that envy is an oral-sadistic and anal-sadistic expression of destructive impulses, operative from the beginning of life, and that it has a constitutional basis.[4]

She expresses her indebtedness to Freud's formulation in *Beyond the Pleasure Principle,* but believes she and others have found independent and decisive confirmation of his hypothesis in clinical observations, especially of children. Moreover, she believes she can describe the actual mechanisms through which destructive impulses manifest themselves from earliest infancy onward.

On the other hand, she cautiously insists that these destructive impulses may not decisively determine subsequent development. In particular, constitutional variations exist which enable some persons to be more, some less succesful in taming these hostile impulses. But these constitutional limits can only be discovered in the case of any specific individual after extensive psychoanalytic therapy. Finally, she emphasizes the extent to which external experience may influence the development and expression of hostile tendencies.[5]

Thus, though certain of the existence of the death instinct and its destructive by-products, Freud's tentativeness is transposed in Melanie Klein's thinking to the level of doubt about the constitutional strength of the impulse in the case of any particular person, and the consequent variation in the possibility of therapeutic aid.

Erich Fromm is probably the best known spokesman for that psychoanalytic school of thought which rejects Freud's hypothesis of a death instinct. In the course of expounding his "humanistic ethics," Fromm argues that Freud's theory is "dualistic," emphasizing the forces that make both for good and for evil in man's nature. Fromm then asks, "Are we to understand this dualism to mean that both the drive to live and the drive to destroy are innate and equally strong capacities in man?" His answer is an emphatic "No."[6] He argues that all tendencies to human destructiveness are due to blocked development of potentialities, and are thus "secondary." Unfortunately, the conditions which block personal development occur all too often in the lives of everyone. Thus the impulses to destroy are universal. But the strength of these impulses varies widely according to the occurrence of unfavorable conditions. Nevertheless Fromm confidently concludes that clinical observations "have shown that man is not necessarily evil but becomes evil only if the proper conditions for his growth and development are lacking."[7] Though he denies the existence of the sort of constitutional limits which Klein and, more tentatively, Freud believed existed, he does emphasize how widespread are the conditions which cause men to become destructive. "Indeed," he writes, "there is less reason to be puzzled by the fact there are so many neurotic people than by the phenomenon that most people are relatively healthy in spite of the many adverse influences they are exposed to."[8]

I do not want to argue for one position or the other, nor do I want to deny the important implications the differences may have for other policy considerations, or for therapeutic practice. What I do maintain is that as far as the problems of democracy are concerned, the views of Freud, Klein, and Fromm have substantially the same implications. Moreover, these implications, while they support the case for a form of democratic organization which protects and stabilizes, in no way rule out the case for a democracy of participation, though they surely weaken some of the power for good which some may be inclined to attribute to it.

A democracy of participation may have many beneficial consequences, but its main justifying function is and always has been, not the extent to which it protects or stabilizes a community, but the contribution it can make to the development of human powers of thought, feeling, and action. In this respect it differs, and differs quite fundamentally, from a representative system incorporating all sorts of institutional features designed to safeguard human rights and ensure social order. *This distinction is all-important*. The fundamental error many critics of democracy make consists in failure to recognize that different institutional forms of democracy may be and are defended on the basis of different functional consequences.

Clearly, the three views considered all support the position of those who insist that a representative system of some sort is desirable. Whether one agrees with Klein in maintaining that there are instinctual destructive impulses, or with Fromm who denies this, all would agree that the conditions which make for and support the growth of destructive tendencies are very widespread. The Platonic-Calvinist belief that there is a class of men, the philosopher kings or the elect, who can early and easily be identified as possessing special exemption from destructive urges, has been shattered once and for all by Freudian discoveries. Surely Freudianism does weaken the case for aristocratic theories (though Freud himself tended to be an élitist, a fact which is admirably discussed and analysed by Fromm).[9]

On the other hand, while Fromm and Klein disagree about man's native constitution, they would agree that the possibilities of personal development are difficult to determine, and, in any case, generally great. Nothing in what either of them says precludes the possibility that participatory democracy may play an important role in enabling a person to develop his constructive and creative powers and achieve greater happiness. True, we can no longer accept the buoyant optimism of the Enlightenment concerning the potentialities for purely social reform. And assuredly underlying Rousseau's classical defense was a very great faith in the power participation has to effect personal development. We must admit that these institutions are not quite as important as Rousseau himself supposed, but this does not imply that they are not vitally important. The issue must be decided independently of Freudian theories of human nature, on the basis of the relevant evidence.

Participatory democracy has also been attacked on the grounds that most men are constitutionally lacking in intelligence. The scientific evidence for this claim is based primarily on the cumulative record of intelligence testing. A very able criticism of the anti-democratic conclusions sometimes drawn from these results has been given by David Spitz.[10] I will restrict myself to a few observations.

First, the score of 100 I.Q. has come to represent the threshold of adequate intelligence in the popular imagination. It is too often forgotten that this score is a relative figure, and implies little about the basic capacity to exercise political responsibility. Second, I.Q.'s are not irrevocably determined by inheritance. There is much evidence for the view that whatever it is that intelligence tests may be greatly affected by environmental changes. The more we learn, the more does nature seem to give way to nurture as a determining influence in human affairs.[11] Third, participation may be an important if not an indispensable condition of a person's fully developing his inherent powers of intelligent thought and action. Fourth, the suffrage in advanced industrial democracies is, in any event, going to be almost universal. It may well be that participation is one of the most important ways of ensuring that those who vote will make their decisions intelligently. In a political democracy the important thing is not that the voter always vote for the best man, but that he never vote for a stupid, irrationally bigoted, or demagogic person.

Which brings us to the fifth point. No one has ever demonstrated a connection between virtue and intelligence. As Carl Friedrich has put it, "In the forming of political judgments, character is more important than intellect."[12] And, as one psychoanalyst has written, "Undoubtedly there are children and adults with a defective guilt sense, and such defect is not specifically linked with intellectual capacity or incapacity."[13]

The results of intelligence testing, while they may induce more realistic expectations, do not seriously harm the case for participation. Nor does the fact, and I accept it as a fact, that all men are irrational a good deal of the time.

Joseph Schumpeter has argued that what he calls the "classical doctrine of democracy" (by which he seems to mean a rather vague synthesis of Rousseau's views and the naive utilitarianism of the worst classical economists) is untenable because men are demonstrably irrational. In defending his conclusion he mentions the theories of many men, Freud among them, as well as the results of contemporary empirical economics. All of these sources, he argues, tend to confirm his belief that men are very irrational, much more so than classical democratic theorists ever suspected. Schumpeter's argument has greatly influenced prominent intellectuals (e.g. Seymour Lipset and Kenneth Galbraith), so one approaches it respectfully. But in the final analysis his argument against participatory democracy is puzzling and incoherent, especially those parts which bear on man's irrationality. Yet it is sophisticated and entirely representative, so I will use it as a peg on which to hang criticism which I believe to have more general validity.

I must abbreviate Schumpeter's argument, but that part which is relevant can be sketched easily enough. Schumpeter wants to disprove the fundamental assumptions on which "the classical doctrine of democracy" rests. That doctrine affirms that:

The democratic method is that institutional arrangement for arriving at political decisions which realizes the common good by making the people itself decide issues through the election of individuals who are to assemble in order to carry out its will.[14]

The psychological presupposition of this doctrine is, according to Schumpeter, the belief that "every normal person can be made to see (the common good) by means of rational argument," and that, therefore, only ignorance, stupidity, and anti-social interest prevent the common good from being realized. The classical democrat is thus placed "under the practical necessity of attributing to the will of the *individual* an independence and rational quality that are altogether unrealistic."[15] For, even supposing there are no widespread anti-social interests, the argument presupposes that everyone knows exactly what he wants to stand for, has the ability to sift information and, in so doing, to select the most rational means to an end. But, says Schumpeter, the evidence against these assumptions is overwhelming.

It is at this point in his argument that Schumpeter invokes the testimony of Freud and others. His detailed criticism is, however, restricted to mention of the results of investigations of crowd behavior and of economic behavior.

Le Bon and others, in their studies of crowd behavior, have learned that "under the influence of agglomeration," and particularly under the stress of excitement, civilized modes of thinking and feeling break down. There is "sudden eruption of primitive impulses, infantilisms, and criminal propensities."[16] The economists have demonstrated the same curious breakdown of rational intelligence in consumer behavior. Through careful observation they have begun to discover that the wants of consumers "are nothing like as definite and their actions upon those wants nothing like as rational and prompt" as utilitarian economists had supposed. People are so easily influenced and persuaded by appeals unrelated to the nature of the commodity that the economist is forced by the facts to give up his belief that humans decide rationally in an enormously wide range of economic choice.

Schumpeter refrains from pushing his criticisms of the classical assumption to an untenable extreme. He insists, for example, that within limits the consumer does know precisely what he desires, as well as how to select what he wants from among existing alternatives. And, more generally, those decisions which lie within the little field which the individual citizen's mind encompasses with a full sense of its reality" are often made with definiteness and rationality. Nor does this field suddenly vanish as we move away from purely personal concerns. "In the realm of public affairs there are sectors that are more within the reach of the citizen's mind than others."[17] In his consideration of such municipal and national issues the average citizen's degree of interest and realistic assessment may be great. But the number of such issues is much smaller than classical democratic theorists supposed. As the issues grow more remote, a person is more likely to give in to "dark urges," and the group will is more easily "manufactured." Schumpeter concludes,

> All of this goes to show that without the initiative that comes from immediate responsibility, ignorance will persist in the face of masses of information, however complete and correct.[18]

Though Schumpeter fails to do so, in order to complete the picture we must again refer to Freudian theory. For Freud and his followers have given the most detailed account of the way in which an individual's desires are confused, and what he thinks are good means to given ends are dictated, not by rational thought, but by irrational rationalization.

What Schumpeter has written does indeed appear to be a powerful indictment of traditional democratic attitudes—the attitudes reflected most concisely in the motto *Vos populi, vox dei*. Nevertheless, Schumpeter, far from repudiating the essential elements of the classical doctrine he attacks, actually supports what is central to it; moreover, his general line of argument *cannot* weaken that doctrine.

To begin with, Schumpeter commits what I have already suggested is the fundamental error of all such critiques; he confuses the functions of direct participation with the functions of a representative system within a framework of countervailing institutional power. The first has more to do with what can be done *to* men, with the development of distinctively human powers; the second with what can be done *for* men, with protection against tyranny and establishment of social order. *This distinction is absolutely essential to any clear thought about democracy and its implementing institutions.* For corresponding to the distinction are two different, though overlapping, sets of institutions. Differences between institutions are inevitable when we are trying to implement different and possibly incompatible general aims. In the course of making his case for democratic processes of one sort, Schumpeter has inadvertently suggested the case for institutions of the other sort.

Schumpeter also seriously confuses popular rhetoric and popular beliefs. Primarily preoccupied with the economic theories with which he is familiar, his description of what he calls the "classical doctrine" is a caricature. But, for the purposes of discussion, let us assume that he has accurately described what the classical democrats believed.

Does Schumpeter's argument weaken the case for extension of participatory institutions? In a passage already quoted Schumpeter writes, "without the initiative that comes from immediate responsibility, ignorance will persist." If we admit that participatory institutions ought not to be extended to embrace all social decisions, then the question becomes, how much should they cover in order to make democracy, in the sense of free competition for leadership, function well? For, as Schumpeter himself admits, it is only when men acquire direct responsibility for a certain range of decisions that social imagination breaks through its parochial barriers and envisages larger possibilities. Where Schumpeter errs, or where he at least does not even begin to prove his case, is in supposing that a man's sphere of direct responsibility must be confined to the rearing of children, the purchase of butter, and the construction of sewer systems.

Let me put the points that emerge in the form of two hypotheses. In modern industrial societies men can successfully assume responsibility for the direction of many affairs which today they regard as largely irrelevant to their lives because these affairs seem so remote. Moreover, in the case of those types of decision which it is best, for other reasons, to put into the hands of delegated agents, the best agents will be selected when those who make the selection have direct responsibility for decisions which are similar to those with which the agent will be entrusted.

Schumpeter insists upon the role of leadership in modern industrial societies. "Collectives," he writes, "act almost exclusively by accepting leadership—this is the dominant mechanism of practically any collective action which is more than a reflex."[19] Assuming this assessment of the role of leadership is sound, Schumpeter gives us no hint as to how good leadership is to be ensured. The only aspect of his analysis which suggests what those mechanisms might be is what he says about direct responsibility. I wish simply to state more explicitly and emphatically what Schumpeter very reluctantly suggests even though his suggestion conflicts with the main thrust of his analysis. The most important condition of the emergence of good leadership in modern industrial societies is, for the great mass of human beings, direct responsibility through participation. A nation can be lucky. Perhaps France has been lucky in its choice of a strong man. But a nation can be unlucky. Germany was. The stakes are too important to trust to luck. If this is true of the nation, it is no less true of all the collectives within the nation. Like Lippmann, Schumpeter wills the end, but not the indispensable means.

If what I have been arguing is sound, it is because an empirical case can be made for participatory institutions. That is why I have put my main points in the form of hypotheses, unexamined hypotheses up to this point. For this reason it is important to emphasize that I have shown only that Schumpeter, rather than ruling out an extension of participatory institutions, has by implication suggested that direct participation is essential for the proper functioning of democracy in his restricted sense. What remains to be shown is that direct participation is an effective and indispensable condition of diminishing the extent to which men think irrationally about all things.

Can an empirical case be made for participation? This is not a question which the great advocates of participatory democracy have ever faced seriously enough. Usually they have simply assumed that participation will make a vital contribution to the development of human personality.

In this connection, it is interesting to note a change in the tactics of participatory democracy's critics. The heart of Plato's attack on democratic participation was the claim that it turned men into beasts, incapable of restraining the pull of either appetite or passion. In short, Plato thought that democracy makes monsters of men. Echoes of the Platonic critique persist, e.g., in the writings of Russell Kirk. But the most effective critiques are today tinged with a sad "would that it could be" reluctance to draw the awful conclusion. Those who base their rejection on a pessimistic conception of human nature do not deny that participation can be, in itself, beneficial; it is simply that in balance it is pernicious. We cannot take the chance of permitting men to devour or injure each other through stupidity, however much it might contribute to personal development. Others, shortly to be considered, reluctantly conclude that participation is impossible in advanced industrial societies. The point is that, whereas Plato met the democratic case head-on, simply contradicting Pericles' famous defense, today critics try rather to outflank the advocates of participatory democracy.

Thus, though there is general agreement with the proposition that participation contributes to personal development, it is both valuable and necessary to make the empirical case. This has never really been done adequately. Neither G. D. H. Cole nor John Dewey, for example, ever developed an empirical defense. An adequate philosophy of participatory democracy demands a more systematic approach to the problem. But in this paper I can make only a few suggestions.

The first step in the fulfillment of an empirical program must be a much more precise definition of participation than theorists usually work with. In a 1957 symposium which dealt with Workers' Participation in Management, the symposiasts were able to agree that at least three different forms of participation had to be distinguished: formalized direct participation, formalized indirect participation, and informal participation.[20] But what is essential to all these forms of participation? The suggestion I should like to make, though not argue for in detail, is that participation essentially involves actual preliminary deliberation (conversations, debate, discussion) and that in the final decision each participant has a roughly equal formal say. While this does not imply majority rule, it does preclude rule by a minority of those sufficiently interested to participate. Nor does it imply that each person has influence equal to that of those who have the equal power of formal decision. The distinction between power and influence is vitally important. If someone is especially influential because he has special knowledge about a problem or because he thinks more clearly or more imaginatively about certain issues, his influence is compatible with equal participation in the sense intended. (This is the confusion on which Schumpeter's conclusion about the inevitability of leadership in collectives is based.)

If we have an adequate conception of participation to work with, we can then proceed to examine the evidence for the key hypothesis—that in advanced industrial societies participation is, in balance, beneficial because of the contribution it makes to individual personal development. This implies that side effects do not have long-term detrimental consequences which more than outweigh momentary benefits. Empirical investigation thus gets very complicated. But concern with empirical complexity is all the more necessary. It is necessary not only in terms of justifying participation, but, just as important, it is by acquiring this kind of systematic knowledge that we will be able to implement participation in a way which minimizes harmful consequences. The results of participation are not the same in very different situations.

I will give only one example of the sort of investigation I have in mind. The syndicalists have traditionally supposed that workers could assume managerial functions with good results both for the workers themselves and for the larger society. But careful sociological analysis of the results of experiments in Germany, Yugoslavia, Poland, and elsewhere seem to indicate that this optimism is not justified. One symposiast concludes, "Any form of participation that is based on the appointment of workers to managerial or quasi-managerial positions is bound to defeat its own ends."[21] Another, more optimistically, considers the possibility of eliminating conflict through an extensive rotation of managerial jobs. All agree that the issue is fundamental for the future of workers' participation.

There are many problems that the symposiasts do not go into. For example, one difficulty seems to be due to the jump in income enjoyed by workers' managerial representatives. This tends to destroy their ability to represent their rank and file in a mutually satisfactory fashion. The differences between modes of selecting workers' representatives, the way in which their accountability is ensured, and so on—in short, the truly participatory element in the whole business—is extremely influential in determining the outcome. My point is simply that these are the concrete details of various types of participation which must be seriously considered by those who advocate its implementation in different spheres. The unargued presupposition of this paper is that participation is immensely beneficial. The burden of my argument to this point has simply been to prove, first, that what we know about human nature does not force us to conclude that participation is either pernicious or useless. In the last few paragraphs I have indicated that what we know about the effects of participation indicates that it has a role to play in such improvement, but its role is immensely complex. Much empirical study is required both to prove that participation is beneficial and to clarify the way in which it can best be implemented in specific spheres.

Important as these empirical considerations are, there is more to the perennial debate concerning man's nature and the consequent desirability of participatory democracy than can be embraced by a strictly empirical approach. There is something which Freud hints at in a passage quoted earlier. In thinking about the great problems of man's goodness or evil "each of us is governed . . . by deep-rooted internal prejudices, into whose hands our speculation unwittingly plays." This is profoundly true; and no discussion which ignores it can be adequate. Beliefs concerning man's basic constitution and the consequent possibilities of personal development cannot be defended or explained on empirical grounds alone. The *something more* involved concerns the relation between belief and effort.

William James, in his much maligned essay *The Will to Believe,* illustrates one of the dimensions of belief with which he is concerned by describing a lover who wins the one he woos by *believing* that she loves him. James was, I presume, trying to say that often making the effort to achieve a possible good depends on our belief in the possibility of that achievement—that the very nerve of our effort to achieve a good may be cut by premature admission of its impossibility. Surely, the lover who *believes* courts disappointment and defeat—disappointment and defeat which may be all the more disillusioning because he has, so to speak, lowered his defenses in an act of faith. But, and this is James' central point, the defensive posture, while it protects, precludes achievement.

James goes on to misuse this point about the relation between belief and effort in discussing the existence of God. But it does have relevance to our problem. For surely the belief in the possibility of personal development is an important condition of its achievement.

All-or-nothing conceptions of human endowment are definitely disconfirmed by the relevant evidence. That which is most certain about our knowledge of human nature is the extent of the variation over which a person's destructiveness, irrationality, and stupidity may range. It is impossible for anyone to know the upper limit of potentiality for any human being with much accuracy unless he has a good deal more knowledge than is available even to a parent, an intimate friend, or an intimate enemy. It is, in general, a supreme conceit to think that one has the intellectual power or the moral justification to describe the fixed frame of human potentiality for any individual. It is desirable, without blinding oneself to existing defects, to assume that remedial action is always possible. This is the essence of the optimistic conception of human nature. Far from being "naive" or "unrealistic," it is the only assumption that makes realistic sense in an imperfect world whose inhabitants' will to

perfect themselves is so easily undermined by pessimistic beliefs that are not justified on the evidence.

It has been argued that Condorcet is misinterpreted if we
regard his doctrine of the perfectibility of man as implying that
man is or ever can be perfect.[22] Condorcet meant only that one
cannot at any given time say with reasonable certainty that the
upper level of possible achievement has been reached. Given
any level of development, through effort more can be achieved.
With the sobering empirical qualifications already described,
this faith of the Enlightenment is sound today. In the final
analysis pessimism, while it protects us from disappointment,
blinds the individual to possible lines of advance. It is necessary to encourage and renew man's efforts to improve himself
and his world, not wither the will to try, by subjecting it to a
bombardment of sophisticated and somewhat cynical arguments
which never actually prove the extreme conclusion they either
affirm or, more likely, insinuate.

Of all that has gone before a critic might remark, "What
you have written is infused with commendable moral concern.
If the world were the kind of place in which participatory democracy could exist on any substantial scale, I would be all for
it. Unfortunately we must face hard facts. And the hard facts
are that participatory democracy, and even majority rule, are
not possible in modern industrial societies, however desirable
theoretically. If you want to avoid wasting your time, bend
your efforts to the achievement of possibilities, not ideal im-
possibilities." The view that democracy is impossible is identified with the names of Mosca, Pareto, Michels, and in the
United States, James Burnham. *The Iron Law of Oligarchy* is
its slogan.

Many have criticized important claims made by these élite
theorists.[23] But few of the élitists' critics have tried to defend
the position these men were actually attacking. For it is clear
that it was against Rousseau that they aimed their sociological
darts. For example, Mosca wrote:

> . . . the modern democratic theory, which had its source in Rous-
> seau, took its stand upon the concept that the majority of the

citizens in any state can participate and in fact *ought* to participate, in its political life . . . We shall not stop to refute this democratic theory here, since that is the task of the work as a whole.[24]

The most systematic and empirical sociological case against
the possibility of participatory democracy and majority rule is
made by Robert Michels. That it is against Rousseau's views
rather, say, than those held by James Madison or even John
Stuart Mill, that Michels directs his argument in the book,
Political Parties, is most clearly revealed in a chapter entitled
"Mechanical and Technical Impossibility of Direct Government
by the Masses." There Michels writes:

> A mass which delegates its sovereignty, that is to say transfers its
> sovereignty to the hands of a few individuals, abdicates its sover-
> eign functions. For the will of the people is not transferable, nor
> even the will of the single individual.[25]

This passage is almost a paraphrase of a basic passage in Rousseau's *Social Contract*.[26] But, unlike Rousseau, Michels goes
on to argue that only representative democracy is possible in
mass organizations. That proposition is the essence of his *Iron
Law of Oligarchy*.

The first thing one should note about Michels' book is that
his desire to debunk socialist pretensions permeates the whole.
He wants to prove that socialist organizations can be neither
democratic nor revolutionary. A sense of passionate disillusion-
ment leads Michels, like so many contemporary sociologists, to
see in sociological analysis a way of purging himself of his
earlier socialistic commitment, now felt to be naively optimistic.

The actual argument must here be pared down to its barest
essentials. Political effort based on mass discontent must, he
contends, be organized if it is to be effective. Organization implies specialization of function, which implies the existence of
leadership. The imperatives of technical expertise together with
the imperatives of leadership in a situation of deep social conflict inevitably increase the remoteness of the relationship between membership and officials. Reinforcing these sociological
forces are certain basic psychological tendencies. Custom, apa-

thy, the primary need for authoritative direction, political gratitude, ignorance, and deficient intellect all reinforce the drift
toward oligarchical domination. Moreover, officials have a basic
desire for power as well as a great tendency to satisfy their
self-interest. These sociological and psychological forces give
rise to a generalization which holds universally—the iron law
of oligarchy. "Thus the majority of human beings, in a condition of eternal tutelage, are predestined by tragic necessity to
submit to the dominion of a small minority, and must be content to constitute the pedestal of an oligarchy."[27]

Now the argument I wish to suggest, but cannot fully defend,
is that the organizational imperatives to which Michels attributes
such importance must control organizational development only
at a certain stage in the development of industrial societies.
The relevance of Michels' psychological assumptions to democracy have already been considered. Therefore, the impossibility
of participatory democracy or of majority rule is not proved by
his argument. Michels' claim that organization implies specialization of function and leadership need not be disputed, for it
is tautological. The question is, does specialization and leadership imply minority rule and the impossibility of participatory
institutions on any substantial scale? Does it imply oligarchy,
in Michels' sense?

At this point it is necessary to emphasize that Michels is primarily concerned with political parties and trade unions, both
of which have been traditionally engaged in fierce competition
for power. It is this element of unceasing and deep conflict
which gives Michels' sociological hypotheses their basic credi-
bility. *To the extent that conflict abates or does not run so deep,
participation and majority determination of basic policy becomes possible.* But I believe that long-term social tendency
both within and among societies is toward harmonization. Social harmony is not inevitable, but it is possible and there are
forces which powerfully support this tendency. The basic instrument of harmonization is law. Through law the resolution of
the major forms of conflict are regularized. It seems quite likely
that in the not too distant future industrial relations in advanced
industrial societies will be entirely governed by law. As regards

political conflict, through affluence the main causes of deep conflict, *though not of personal discontent*, can be progressively eliminated. This development is not inevitable, but it is possible. The historical epoch through which we are passing, an epoch which has been marked by such deep social division, is not necessarily a permanent thing, though man could conceivably perpetuate it through stupidity and bad will. And so we return to our starting point. At the base of the sociological pessimism to which Michels and the other élite theorists subscribe, is a pessimistic assessment of man's nature. As James Meisel has written:

> Elitism is a defensive doctrine, a new Dismal Science aimed at the naive optimist of eighteenth-century enlightenment . . . Confidence in the wisdom of the common man was misplaced; therefore its rationale, the doctrine of popular sovereignty, had to be expunged from the middle-class canon.[28]

But, for reasons already given, the psychological pessimism which lies at the root of the élitist doctrine is an inadequate ground on which to base rejection of either the possibility or the desirability of participatory institutions.

The main justifying functions of free competition for leadership are maintenance of order, protection against the tyrannical exercise of power, and fulfillment of actual human preferences without unduly sacrificing the values of efficient decision and expert opinion. The main justifying function of participation is development of man's essential powers—inducing human dignity and respect, and making men responsible by developing their powers of deliberate action.

How can both sets of aims be achieved? By developing two sets of institutions which are able to coexist. This cannot be done without conflict or sacrifice. But rather than focusing exclusively on the drawbacks, the social cost of permitting a greater degree of participation must continually be weighed against the human cost of denying such extension. Obviously no precise quantitative judgments are possible. These are decisions which are at best based on reasoned hunches.

But to destroy the nerve of effort by preaching psychological and sociological despair when remedies are at least possible is unrealistic folly. If the possible remedies are never employed, then these doctrines will themselves be an important cause of their own fulfillment. For the persistent truth is that participation is an essential condition of the good society and the good life.

REFERENCES

1. Walter Lippmann, *The Public Philosophy* (New York, 1955).
2. This, of course, presupposes criteria of badness which need not themselves be empirically determined.
3. Sigmund Freud, *Beyond the Pleasure Principle* (1950), p. 82. Italics added for emphasis.
4. Melanie Klein, *Envy and Gratitude* (1957), p. ix.
5. Melanie Klein writes (*ibid.*, pp. 81–83), "Freud early accepted that some individual variations in development are due to constitutional factors. . . . I have previously suggested that greed, hate and persecutory anxieties in relation to the primal object, the mother's breast, have an innate basis. In this book I have added that envy, as a powerful expression of oral- and anal-sadistic impulses is also constitutional. The variations in the intensity of these constitutional factors are in my view linked with the preponderance of the one or the other instinct in the fusion of the life and death instincts postulated by Freud. . . . Another factor that influences development from the beginning is the variety of external experiences through which the infant goes. . . . The existence of the innate factors referred to above points to the limitations of psychoanalytic therapy. While I fully realize this, my experience has taught me that nevertheless we are able in a number of cases to produce fundamental and positive changes, even where the constitutional basis was unfavorable."
6. Erich Fromm, *Man For Himself* (1947), p. 214.
7. *Ibid.*, p. 218.
8. *Ibid.*, p. x.
9. Erich Fromm, *Sigmund Freud's Mission* (1959).
10. David Spitz, *Patterns of Anti-Democratic Thought* (1949), pp. 163–90.
11. Spitz summarizes the evidence for this conclusion in *op. cit.*, chap. 7.
12. Carl J. Friedrich, *The New Image of the Common Man* (1950), p. 16.
13. D. W. Winnicott, "Psychoanalysis and the Sense of Guilt," in *Psychoanalysis and Contemporary Thought* (1958), p. 16.
14. J. Schumpeter, *Capitalism, Socialism and Democracy* (3rd ed.; New York, 1950), p. 250.
15. *Ibid.*, p. 253.
16. *Ibid.*, p. 257.
17. *Ibid.*, p. 260.

18. *Ibid.*, p. 262.
19. Schumpeter, *op. cit.*, p. 270. I agree entirely with the following description of Schumpeter's position by James Meisel, *The Myth of the Ruling Class* (1958), p. 353: "Essentially, Schumpeter's reappraisal amounts to an integration of élitist elements into a democratic framework which is much more modest than the structure built two hundred years ago, more diffident and more complex, but basically still within the classical tradition."
20. Most of the papers read at this symposium, which was held at the 1957 meeting of the International Sociological Association, are reprinted in the *International Archives of the Sociology of Cooperation*, 2 (1957), 106–820.
21. R. Dahrendorf, in the *International Archives, op. cit.*, p. 163.
22. Cf. Charles Frankel, *The Case for Modern Man* (New York: 1955).
23. E.g., C. J. Friedrich, *op. cit.*; D. Spitz, *op. cit.*; J. Meisel, *op. cit.*
24. G. Mosca, *The Ruling Class* (New York, 1939), p. 52. In another place Mosca wrote, "If by democracy is meant, as Rousseau believed, that the state must be governed by a majority of the citizens, then let us say at once that the new anti-Aristotelian doctrine does not find it necessary to give battle—it simply denies the democratic principle on the ground that it cannot be realized in practice." (In J. Meisel, *op. cit.*, p. 166.)
25. Failure to recognize that this is the position against which Michels' argument is directed has resulted in some misapplications of it, e.g., P. Magrath, "Democracy in Overalls: The Futile Quest for Union Democracy," *Industrial and Labor Relations Review*, 12 (1959), 504ff. See also Part II, chaps. 6 and 7 of *Political Parties* (New York, 1949). There Michels describes the fierce struggle that goes on among leaders in socialist parties and trade unions; how, for example, they reflect important regional differences (hence, corresponding regional majorities). Yet he considers all of this competition for leadership proof of his own basic thesis!
26. Rousseau, *Social Contract*, Book III, chap. 15.
27. Michels, *op. cit.*, p. 407.
28. Meisel, *op. cit.*, pp. 10–11.

Participatory Democracy: Ten Years Later

ARNOLD S. KAUFMAN

The foregoing essay was written at a time when few Americans defended participatory democracy. Ten years later the concept and the cause have been moved to center stage. What has brought the change about?

Paradoxically, the main causes are two spectacular American achievements: the prevailing system of coalition politics and the existing industrial order.

Nowhere else in the world have so many powerful but disparate groups combined to produce a society as democratic, stable, and prosperous as ours. Never truly a melting pot, the genius of the American social and political system has lain precisely in its ability to harness an extraordinarily heterogeneous people to mutually acceptable goals. And this has come about, not by accident, but by design. In the *Federalist Papers,* especially Federalist #10, James Madison provided a scheme for just the kind of system that has evolved; a political society

From *La Table Ronde*, No. 251–252 (December–January 1968), 216–228.

composed of many groups which combine into unstable, shifting coalitions that, partly because of the political instability of the component coalitions, produces a transcendent social stability.

The astonishing affluence of American society—the United States has about six per cent of the world's population but more than a third of the world's productive resources—has provided the firm material underpinning for political stability.

Yet these very achievements have been secured in a way that has had a most oppressive impact, economically and politically, on vast portions of the population. Large segments have been excluded from equal access to, or participation in, the benefits of the system.

In the game of coalition politics, some interest groups have been more equal than others. Ethnic and racial minorities, but other groups as well, have been denied effective access either to a mounting cascade of commodities or to instruments of power. And quite understandably many in the excluded components of the old coalitions, those who despite a trickle of benefits continue to be despised underdogs, have turned sour on The System. They have become the severest critics of the countervailing system of coalition powers. In their despair—a despair intensified by the very magnitude of the political and industrial achievements mentioned—exploited and oppressed people demand a more participatory control over their destinies. They want relief from the banal fanaticism of these moderate and respectable people who, having made it, ceaselessly incant, "America may not be perfect, but it is the best system the mind of man has ever been able to devise." Even if true, it is small comfort to the submerged citizens who correctly think that what is the *best yet* is not remotely good enough.

Meanwhile, on the other side of the tracks, many of those who chiefly benefit from our social marvels have been rearing a generation of affluent but rebellious youngsters. They bite the hand that feeds them. And with good reason.

For, all the devotion, energy, creative imagination that have been bestowed on material things have tended to turn people into human things. And this has happened even while the desire for a human existence has been nourished and has grown. Spiritual ideals that once partly functioned to contain danger to the power and prerogative of the advantaged few have been converted into rallying cries by the progeny of the advantaged many, slogans whose thrust is directed right at the heart of the prevailing system of inequality. Young radicals proclaim, "If this is the good life all your sweat and tears have brought us, then your work and your sorrow have been in vain." The parents cringe and grow admiringly furious. For, though they are dimly aware that their sons and daughters answer to their discontent, they resent the immense amount of blame and disorder these young people produce in their frustration.

The radical young demand an end to the powerlessness of the "powerful"; an end to the isolation of those who frantically practice being together. In SDS's Port Huron Statement, the first New Left manifesto, the authors proclaimed:

> We would replace power rooted in possession, privilege or circumstance by power and uniqueness rooted in love, reflectiveness, reason, and creativity. As a social system we seek the establishment of a democracy of individual participation.

So some have come to view participatory democracy as the single most important remedy for the accumulated ills of poverty, apathy, slavishness, inauthenticity, incompetence, manipulation, and, above all, powerlessness. These evils are the by-products of a system that has, quite superbly, devoted an enormous amount of attention and energy to the task of mastering the problem of acute economic scarcity without destroying social order. But those who operated that system have tended to ignore what should have been the overarching purpose of all the furious activity; promotion of a truly human existence for each and every human being. In demanding something radically different, advocates of participatory democracy have tried to replace Madison's pessimistic assumptions (on which he reared his constitutional proposals) with an affirmation of man's potentialities for creative, moral existence.

But the very passion and energy of the new affirmation, the intense frustration and anger that underlie it, have obscured the nature and limits of a democracy of participation. For if participation provides an answer to many problems, it does not answer every problem; nor does it serve in any old form. In any event, it is with the limitations and nature of participatory democracy that I want principally to deal in this essay.

It hardly needs to be said that advanced industrial societies cannot come anywhere near being fully participatory. Curtail bureaucracy as you will, bureaucracy there will be. For it is impossible to conceive of an industrial system in which important decisions are not made at various levels by considerably fewer than all those affected by the decisions. At best, certain kinds of managerial decisions can be made in ways which are responsive to those affected. At best, the effort to increase the participatory elements can make new inroads, bring within the ambit of direct democracy some important kinds of decisions previously subject to executive command. For example, workers' control in Yugoslavia limits, but does not eliminate, the power of managers.

But beyond the fact that it may be organizationally impossible to achieve pure participatory democracy without paying an absurd price in terms of the values the organization aims to realize, there are certain other factors that sometime make it undesirable even to try to bring decisions under direct control.

National problems often require national solutions; state problems, state solutions. A comprehensive federal health insurance act that requires maintenance of universal uniform standards throughout the union is highly desirable. For in the absence of a universal legal right and specification of standards, the present anarchy of the medical market place will prevail. And, if resources permit—as they certainly do—the health of individuals should be removed from the caprice of supply and demand. Moreover, as Gunnar Myrdal has argued, to increase the amount of participation involved in administering programs, to increase participation at the municipal level, may require that a frame be provided at the national level. Myrdal writes that in the transitional phase of the development towards a more perfect democratic Welfare State, while coordination and planning are becoming gradually more thorough, under the pressure of the continually growing volume of intervention . . . it often happens that people confuse planning with direct and detailed state regulations. The opposite, however, is true; there is still such a large volume of intervention because the measures are not ideally coordinated and planned.[1]

Once better planning occurs, there can be "an intensified citizens' participation and control." In other words, *federal* planning should have, as one of its aims, increasing the element of *municipal* participation.

In addition, and this is partly implicit in the preceding point, decisions at higher levels may be the most effective way to counter municipal tyranny. Participatory democracy is one way to decentralize decision-making; but like other forms of decentralized control, it may function tyrannically. It may be necessary, therefore, to apply more centralized counterpower to devolved, participatory power. Certain Southern communities have a greater element of participation than one encounters in the North. But because white men constitute a decisive, tyrannical majority, black men in those same communities may understandably be a mite cynical about the blessings of Southern grass-roots democracy.

Finally, some problems are constituted or generated by unjust distribution of resources. Some cannot be solved unless tax revenues are obtained from municipal areas where industry happens to be concentrated. Collection and redistribution of such funds require non-participatory institutions. On average, the black residents of Lowndes County, Alabama, earn about one fifth of what whites earn. Few in Lowndes earn very much, in any event. It is absurd to suppose that distributive justice can be achieved unless resources obtained from more prosperous segments of the national community are transferred to Lowndes. Similarly, the auto industry that is so heavily concentrated in Michigan should be federally taxed, and the benefits transferred to less industrialized states.

To summarize, the principle of participation may have to be modified for any of the following reasons: the imperatives of desirable bureaucracy; the dangers of municipal tyranny; the effort to make expanded participation more defensible; and the existence of unequally distributed wealth and revenues.

Description of these limitations may strike some readers as a mere catalogue of truisms. But the uncritical exuberance with which many advocate participatory democracy makes it important to recite these truisms. At the same time, the emphasis on these limitations is in no way intended to undercut my basic claim: that it is both possible and desirable vastly to extend the frontiers of participatory institutions in many areas of our social and political life. As usual in dealing with the great social and political issues, optimal solutions cannot be achieved according to formulas that demand all or nothing; there are matters of discrimination and degree involved.

Turning next to the nature of the participatory process, I argued in my earlier essay that "the main justifying function of participation is development of man's essential powers—inducing human dignity and respect, and making men responsible by developing their powers of deliberate action." But if the conclusion is sound, a paradox is generated: participation must begin by being unsuccessful if it is to fulfill its principal function. For, by hypothesis, participation is typically an essential condition of making men competent and responsible. But individuals who are incompetent and irresponsible will not make good decisions. They will be neither effective nor wise. Therefore, before participatory decisions can become sound, they will be unsound—necessarily. (The saving grace in this paradoxical situation is that when wrong decisions are made they will typically be implemented ineffectively.) Let us call what has just been described *the paradox of participatory democracy*.

Rousseau was acutely aware of the paradox. He tried to take account of it by providing for an agency—better, a function—which he confusingly called *the legislator* (confusingly because Rousseau specified that his legislator has no legislative powers). The legislator's function is to shepherd, by noncompulsory means, those who lack competence and wisdom until, through participation, they become capable of shepherding themselves. The legislator must have remarkable qualities, and is free to rely on any of the arts of influence. As those he seeks to influence lack competence, "he must have recourse to an authority of another order, which can bear men away without violence, and persuade without convincing them." In brief, he must "make the gods speak" to superstitious people. Rousseau realized that any emerging social order that was actually guided by so remarkable an agency would have to be very lucky.

That there is a discernible difference between competence and incompetence, responsibility and irresponsibility, is presupposed by this line of thought. With Hegel, Rousseau might have marvelled at those who think that "that only is true which each individual allows to rise out of his heart, emotion, and inspiration about ethical institutions, especially about the state, the government, and the constitution." And Hegel adds, "in this connection what a lot of flattery has been talked, especially to the young!" Amen!

But Rousseau is wrong in one respect. Whether a participatory group is able to surmount the problems of incompetence and irresponsibility prior to the time when participation has worked its benefits is not entirely in the lap of the gods. For through prior education, sound political theory, and appropriate modification of the institutions of participatory democracy, the likelihood of calamitous decisions can be diminished. In particular, participators should learn to appreciate the fact that, even within predominantly participatory arrangements, there is a place for *leadership* and *representation*.

The foolishness of failure to identify competence, to accept leadership, has been sensitively described by Kenneth Keniston in the *Young Radicals*.[2] Keniston interviewed young radicals who participated in Vietnam Summer, an anti-Vietnam War project. He discovered that they were terribly fearful about problems of leadership and authority. Sometimes they knew that the effectiveness of their actions depended on drawing the distinction between competence and incompetence, upon investing those who clearly possessed greater competence than others with non-coercive authority. Nevertheless, they so feared that they would commit the Great Sins—being manipulative or authoritarian—that they frequently sacrificed the effectiveness of their program for the sake of "moral purity." Hence, participation came to bar the way to achievement of their stated goals.

For example, at one point some secretaries who had had no previous experience in the Movement were taken into the decision-making structure of the organization. They were given *glamour* as well as menial jobs to do. The results were generally detrimental from the point of view of the group's basic aims.

Perhaps the sacrifice was worth making. The crucial point is that the costs were never really calculated before the decision to empower the secretaries was made. Incantation of "participatory democracy" gave reason enough.

The competent individuals had such severe hang-ups, the lack of self-restraint and experience of the incompetent was so acute, that "the distinction between rational authority based on competence and the authoritarian exploitation of power" was typically blurred. The situation became so bad, that " 'natural' leaders with the greatest experience, the best ideas, and the surest grasp of facts sometimes deliberately refrained from voicing their opinions lest they appear to dominate." Even worse, so insistent were those who favored more militant tactics, that those who knew better permitted their judgment to be swamped by the participatory equivalent of mob action.

Keniston's own core value is clear.

> No matter how incomplete, the emerging styles that cluster around the concept of participatory democracy illustrate an important effort to devise new forms of organization and action that will humanize the organized and vitalize the actors. [But he also notes that] the extent to which it is possible to retain an unmanipulative and participatory style, and yet mount an effective program on a national scale, is one of the unresolved questions of the New Left.

The problems Keniston's young radicals encountered are typical. And an important reason for their inability to cope with them is that they had a wholly unanalyzed, undifferentiated conception of the nature of participatory democracy. Had they been acquainted with the paradox of participation; had some preliminary attempt been made to discuss the nature of competence and of suitable leadership; had their hang-ups about manipulativeness and authoritarianism been openly, candidly, and even therapeutically discussed; had they been somewhat innured against *manipulative* attempts to use participatory rhetoric to induce guilt and equivocation; then they would all have been more able to act with greater fidelity to organizational goals, with greater sensitivity to the uses and misuses of participation.

There is another problem to which too many participatory democrats are oblivious. As Michael Walzer has pointed out, many good citizens will find time to "take long walks, play with their children, paint pictures, make love, and watch television," even if doing so means taking time away from valuable meetings. For them, participatory democracy simply takes too many evenings.[3]

Others choose, at great personal sacrifice and out of a genuine sense of civic responsibility, to attend *all* the meetings. They give up so much that they quite understandably come to think that they are the vanguard of good citizenry of the future. They, and they alone act for the many who miss the meetings. They view themselves as the political incarnation of the General Will. The proprietary attitude some activists develop toward the organizations in which they participate has to be experienced to be believed. Normally sensible people become infused with a demonic possessiveness only thinly masked by rectitude. They succeed in converting the adult equivalents of having a tantrum and pouting into the main instruments of organizational efficacy.

But those who miss the meetings may have good reason for doing so. In any event, they have rights that even participators are capable of abridging. They are therefore entitled to have their interests and concerns adequately represented.

How is adequate representation to be achieved without abandoning substantial reliance on participation? As in the case of competence, mere awareness and acknowledgment of the problem provides only a partial remedy. This is not just an abstract possibility. I have been in meetings where the views of those not present were well known to all the participants; and by making a fuss on their behalf, those absent voices did influence the course of events. But beyond mere awareness, there are institutional possibilities that are worth exploring. Inventive use of committees, decision by more than a majority vote, creation of special offices, perhaps even plural voting, may provide partial answers to the problem of representation. (Those who cringe at the idea of plural voting should be reminded that this is precisely the direction in which many liberal organizations are, in effect, moving in an effort to involve their mostly absent black brothers in more meaningful ways than before.)

In any event, my aim is not to provide a blueprint. The important thing is that the problems of effectiveness and representation be taken seriously, both by those upon whom the responsibility for designing participatory arrangements devolves, and by those who eventually participate.

My purpose has not been to debunk participation. I defended a democracy of participation against critics when the New Left was only a gleam in the eyes of its founders. The essay reprinted in this volume expresses ideas which I still substantially accept. But the mindless way in which some now apply the principle of participation is disconcerting.

The fact is, participation is no panacea. Nor is it even the only form of decision-making that is worth defending. It is only an instrument of political change and accountability, and not necessarily the most valuable one. Participation does not even always produce desirable or radical results.

This last should be clear from the ease with which many who are not radicals deploy the rhetoric of "participation," and sincerely urge its practice. Richard Nixon calls for "expanded democracy" based on increased participation. General DeGaulle urges the French Assembly to adopt a "policy of participation" for French workingmen. He wants laborers to have a greater voice in the business organizations that employ them, even in major management decisions.

But men like these propose participation, not primarily to encourage change, but principally in order to allay discontent. It is not difficult to see how participation can become an instrument of co-optation. For participation encourages one both to identify with the agency or organization in which he participates; and, by becoming more aware of "complexities," to identify with "management" in ways that those previously excluded from access to the centers of powers would have regarded as unthinkable. Consider most American trade union leaders as cases in point.

The result of such participation might well be the disappearance of outside critics—those who possess the cool detachment and ability to calculate consequences that come with having little identification with the organization, no axe to grind, no piece of the action.

(One of the most curious and, to my mind, irrational positions taken by some men of the Left is the view that people who do not participate, who do not express solidarity, forfeit the right to criticize, a right possessed primarily by those who do participate and act.[4])

Hence participatory democracy is a double-edged political instrument. Used one way, it can promote radical change. Used another it can hamper all change. It can invigorate and improve both participators and their decisions. It can also erode sentiment, destroy effectiveness, function in ways that abridge rights. All I have tried to do in this essay is continue the efforts made by theorists like Walzer and Keniston to deepen and clarify our understanding of participatory democracy as it actually operates—especially in advanced industrial societies. But beyond any critical thrust lies a basic conviction, that vast enlargement of the sphere of participation is *one essential condition* of a decent society.

REFERENCES

1. *Beyond the Welfare State* (New Haven: Yale University Press, 1960), p. 93.
2. *The Young Radicals* (New York: Harcourt, Brace & World, 1968), p. 171.
3. "A Day in the Life of a Socialist Citizen," *Dissent* (May–June 1968), 243–247.
4. Cf. Herbert Marcuse, "Repressive Tolerance," in Wolff *et al.* (eds.), *Critique of Pure Tolerance* (Boston: Beacon Press, 1965), p. 117; and Hillary Putnam, "In Defense of Resistance," *Dissent,* January–February 1968.

9: The Politics of Social Change: The Relevance of Democratic Approaches

DAVID KETTLER

> Democracy is not simply a political system like any other; its essence consists in the execution of large-scale social changes maximizing the freedom of man.
> —FRANZ L. NEUMANN[1]

Twelve years ago, C. Wright Mills was almost alone when he rebelled against the "conservative mood" and its largely mythical "theory of the balance."[2] Today, thanks in part to his courage, sustained and intensifying critical attack erodes the pretensions of the ideological Pluralist account of American political arrangements.[3] Mills' picture of "power elite" and passive mass now seems too crude and static to serve as adequate interpretation of the situation, but the caricature helped to break a spell of acquiescence and to reopen serious inquiry into the American power structure. There is more, however. Often overlooked in discussions of Mills' work is a major theme which actually caps his argument: in Mills' view, the most important truth about the ruling elite he identified is not that their rule contravenes democratic principles of self-rule or accountability; it is, rather, that an elite constituted like this one is congenitally incapable of making genuinely realistic and therefore morally responsible decisions, especially about

213

international conduct in a revolutionary world. The habits of mind and picture of the world required for ascending in the system he described, reinforced by the effects of ruling in such a system, he argued, cannot comprehend a real world of disorderly but goal-oriented conflict, in which whole populations function as self-impelled actors, and in which no convenient deals can be made with a competing but congenial elite. The incapacity has persisted during the twelve years since Mills wrote, and its frightening consequences have multiplied, so that we must press Mills' search for the structural sources of "the higher immorality." It is not enough to remark that the American political order is biased and not, as the ideological Pluralists contend, the neutral arbiter among equal contestants or the willing instrument of shifting temporary majorities; it is also necessary to see that the bias tends to produce irrational policies and actions.[4]

With the refinement and modification of Mills' bold interpretation of the American power system, then, it also becomes necessary to develop a more satisfactory account of the ways in which the arrangements militate against rationality. The distortion must be seen as permeating a complex but biased power system, rather than as concentrated in deficiencies peculiar to an integrated elite. Correspondingly, the effort to correct distortions need no longer be linked to self-condemned attempts to convert the elite or all-or-nothing injunctions to destroy the elite.[5] Proceeding through a critical survey of conflicting models of democratic theory, this essay undertakes to identify an approach to contemporary irrationality less rigid than Mills'. But first, because of the confusions surrounding the term "rationality," the central issue had best be restated in language less dependent on continental philosophical traditions.[6]

Political theorists drawing on one strand of American pragmatist thought have ascribed to the American political system of "partisan mutual adjustment" a unique capacity for coping with the problems raised by the always conflicting aspirations of diverse actors within the social system and by the continuing need to adapt social arrangements to a constantly changing environment. Such capacities of the system for homeostatic adjustment, moreover, are also said to yield results approaching an optimum, when measured by such standards as liberty, equality, public interest, and the rest.[7] Challenge to the ideological thrust of this Pluralist story builds ultimately upon profound criticism of the actions carried on by the political agencies whose operations are prettified and justified by the doctrine. Not general theoretical considerations impel us to uncover the fallacies in the theory, but recognition of and involvement in the fatal crises of our time. Irrationality is not a metaphysical specter; it is manifested in policies which intensify threat and suffering, instead of countering them.

Present purposes do not require us to adjudicate the philosophical issues in dispute between the distinct lines of attack whose convergence constitutes the challenge to Pluralist orthodoxy.[8] One intellectual strategy, congenial to most Americans, posits a complex of humanistic "values" or "needs" and then shows the disparities between these "values" or "needs" and the outputs of the social system as a whole. The alternate critical approach, drawing on Hegelian or Marxist or Comtean intellectual traditions, formulates its objections quite commonly as a "diagnosis of crisis": the political or other social arrangements are shown to be no longer able to meet certain requirements objectively set by historical or general forces, and the inability is said to be increasingly revealed by mounting signs of crisis.[9] In either case, writers often begin by interpreting key events and circumstances of our time as symptoms of major crisis: the writers in the first group will cite riots and other signs of disaffection or stagnation as indications that intensely valued objectives are neglected; those in the second group will read these signs as manifesting a failure of the system, in some objective sense of the term. Both groups charge at least proximate responsibility for the crisis to some basic deficiency or malfunctioning in the American governmental scheme, and both accuse the Pluralist account of that scheme of obfuscation.[10]

In this, recent discussion continues along the lines developed by Mills. He accused the "power elite" of oppression, of accelerating social trends toward dehumanization, of pressing steadily toward catastrophic war; he did not indulge in the clerkly exercise of caviling at the rulers' credentials, at their authority to voice commands which we are morally obligated to obey. Despotism, from this point of view, is above all a matter of oppression and not of illegitimacy. The criticism and displacement of despotic rule require an understanding of and attack upon the factors which lead it to act as it does. Condemnations of the regime's claim to authority play a distinctly subordinate role in this strategy of inquiry and action.

Reviewing the argument, then, it appears that the work of political theory in which we are associated specifies certain conditions of freedom and justice which must prevail in men's social experience, and it ascribes to the political arrangements of society the responsibility for bringing actual circumstances into the closest possible alignment with these conditions (although political arrangements may not themselves receive blame for creating disparities between norm and fact). Criticism distinguishes between the social system in all its manifestations and the political arrangements as such, but sets itself the task of working out the interrelations between them. In America today, many are subjected to hurt by the normal operations of the society; many more outside the territorial borders assigned to that system are victimized by forces arising within them; and any sober projection of present trends sees an intensification of such consequences. Notwithstanding the ideological claims of American Pluralists and the hopes of all democratic thinkers, the political arrangements within the society do not labor effectively against these grave injuries; they help to inflict them. In canvassing the prospects for change, this essay addresses itself to the political arrangements, seeking to identify political strategies which can so alter the distribution and constitution of political power that this power comes to serve freedom and justice—or, at least, that it does less to reflect and to strengthen anti-human forces. The essay does not pretend to radical novelty; instead, it seeks to put together information and considerations widely shared in the informal literature of recent political movements and in some of the newer academic writing as well. It is designed to foster consciousness about where we have been going, and not to set us off in some altogether new direction. Consequently, the paper encompasses a broad sweep and necessarily asserts rather more than it can prove or otherwise support with detailed argument. The obligation to remedy these shortcomings defines a collective task for our generation.[11]

THE POLITICAL CRISIS

Diagnosing a situation as crisis is a risky business, mostly because the term has so often been used to beg the crucial political questions. Writers working in what may be called a Platonist or Elitist mode of thought often proceed as if a crisis could be counted on to suspend all the structural factors which give shape to the political problems and set the peculiarly political tasks, so that guardians presumed to be both wise and beneficent can go ahead to carry out whatever fundamental changes are seen to be required.[12] In reality, however, the situation is normally quite different. The role as crisis-leader of an ongoing system commonly limits available options even more narrowly than does leadership at other times, although the restrictions may be different. Crisis-government tends to be protective of existing order, repressive, and essentially conventional in every respect save the immediate adjustments felt necessary to control the crisis. The politics of social change may possibly gain impetus and opportunity in a time of crisis; but the politics must be thought and worked through, and the fact of crisis cannot itself be expected to solve the political problems. A closely related misuse of the crisis-concept occurs among commentators writing in quite a different political tradition. Some who consider themselves proponents of popular revolution and not of elite manipulation have a wholly apocalyptic conception of crisis, imagining that crisis necessarily signals total collapse of some altogether rigid "system" and that such collapse necessarily ushers in "The" revolution. But revolutions are political and not magical occurrences, and the complex political problems of revolutionary movements—direction, efficacy, integrity

—must not be hidden from view in the visionary flare of some chiliastic expectation. When we speak of crisis here, we expressly do not intend any such misleading consequences.

Although it offers no guarantee of elitist remedy or of revolutionary renovation, there is indeed a crisis in American political life. The situation must be labeled a crisis because the warmaking in Vietnam, the safeguarding of forces whose operations drive black Americans to despair, the steady worsening of untended technological and bureaucratic dangers to lifestyles and even to life itself are all products of the normal and deeply embedded structural biases of the political arrangements. They also generate increasingly bitter and destructive conflict in the society; while the normal responses of the political agencies either prove altogether irrelevant or cope with one aspect of the problem by creating inner tensions and disruptions at another point. Many segments of social life are swept by new threats and new promises, and the political processes cannot respond adequately to either, so long as they move in accordance with the rules now established. The reserve resources within the political constitution for revising the rules, it must be feared, will devise responses whose effectiveness will be purchased at a terrible sacrifice of human goods. Without a radical reorientation of the political system, in other words, American political power will respond to present disintegrative threats with repression and not with innovation. The experiences of various total systems of rule within this century must dispel the last illusion that political bankruptcy necessarily leads to a progressive receivership.

The crisis dramatizes the need for change and makes it urgent; the task is to develop a political strategy for change. Marx and other revolutionary writers envision radical change, of course, but they are notably unhelpful with specifically political problems, largely because they count—almost certainly overmuch—on revolutionary tendencies and movements already in being and under way. If it were indeed the case that politics had been simplified and polarized to a choice between two coherent forces, with the movement challenging the status quo fully able to function as an ordering and integrating force in a society able to continue meeting expanding needs and wants, then the political problem might well be reduced to the simple question of who has the power to control. But lacking assurance about the reality of such a revolutionary spirit, both rational and potent, political questions must appear far more vexing. Even within the revolutionary movement historically rooted in Marx's conception, the primary difficulties and conflicts have turned over the years upon conflicting efforts to remedy the deficiency in political clarity characteristic of Marx's own work: struggles over party organization, concentration and control of state power, forms of revolutionary struggle, and the rest. And in these discussions, the revolutionary writers have found themselves engaged in extensive critical commentary on the literature of democratic political thought. This literature still offers the appropriate starting point and frame of reference for serious discussion of political problems.[13]

As formulated by the great classical writer of liberal democracy, John Stuart Mill, the doctrine clearly addresses itself to each of the major political problems identified in modern times, and it offers an approach to each of them which merits some attention, although none can be accepted as wholly adequate.

Four basic problems have preoccupied political thinkers since the sixteenth century.

1. *Securing minimal conditions of domestic tranquility within territorial boundaries given by nationality or some other similar principle, with special stress on eliminating competitors to a "sovereign" complex of governmental offices.* This problem, which can be restated as the problem of generating sufficient power to constitute an order, has been explored most profoundly by Thomas Hobbes and his followers. Without accepting Hobbes' stark answer to the questions involved, the liberal democratic tradition takes the matter extremely seriously and recognizes that society cannot dispense with coercive controls and political power, and that the presence of conflicting coercive authorities within a given territory heightens the danger that coercion will be more unpredictable and violent than otherwise. John Stuart Mill relegates the basic problem of establishing the state with its order to an historical stage earlier than

his own, and he sees his own society as beneficiary of habits of obedience inculcated over the years by force and reward and by the sheer momentum of repetition. Corresponding to this, in Mill's view, are habits of command in the political class, a sense of security which permits them to dispense with much of the reliance on threat considered indispensable for the Hobbesian monarch.[14]

2. *Channeling and restricting the exercises of political power through constitutional safeguards.* John Locke and others commonly classified as Liberal or Constitutionalist writers have developed the modern statement of the issues involved in harnessing the power, to lessen the likelihood of its being used to violate prime constituents of human identity and of relationships among men. Usually conceptualized as a matter of rights and rule of law, the approach has been more or less incorporated within democratic doctrine. In J. S. Mill's formulation, constitutional safeguards are to be built into the political arrangements themselves (rather than standing, as in Montesquieu's conception, largely outside the clearly political sphere): requiring all government officials to answer to a wide electorate and allowing the formation of political opposition competing for these offices are the two features which are to give primary protection to constitutional liberties, especially where these have been already historically established. Responsible representative government, Mill believed, served to secure basic rights.

3. *Maximizing the chances that governmental actions and policies will be "rational"; i.e., that appropriate responses are made to the complex tasks set by the changing environment and circumstances, or at least avoiding those errors of policy which could seriously endanger social life.* This concern dominated the work of most of the writers whose collaboration produced the *Encyclopedia*, as well as that of Jeremy Bentham and his associates. In this matter, too, Mill supposes that much will have been accomplished during the periods before liberal democracy becomes relevant or possible. Thus he cites the high level of civilization and wide diffusion of knowledge, which he considers to be preconditions for representative government. But he also sought devices to strengthen the political influence of the "spec-

ulative class," which he saw as the special carrier of political rationality. Accordingly, he advocated multiple votes for the university-trained, open balloting (to limit the presumed depravity of the poorest and least educated through the influence of public scrutiny by the respectable and informed), proportional representation (to assure some places in Parliament and hopefully the balance of power to the intellectuals), and categorical guarantees for those liberties which he considered essential to the progress of rationality.

4. *Fostering the qualities of moral community within the society.* In the democratic literature as such, the writings of Rousseau above all dramatize the problems of "virtue" in society—overcoming the sense and the reality of powerlessness among citizens and developing an authentic condition of community. Mill's proposals for a broad franchise and for representative government were at least in part designed to generate the sort of public-spiritedness which the radical tradition represented by the Jacobins, for example, also stressed: participation in public matters was seen as stimulus to an "active" virtue. He also insisted on the moral impact of education, and sought to protect educational arrangements against possible democratic excesses which he feared might jeopardize their elite character and high-mindedness. To counteract the extreme social inequities which breed bitterness, he turned to measures like encouragement of cooperatives, to give workmen pride and proprietary interests in their work, and the emancipation of women.

So stated, the problems are very general, and the catalogue cannot pretend to offer more than the beginnings of a checklist. And the references to Mill are not intended to do more than indicate that the liberal democratic tradition, in its strongest statements, relates to the items on the checklist in a nontrivial way. As is clear from the listing alone, the problems are intertwined, and it must often happen that priority must be given to one at the expense of others. A comprehensive approach, however, must understand the consequences of such adaptations and anticipate the rectifications which shall have to follow. Later versions of the democratic approach, as will be shown, proceed in subtler ways than Mill to comprehend the problems, especially those aspects of all the problems most directly pertinent to the politics of social change.

But before that discussion can be pursued, it is necessary to meet the sweeping contention that the attention to liberal democratic approaches is quite beside the point, because—whatever the past merits of liberal democratic interpretations and strategies—democratic doctrine has become an anachronism. The point at issue must be rightly understood. The critics do not mean to limit themselves to pointing out that the present American political system fails to meet liberal democratic standards; many democrats accept that judgment. The distinctive issue is whether the whole set of questions and emphases which constitute the liberal-democratic interpretation has any important bearing at all on the conditions of contemporary societies, whether it is at all interesting to inquire whether liberal-democratic standards are met. To say that a doctrine is anachronistic in this sense, then, is to say that it answers questions which are no longer asked, that it offers guidance concerning matters which do not appear problematical in the way that it expects or which do not appear at all in the real world. Resisting unfeared dangers, pursuing unsought goals, honoring noncompelling rules, such a body of ideas strikes the generation which condemns it as a dubious exercise, amusing or disgusting. We are challenged to show, in brief, whether any adaptation of the liberal democratic approach can orient men in their efforts to make sense of our present circumstances and activities.

THE RELEVANCE OF DEMOCRATIC CHANGE

It must come as a surprise to discover that within the past ten years there has developed a far from universal but significant trend toward treating democratic theory as an anachronism in serious discussion about the most urgent political themes. Only a few years before, the challenges to the intellectual dominance of the democratic frame of reference seemed smashingly discredited in the moral and intellectual debacles of fascism and

Stalinist communism.[15] But some illustrations will suffice to show that, in considering the charge of anachronism, we are not pursuing a phantom problem. George Lichtheim is only one of the better-known commentators on European integration to treat with derision the objection to the leading roles assigned to politically nonaccountable technocrats within this process. He and others have also defended the French Fifth Republic against similar objections. Jo Grimond, only recently resigned as able leader of the English Liberal Party, has written on the "End of the Party Game" and has urged careful study of Yugoslav political innovations, which appear to abandon the democratic doctrine. With the exception of some American political writers, notably Edward Shils and Seymour Martin Lipset, very few observers consider the language or preoccupation of democratic theory appropriate to the interpretation of either present conditions or future prospects in the so-called developing nations; and the uses to which the Americans frequently put the democratic language in these contexts raise serious doubts about the extent to which ideological rather than intellectual considerations account for their proceedings. In the study of international relations, the situation appears even more striking: the idea that democratic political categories can orient men to the world of international conduct is widely viewed as the pernicious illusion of "idealism."[16]

Discussions of the most pressing American political topics also show increasing signs that the frame of reference given by democratic theory is not seen to offer the conceptual tools for clarifying problems and proposed solutions. Numerous writers, including Hans Morgenthau and Theodore Draper, have come to speak of the warmaking in Vietnam in terms of a crisis in the American political system; but they do not find that the democratic interpretation of that system aids materially in defining the nature of the presumed crisis or in assessing the prospects for its resolution. Similarly, attempts to comprehend within the democratic language the issues and instruments of the conflicts generated by recent assertions of claims by black Americans are increasingly displaced by groping or strident efforts to make do with concepts of "revolution" or "criminal

disorder." A third vital sphere where democratic theory does not appear to offer much help to orientation is the vast domain where men discuss the supposed functional requisites and imperatives of the technical-economic apparatus, the vast and radical innovations said to be required for civil survival. Complementing such growing indifference to democratic categories is persistent and mounting criticism of the academic literature of political science (which does by and large continue to select and define its topics for inquiry in terms of a sort of democratic interpretation, as is clearest from considering the tremendous energy and imagination expended on study of parties and elections in the United States). The charge of "scholasticism" becomes credible when we contrast the concerns of political scientists with the topics which define the crisis of our times. These allusions and illustrations cannot give quantitative or qualitative assessment of the trend toward treating democratic theory as an anachronism; they suffice to indicate, however, that the phenomenon is not negligible and is by no means restricted to marginal intellectual groups.[17]

In thinking about the sources of such a shift away from democratic theory, a comparison may prove helpful. Some time between the work of Marsilius of Padua and that of Thomas Hobbes, the medieval conception of monarchy became an anachronism. Without venturing into the risky terrain of determining causes, we can identify some of the key elements in that change. The traditional gradation of ranks intertwined by a complex network of mutual expectations and common symbols presupposed by the doctrine of monarchy had ceased to exist; the tasks and instrumentalities of government had been radically altered; standards of legitimacy were radically redefined; the Aristotelian way of disciplined thinking was largely exploded; medieval formulas were considered as nothing more than sly efforts to justify clerical or feudal powers and privileges. Under the new circumstances, an effort to work with the old categories—especially with the distinction between king and tyrant which stood at the center of the doctrine—would lead to the disorienting conclusion that prevailing conditions were utterly without meaning, that all existing political institutions were equally illegitimate and fundamentally antithetical to human purposes. In saying this, we are speaking, it should be noted, about a genuine effort to orient oneself to the world in these terms, and not about the ideological manipulation of authoritative symbols, which continued long after the doctrine had been discarded as a guide to thought. The atmosphere of "Machiavellism" is the normal concomitant of transitional periods, when there is a radical disparity between what might be called the operating doctrine of the politicized segment of the population and the myth of authority professed by them and inculcated in the population as a whole.

In this respect as in others, there are unquestionably enough striking similarities between that time and the present to make understandable the recent parallel discarding of established interpretative doctrine. Despite these similarities, the parallel is not as strong as many contemporaries suppose it to be. The conviction that democratic doctrine is now as anachronistic as medieval monarchism had become by the sixteenth century rests on a number of key errors which exaggerate certain features of the situation. In the brutally condensed survey of the post-Medieval developments above, we referred: (1) to certain socioeconomic changes, structural changes in the social system as a whole; (2) to a radical reconstitution of government (i.e., the emergence of the so-called modern state); (3) to a change in the conceptions of authority and legitimacy; (4) to basic revision in the norms defining knowledge; and (5) to a widespread discrediting of the old doctrine as mere particularistic ideology. Such a general listing will doubtless call to mind some of the more familiar themes in contemporary discussion, touching on the same elements: (1) the literature of "mass-society";[18] (2) the new emphasis on planning and coordination functions of government; (3) the disarray concerning problems of authority and disobedience, especially the literature of "alienation"; (4) the widespread denial that disciplined thinking can or need be carried on about matters of doctrine—a rejection joined, for different reasons, by those morally committed to political life as well as by proponents of rigorous knowledge; (5) and the stark increase, in this country and abroad, of contentions that democratic doctrine simply serves as an ideological weapon for propping up the national or international "Establishment." The question before us is not whether these intellectual tendencies have any justification; the question is whether the justification is sufficient to permit dismissal of democratic theory as anachronism. Three interrelated errors exaggerate and distort the findings.

The first error is a flight from politics, a tendency to misgauge the complexity of political relationships and to misjudge their effects. This takes several forms, among observers who disagree with one another, but their joint impact helps to make democratic categories appear more irrelevant than they are. One form is "culturism"—in revolutionary or in conservative varieties—which may be used to designate the mistaken conception that analytical categories calling attention exclusively to the quality of life in a society can comprehend the power dimension of social interaction. This leads to an esthetic canon of social commentary, and the error is common in the literature of "mass-society" and of cultural criticism.[19] A second form of the flight from politics has already been discussed. It can be called Platonism, because it sees the political function exclusively as the application of disciplined intelligence to the rational solution of problems put before society by its objective circumstances. This can be found in some of the more general literature on "planning," but is implicit in much writing about policy, which ignores the relationships between policies and political processes. In its third form, this error is commonly found in literature reacting against the first two types: here the complex political problem is reduced to the rude (and therefore occasionally wholesome) question: "Who has the power?"; and the complex of political action is reduced to the seizure of power. Democratic theory at its best, as will be suggested below, has a far more adequate conception of politics than has any of these.

The second class of fundamental error likewise involves a curious symbiosis, a mutually beneficial "collaboration" among advocates for views which appear to clash sharply. What is involved is a discrediting of the activity of disciplined interpretation. In academic circles, we have the tedious confrontation between the simplistic scientizers for whom the literature of interpretation is simply a repository of "values" or "ideologies" and, on the other side, philosophical knights of the *ipse dixit*, who scorn any adaptation of interpretations to emerging reality, as observed by empirical inquiry.[20] The third partner and beneficiary is an anti-intellectualism among activists—conservative, moderate, or radical—who make a fetish of a supposed practicalness and hostility to doctrines or "ideologies," when they do not caricature the other academic strategy of setting up some preferred doctrine as unassailable. The net effect of all this is not, of course, the abandonment of interpretation; it is simply a disparagement of efforts to assess and revise interpretative doctrine in a rational way. Thus, the political scientists, as has been noted, continue to govern their inquiries by the categories of democratic theory; but they come to treat those categories as a fixed canon, not as elements in a flexible strategy of interpretation.[21] Among the political, this error feeds the misconceptions of politics noted above and protects the errors from critical scrutiny. In part, then, democratic theory is victim of a general contempt for interpretative doctrine, which actually heightens doctrinal credulity and rigidity.

Intimately tied to this is the third error, the perception of all interpretative doctrine as nothing more than ideology. On the one hand, decades of war and cold war have seen an ever more cynical manipulation of democratic categories as weapons of conflict. The meanings of terms were trimmed and adapted to the exigencies of political objectives and came to operate at times as an Orwellian rhetoric of justification. "Freedom" and "democracy" have been the prime victims. On the other hand, political opponents of these political trends helped to cripple themselves intellectually by putting their own views forward as "counter-ideologies" and by refusing to seek out the rational kernels in the doctrines whose distortion for ideological purposes they properly scorned. Or they sought refuge in purely private modes of encountering the political world, supposing these to be uncorruptible if not publicly articulated. The concepts and statements making up interpretations of political meanings do have very special sorts of symbolic weight and are constantly used to serve certain social and political purposes which it has become conventional to denominate "ideological." Awareness of ideology is a capital resource for critical interpretation of the political world, but it causes serious error when permitted to degenerate into a naive or cynical inside-dopesterism. When viewed without the distorting influence of this and the other errors, democratic doctrine proves to be far less self-evidently outdated than critics suppose. Actual developments of the sort listed above offer serious challenges to existing versions of democratic theory; but the insights and resources of the tradition as a whole repay renewed scrutiny, and the theory may well prove capable of the revitalizing which will make it applicable to our circumstances.

STRATEGIES OF DEMOCRATIC CHANGE

The different versions of modern democratic doctrine can be located along a continuum defined at one pole by the traditional liberal preoccupation with the protection of established rights and the limitation of abuses of power, and, at the other pole, by the complicated democratic demand for popular rule within the political community. The third dimension of the diagram is the one most important to the present discussion centering on adapting the political arrangements for service as an instrument to carry through the radical social changes demanded by the present crisis: it is defined by express concern for enhancing the rationality of governmental policy. We shall locate four alternate models of democracy upon this plane and, in the course of the presentation, offer reasons for judging them to be successive improvements upon one another. The fourth model, then, will offer tools for an adequate interpretation of our situation; and this naturally means that it will also offer strategies for change appropriate to our situation—because the need for and movement toward radical change is a circumstance crucial to our whole inquiry.[22]

1. *Old Liberalism.* This is a view whose explication occurs far more commonly in European discussions than in American ones, but which tacitly underlies much that is said by elitist writers. Bertrand de Jouvenel, an outstanding proponent of the old liberal view, has written, "The role of exercising power is widely different from that of combatting abuses, and the two should be kept separate."[23] Rational and orderly government, it is argued, requires rule by judgments not clouded by the need to satisfy popular wishes and desires. The peculiar and special task of popular institutions, on the other hand, is control and prevention of abuses of the power which government must have. Representative legislatures have this mission, but they must not presume to seize power for themselves; and the competition among political parties belongs in this setting. Party competition, then, helps to secure representatives able and eager to voice popular grievances; at most it faces the government with the constant threat of an alternate government, and this threat can be "a trump card in the hands of the citizen who is dissatisfied with the government's policy." But the presence of such a threat is not essential to the task of control, and the threat must not, in any case, be strong enough to force government into actions which it would not otherwise choose. Under some circumstances, government may choose to maintain very close contact with the legislature. As long as representatives in Parliament are men of real influence in the society, de Jouvenel observes, rulers have an incentive to consult with them and to secure their aid, because smooth governing always prefers to proceed through the influence of others rather than through coercion. But at the present time, he maintains, the politicians in Parliament no longer have such standing and are not likely to regain it. As a result, the consultative role will quite properly continue to decline. Modern parliaments, with their party politicians and party discipline, must be seen above all as control agencies, and second as agencies for training and screening aspirants for governmental offices. Parties, in their turn, must be geared to these limited but vital tasks, and must not imagine themselves ever competent to govern or to command govern-

ment: "Representative government means that interests, sentiments, opinions of the governed should be represented *to*
government, not *by* it."

To make such an interpretation of contemporary society hold
up at all, it is necessary either to shut one's eyes altogether to
the fact that a grave crisis exists and that there is no prospect
whatever that some civilized elite could now gain or maintain
power enough to control events—and that any power they
gained would be held only at the progressive cost of that civility
which would presumably qualify them for the office. Or one
can, as Walter Lippmann tries to do from time to time, put
forward the unlikely thesis that present-day problems result
from a democratic corruption of the liberal system, some excess
of "Jacobin" influence.[24] When the political class was small and
fairly well defined and when the power to define social priorities was not seriously contested, a pattern approximating that
envisioned by the old liberals could prevail—even if its accomplishments do not merit all the glowing praise heaped upon
them by writers of this persuasion. But events of the last 120
years have eliminated these conditions. If our society does not
now appear as uniformly or as securely politicized as some
commentators writing twenty years ago believed, it is nevertheless true that there are intensely politicized disadvantaged
groups whose claims to an increased share in power and whose
claims to an order more responsive to their own wants cannot
be denied without recourse to the most brutal and brutalizing
coercion.[25] The objection gains additional weight when we take
into account the actual claimants to elite status in the contemporary world. Mills may have oversimplified the study of their
power, but he was surely right in pointing out that the education of elite groups, in the broad sense, renders them increasingly likely to respond to threats to their order—in domestic
or in international affairs—with the most dangerous policies of
force. The genteel route of the traditional liberalism quickly
leads to the spectacle of Dutch or German or American[26] police
clubbing down student protestors, if not much worse.

2. *Old Democracy.* According to the sharply contrasting old
democratic view, it is precisely the essence of democratic gov-

ernment that political power is commanded by those who have persuaded the majority to entrust them with that responsibility; and the power must be strong enough to enable accountable rulers to follow along the line of policy and renovation which majorities choose. American and French writers sometimes advance a "populist" variant of this democratic argument, according to which true democratic rule requires an elimination of "politics" so that "the" peoples' demands can somehow be translated into action in a more or less direct way. But the more credible approach stresses the place of party competition. The minorities constituting the opposition, from this point of view, play a crucial role. Their rights must be strictly protected and they must be strengthened in their essential work of requiring government to account for its actions and of offering alternatives to voters. These expectations generally imply the following conditions:

a. Voters must be given a reasonably clear choice at elections, with enough clarity about contrasting programs so that they can give a mandate to the party chosen.

b. All members of the victorious party are bound by the mandate, and they must maintain firm discipline in government, so that the weight of full responsibility cannot be evaded or doubted when the voters next come to call the parties to account.

c. For the same reasons, administrators and civil servants must be strictly subordinated to the policy direction of politically responsible officials.

d. To ensure that the range of alternatives offered to voters corresponds to present needs and wishes, the political parties must provide for democracy within their own councils and perform widespread educational work within the community as a whole.

Such a conception of democracy and the place of political parties has been widespread in the British Labour Party, for example, and among other Social Democratic parties.[27] It is also familiar among American critics of American political institutions, although less common today than it was some twelve years ago, when the special committee on political parties of the American Political Science Association published its report under the revealing title, *Towards a More Responsible Two-Party System*—the apotheosis of a critical tradition whose timidity is revealed most clearly by contrast with Mills' *Power Elite,* which appeared a year later. In the American discussions of this sort, criticisms have been directed above all against the Congress, against its alleged short-sighted localism and against the existence within it of entrenched power—especially within the committees—practically immune to electoral pressures and to shifting preferences of most voters in the nation. Objectors have also attacked the inner heterogeneity within each of the two major parties; the lack of clarity in their programs; the president's inability to accomplish any of his purposes without elaborate negotiations and confusing concessions to the host of "barons" and "satraps" in his own administration as well as in the Congress—the so-called New Feudalism—; the resulting incoherence of executive policies accompanied by an excessive reliance on situations of crisis to push proposals through; the uncontrollable influence of private pressure groups on officials not sufficiently responsible; and, finally, the bias toward conservatism and protection of established vested interests built into all this.[28]

As is clear from both of these instances, that of British Labour and that of the recent generation of American reformers, the old democratic conception of parties has been most closely associated with advocates of social changes believed to be blocked by an Establishment, and it has its great history in the socialist movement on the Continent and in other movements for social reform—although American observers were amused or dismayed during the early 1960's to see the position taken over, at least in part, by supporters of Barry Goldwater. In the main tradition, however, the challenges against the old democratic view, where the popular representatives are simply supposed to protest grievances and to protect against violations of rights, are these:

a. The *rationality* and *civility* of rule by an elite Establishment are fictions: such rule is in fact often inconsistent, indecisive, indifferent to major human needs, and strong only in the defense of vested interests.

b. Accordingly, such a government cannot be trusted to remedy grievances, however clearly stated and persuasively urged.

c. Men reacting in isolation, each to his own social circumstances, cannot really articulate their grievances or formulate a claim which could relieve them; correct insights, consciousness of situation and of improvements, depend on the transforming experience of taking part in political organization and political struggle.[29]

These critical insights constitute the most valuable contribution of this version of democratic doctrine, because its account of how the system can reasonably be expected to work is fundamentally deficient. As will be made clearer in the next section, the old democratic theory strongly exaggerates the autonomy of political processes, the distance normally attainable between patterns of established social privilege and power, on the one side, and the biases of political institutions, on the other. Large parties, even when disciplined, will be irresistibly driven to accommodate themselves to prevailing forces—not least because citizens will accommodate their own judgments in this way, so long as they are no more deeply engaged in the political and social process than as passive respondents to opinion surveys or as supporters of candidates. Then, too, such parties acquire leadership closely allied to dominant functional elites and require the financial support of the most calmly calculating of the supporters of the status quo. In the American situation above all, it is moreover an illusion to speak of administrators serving merely to implement the policy directives of the politically responsible. For most of the infinitely complex questions arising today, legislators are wholly dependent on the administrators and technicians for the very statement of the matters upon which they are supposed to decide. The existing incapacity of American political institutions, in other words, cannot be ascribed to deficiencies in the party system, as measured in old democratic terms; nor can it be remedied by some realignment or reconstitution of parties. Such a realignment may at times become a symptom of and then an aid to a process of reorienting the political system; but it can be neither the focus of interpretation nor the center of a strategy for change.[30]

3. *New Liberalism.* Serious defects in the old democratic theory have been uncovered in recent years from quite a different point of view—from the point of view, in fact, of that very pluralism which this collection as a whole takes seriously enough to answer at length. Already in the early 'fifties, a number of American political scientists reacted against the then widely current arguments summarized above and epitomized in the demand for a "more responsible party-system." Their view contends that the most important quality of American political life is precisely the continuing motley competition and mutual adjustment among a great plurality of groups and other political actors, each partisan to peculiar interests; and it maintains that any effort to replace this complex and onflowing process of negotiation, maneuver, and compromise—any pursuit of the phantom of clear-cut choice between clearly distinct political parties as a normal part of the electoral system—threatens the authority and integrity upon which the dynamic equilibrium of the present system rests, without coming at all closer to the presumed objective. Liberal democracy is then at heart a matter of "openness" of political processes, a matter of constantly shifting compromises among conflicting claims, and a matter of allowing every sort of group and legitimate agency in society to struggle for the protection of those rights and the promotion of those interests which it may consider most important. From this point of view, parties and elections are seen to have an important but, as in old liberalism, a severely limited function in the system.

a. They supply politically experienced persons for governmental offices, men who have been trained to develop a "market orientation"[31] and tolerance for uncertainty as well as skill in limited conflict.

b. The fact of competitive election helps to keep channels of access open.

c. The legitimation produced by such elections provides a secure foundation of popular authority for government, and enables it to act decisively should a genuine emergency require it.

Nothing in this excludes the possibility, it is said, that for short periods and under special conditions the political parties, or some one of them, will become the decisive agency for the most important public influences, or that certain specific electoral contests will be "critical" and play a vital part in determining certain issues. But, it is expected, such conditions will be rare, and the absence of such conditions is, at the very least, no defect of democratic theory. Such an argument has come to be widely accepted in various forms by many American political scientists, with the writings of Seymour Martin Lipset, Robert Dahl, and Edward Shils internationally best known. The English political scientist, A. H. Birch, confidently begins his assault on the English Labour Party version of the old democratic arguments with the cool observation: "This idea has never been accepted by Conservatives, Liberals, or independent students of politics," and he concludes that the Labour doctrine "must be rejected not so much because it is undesirable as because it is unworkable."[32]

The new liberal or pluralist argument is, in turn, frequently challenged on grounds of a demand for greater and more certain rationality.[33] Critics argue that the competitive process described works well enough so long as decisions deal with relatively nonurgent matters: in a very rich country like the United States, it might be said, a costly and incoherent economic policy may well be a permissible luxury, especially when such a policy also helps to satisfy diverse influential groups in society. But when hard problems have to be solved quickly, when rational intelligence must be applied and efficiency mustered, then the irrational methods of compromise will no longer serve, it is argued. Many who accept the new liberal viewpoint regarding most things often make important concessions to such objections; they arbitrarily exempt certain spheres of public policy—military affairs and international relations, especially— from the normal operations of the pluralist processes of mutual adjustment; they reserve these spheres for some sort of rational planning and require efficiently coordinated elite-management to secure efficient implementation of planned policy.

Influential writers in the new liberal group, however, have recently refused to make such concessions and have rejected the whole line of criticism. One of the most persuasive among these is the American economist Charles Lindblom, who has worked closely with the philosopher David Braybrooke and the political scientist Robert Dahl.[34] Rational problem solving, he contends, is more likely to proceed successfully through the processes of "partisan mutual adjustment" under conditions of relatively open access, than through centralized and comprehensive planning of any sort and under the centralized coordination supposed to be necessary for effective implementation of comprehensive decisions. Decentralized authority, Lindblom argues, and decision-makers under constant pressure to compromise and to adjust to new factors leads to incrementalist, piecemeal solutions or management of problems, and precisely these are the most intelligent strategies for dealing with most imaginable problems. This strategy does not require superhuman knowledge or omnipotent control over all pertinent factors and consequences; it brings each aspect of a complex whole up for decision in manageable form, and requires constant revision as new aspects come into view.[35]

Fortified in this way or not, the new liberal conception of political parties asks only that there be a competitive pattern of some sort, because that helps to keep channels of access open and adds to the adaptability of the process as a whole; it is, on the other hand, usually hostile to attempts to build the sorts of parties urged by the old democrats. This hostility is justified by the argument that such attempts raise unfulfillable expectations among the public and foster impatience if not contempt for the complex processes of problem-management. At the same time, however, the new liberals agree with old democrats that old liberalism has too rigid and narrow a view of the political process, that it permits inadequate room for maneuver for the diverse forces in society, and that it arrogates to government officials an intellectual and moral superiority for which there is no evidence.

To be taken seriously today, a political interpretation less confident about the outcomes produced by these adjustment processes than are the new liberals must nevertheless deal with the world which these writers have revealed to us. No radical strategy makes any sense which does not appreciate the subtle capacities for adaptation within the system, because it cannot then understand the persistence and pervasiveness of social conservatism. The men associated with the Kennedys represent one instructive effort to develop a political perspective able to cope with crisis. Writers like Richard Neustadt, Arthur Schlesinger, Jr., and the others accept the new liberal account of American political life but amend the interpretation in several significant ways: their work represents the more or less rational kernel within the Kennedy myth and is therefore also helpful for making sense of the men around Willy Brandt or those around Harold Wilson. Although history is not usually prompt in its justice, the steady decline of these figures is doubtless related to the failure of their doctrine.

First, the amended conception stresses that the process of adjustment requires periodic injections of *élan*, a sense of purpose and direction; second, it points out that certain claims having the highest moral urgency and explosive potential (in the United States, the demand of black citizens for equal treatment and opportunities is the example commonly cited, of course) occupy a relatively weak position within the normal partisan adjustment process, and will therefore fail to receive adequate attention in the normal course of things; third, the presidency constitutes the agency in the United States uniquely able to supply the needed impetus; it is structurally inclined, by virtue of its constituency and traditions, to counteract the disparities in power which hamper the most deserving groups and objectives in society. The need, as seen by proponents of this view, is to mobilize the full resources of that office for such objectives, and to move with full energy and skill. In such a campaign, they concede to the Lindblom argument, one does indeed proceed as if one had more complete knowledge than in fact one can possess, and blunders are likely to be monumental; but, they argue, the need for bold leadership justifies the risks, and adroit management can find ways out of the consequences resulting from the inevitable overextension.[36] The Kennedy application of such doctrine—inevitably diluted by other factors—had little time to prove itself, but its limited social accomplishments and the miserable inheritance left by its ventures in Southeast Asia suggest that there are important inadequacies in it.

These inadequacies, in fact, help to point up the continued relevance of democratic frames of reference, because they reveal that "presidentialism" merges imperceptibly with one way of abandoning democratic theory as anachronistic. It approximates to the kind of interim political doctrine which appeals to political insiders during periods perceived to be transitional, when old doctrines are discredited and new ones inchoate. That side of Machiavelli's thought which has come down to us as "Machiavellism" can serve as paradigm case for this, and presidentialism shares some of its crucial weaknesses:

a. Politics is mistakenly seen as manipulative control over essentially inert materials, and as conflict with others similarly engaged.

b. The conception of power is dominated by a myth of decisionism. This systematically underestimates the significance of momentum and feedback; it exaggerates the controllability and reversibility of events and consequently overrates the efficacy of being decisive.

c. The general model of action derives from the experience of "crisis-management," because under conditions of intense crisis, political reality does—within a narrow sphere of action —actually come close to the expectations of the presidentialist doctrine.[37]

d. Despite all the talk of innovation and new departures, the emphasis on purely governmental resources creates an ultimate dependence on prevailing distributions of social power and thus harnesses all that energy ultimately to objectives of system maintenance; that this is disguised as acting out of the logic of the situation or *raison d'état* does not change the fact.

e. Accompanying much rhetoric of responsibility, there is a denigration of the rational content of political discourse, and an increasing reliance on stylish deception or exhortation through manipulation of symbols.

f. And when the unreal expectations are not met, when the supposedly inert materials prove stubborn and wilful and when the system cannot cope with the critical pressures in the old ways, however invigorated, there is a too ready resort to violence and repression as political instruments.[38]

Presidentialism, then, has value as symptom of the insufficiency of alternate democratic doctrines; but its unwarranted generalization from a quite special sort of extreme situation does not provide a satisfactory framework for adequate political interpretation.

4. *New Democracy.* Appearing mostly in the pamphlet and periodical literature of the so-called New Left, there is emerging a new conception of democracy which promises the revitalization needed by political theory. There is a lot of rhetoric and confusion here, and it is far too early to attempt any sort of codification; but it is possible to suggest some of the key elements of this model, and to show its special relevance to a strategy of change. Essentially, it may be said, the new democratic doctrine comprises a set of massive qualifications of established democratic theory, qualifications which are all designed to loosen the ties between practice oriented by democratic theory and the dominant biases of the prevailing structure. The doctrine has been growing out of efforts to make sense out of such developments as the movement for justice to black Americans, the opposition to the Vietnam war, and resistance by students and others to what are felt to be suffocating pressures of bureaucracy and other adaptations to a technological society. With regard to these critical problems, it has become clear, the normal channels of electoral politics cannot be relied upon—partly because, as the new liberal or pluralist writers themselves have shown, they are geared to quite other sorts of tasks, tasks of socialization and incremental adjustment, and partly because, as these same political scientists have also shown, the varying outcomes in elections have little impact on crucial decision-making processes. Critical examination of the presumed "openness" of governmental agencies reveals, more-

240 : *The Politics of Social Change*

over, that access is carefully guarded and that conservative interests enjoy a massive advantage.

From the presidentialist argument, the new democratic doctrine accepts a reminder that imaginative and bold uses of political power can have creative impact. This serves as useful corrective to the dismal prospect for social change usually discerned from the old democratic perspective: the prospect of somehow having to persuade a huge disoriented and distracted population to accept some complete package of new institutions and arrangements before political institutions can begin to cope more rationally with the crisis in society. Men respond to situations much more than to arguments, and the stroke which redefines the situation need not be an act of violence or *coup d'état*. There is no serious reason for believing that the presidency is peculiarly equipped with either will or capacity to move in these ways, of course, and the new democratic argument parts with presidentialism at this key point. As indicated by such slogans as "Black Power" and "Student Power" the emerging new democratic interpretation is intensely aware of the political system as a purposive structure of power. It sees the capacity to shape events or at least to protect preferred conditions as a consequence of certain key resources very unequally distributed in the population and among groups: wealth, strategic position within key institutions, authority, coercive force. In the New Left pronouncements, this structure is often characterized as a monolithic elite to be overthrown in its entirety; but New Left practice presupposes the possibility of cracking this monolith at certain vulnerable places, when counter-power is carefully mustered and strategically employed. In this sense, the new democrats are striving for radical reorientation of the system and not for revolutionary overthrow in some literal sense of the term. In the long run, it may well happen that efforts to change conditions in areas most manifestly critical today will open the way to even more fundamental changes in society; but revolutionary rhetoric and even revolutionary determination cannot create revolutionary conditions or justify senseless bluster or violence. The task is to make politically effectual the forces striving for social changes leading out of the present critical impasse, and these forces are not embodied in a powerful revolutionary army in search of a vanguard. Even when properly mustered, the power resources are far more slight: a wary trust of bitter and often incoherent elements victimized by the ongoing rules, fresh ideas for working out of crisis, support in some important places, like the universities which play such an important economic role in the technological society, a political strategy, and occasional allies.

The new democratic approach presupposes much of the pluralist account of the political world, although it adds to that account an appreciation of the structural biases which limit the political arrangements in their normal operations and an understanding, derived ultimately from Marx, of the sources of that bias in the imperatives of the social system as a whole. On this basis, it builds a political conception out of five central contentions:

a. *In certain key areas, radical innovation rather than incremental adjustment is the politically apt mode of conduct.* Despite all likelihood that grave errors will be made, it is necessary to depart with bold abruptness from deeply established patterns of conduct. The structural bias toward degrading and exploiting the great mass of black Americans who are poor is so strong, for example, that only the most dramatic shift in policy can help to create a sustainable new pattern. Commitment to such new courses must be overwhelming if the commitments are to have any reality. A political system geared to change, as democracy purports to be, must therefore be capable of radical change.

b. *Because the rules which constitute order at any given time and which define the limits of the political game are in practice always partial to existing distributions of power, techniques of political conflict considered disorderly and disorienting by existing rules will be necessary for producing structural changes.* In practice, if not in principle, this is the most difficult and controversial portion of the argument. Obviously it cannot be a plea for unbridled violence and arbitrariness, because the basic accomplishments of liberal constitutionalism are cherished. What is involved, rather, is the reinterpretation of basic liberal principles as a pattern of presumptions instead of as a rigid code. Then, traditional codifications of these presumptions are tested, through deed and critical thought, to separate the aspects having good claim to universal value from the aspects reflecting a given allocation of goods and power peculiar to a certain society at a certain time. Even the more nearly universal presumptions are sometimes overridden, without as within the legal system, so that, for example, acts of violent coercion take place and even the autonomy of such institutions as university and press are violated. In those cases, the hard questions are whether the departure from respected norms is really justified and whether that departure is carried on in a way maximizing the possibility that a return to the norms will take place as directly as possible. The approach does not play casuistic games with presumptions; they are deadly serious inhibiting thresholds in a badly distorted world. The most important consequence of this reinterpretation of constitutional rules, however, is the empirical search for functional equivalents to traditional institutions. A certain way of organizing the work of governmental agencies, for example, may have once served as a safeguard for predictability and control; under new conditions, some altogether new principle of organization may be needed to create that effect. Student demonstrators may breach established rules of "law and order"; but their conduct may reveal the operation of different and better restraints, by virtue of who and where they are.[39] Such an experimental attitude toward law is common to discussions of international law; its application to other sorts of conflict-realities requires much more work.[40] But the fact remains that even a liberal system of law acts to secure existing expectations and to conserve established patterns of order. Implicit in this observation is grave doubt that a theory of civil disobedience can adequately comprehend the techniques of conflict which may have to be legitimized, in the conditional way in which any such legitimations take place. Most specifically, what this means is that political techniques which are in fact coercive come to play an increasing part—in the forms of "direct action" or "confrontation" or "resistance" —and the task of keeping that coercion from spinning out of control into wanton brutality and arbitrary deprivations of rights is entrusted more to political and social processes internal to the political movement and generated by informal relations between that movement and the social environment than to supposedly impartial and authoritative law-enforcement, at least in the areas of critical conflict.[41] The problem is to authorize enough leverage to outmaneuver the biases which preclude needed social change without licensing self-aggrandizing adventures and meaningless violence. If constitutionalism is understood as a complex of political techniques and not as word-magic, it ceases to be an anomaly or imposture to speak of limiting abuses of power by checks within political movements for change. The question becomes an experimental and empirical one.

c. *To avoid the usurpations which have characterized movements engaged in massive revolutionary struggles,* even when resources and justifications were more clearly available than they are likely to be in the American situation within foreseeable time, *the basic strategy for change is to concentrate available power upon the securing of "strategic enclaves" within the existing system.* Although that formulation is redolent of guerrilla jargon, the idea is much less bombastic. If imaginative and intensive political action can deliver a concrete policy in some important aspect of one of the critical problem areas, then a breakthrough may be possible toward reorienting the structural bias itself in that regard. Here repeated mistakes and disappointments must be expected, because the capacity of prevailing forces to recapture activities and programs which begin by being antithetical to them cannot be underestimated. But if the programs promoted also have some intrinsic short-run value —such as improving living conditions for some oppressed people or giving them some confidence in their potency—then the fact that the enclaves prove not to be strategic will not be so bitter. Strategic action of the sort envisaged here proudly seeks radical objectives but soberly recognizes that struggle against prevailing biases is hard and that determination alone does not suffice to subdue superior power. Radical politics without chiliastic expectations is the goal.

d. *Since conventional political arrangements are often structurally condemned to irrelevance in the key areas, institutional innovations are required, especially those which return appreciable measures of control over their own affairs to disadvantaged populations.* Participation is a central democratic objective which serves multiple purposes, and new democratic commentators have placed great stress on "participatory democracy" as a counter to political alienation and bureaucratic usurpation.[42] Especially where men have been degraded and exploited, the very fact of recapturing command over important affairs may make a crucial difference. But politics remains a matter of conflict and coercion and scarce resources, including time and skills. To say that the privileged will run their affairs and the disadvantaged theirs is a bad joke, and it is too romantic to suppose that the beneficiaries of a biased system will be so ennobled by the experience of self-government that they will abandon their privileges. We begin by supplementing existing electoral and pressure arrangements with new forms and units of self-government and with new forms of opposition; this requires imaginative re-examination of various schemes of representation and diverse ways of structuring conflict. The sociology of leadership roles must be focused on the problems of minimizing self-aggrandizement. No shibboleth is secure, not even the formula of "participatory democracy." The process remains an interplay among militant initiatives, participant responses (and restraints), and reality-testing against established patterns of power and against concrete consequences. It is a politics of forays and institutional experiments, not of formulas.

This last approach to democratic theory, then, treats the new liberal account as deficient in its analysis primarily in failing to see the tendencies toward ossification and bias within a prevailing pattern of mutual adjustment, and it argues that a crisis like the present requires an extension of the means and objectives of political conflict, until the sources of that bias are overcome. Much of the emphasis and energy of the argument derives from the old democratic insistence that human choices rather than established patterns of privilege must shape the destinies of society. Considered at the highest level of generality, the "principles" of democracy remain intact: the democratic tradition is ultimately defined by a set of emphases, a shared conviction that a certain set of questions—about power, authority, rationality, and community—are decisive questions. Moreover, certain political patterns remain the starting point for discussion; i.e., the nation state, constitutional government, accountability, voluntarism. But the questions are reformulated, to bring them to bear upon our circumstances, and the actual significance of the traditional democratic patterns is critically restudied, so that corrective supplements and functional replacements appropriate to our circumstances can be uncovered. To think of democratic doctrine as merely an ideology to be inculcated because that may have beneficent consequences is unworthy of critical intelligence; to think of it as a set of abstract norms for the imperious judgment of human affairs is an abdication of intellectual responsibility for enhancing the consciousness of acting men. From our standpoint, then, the democratic tradition as historical artifact can quite properly be described in terms of principles and institutions. But what matters to every generation is the substance of democracy, its impact on men in their lives together, and not a canon of forms.

REFERENCES

1. Franz L. Neumann. "The Concept of Political Freedom," *The Democratic and the Authoritarian State* (Glencoe, 1957), p. 153. Returning to problems of democratic theory after a number of years, I realize how abiding is my debt to my teacher Franz L. Neumann, and how much he packed into his rich essays. This is not to say, however, that he would have approved my views concerning many of the matters to be discussed. Cf. David Kettler, "Franz L. Neumann: Dilemmas of Radicalism," *Dissent* (Autumn 1957), 386–392.
2. C. Wright Mills, *The Power Elite* (New York, 1957), especially chapters 11 and 14.
3. See the essays collected in this volume and the bibliography. Other relevant collections are Charles A. McCoy and John Playford (eds.), *Apolitical Politics* (New York, 1967), and Maurice Stein and Arthur Vidich, *Sociology on Trial* (Englewood Cliffs, N.J., 1963).
4. Mills' concepts of responsibility and rationality derive from Max Weber and Karl Mannheim. See Hans H. Gerth and C. Wright Mills, "Introduction: The Man and His Work." *From Max Weber:*

Essays in Sociology (New York, 1958), pp. 61–65, and the work there cited. See also Karl Mannheim. "Competition as a Cultural Phenomenon," *Essays in the Sociology of Knowledge* (London, 1952), pp. 191 ff., and "Prospects of Scientific Politics," *Ideology and Utopia* (New York and London, 1946), pp. 97ff. Mills builds on these views in *The Sociological Imagination* (New York, 1959).

5. C. Wright Mills, *The Causes of World War III* (New York, 1958), comes close to the former of these: his *Listen, Yankee* (New York, 1960) approaches the latter. Two of the most interesting criticisms of Mills' approach are E. V. Walter "[Review of] *The Power Elite*," *Dissent* (Fall 1956), 393–398; and the essay on power by Robert A. Lynd in Arthur Kornhauser (ed.), *Problems of Power in American Democracy* (Detroit, 1957).

6. For a persuasive account of the problem in the older language, see Max Horkheimer, *The Eclipse of Reason* (New York, 1947). Better known but more difficult are Herbert Marcuse, *Reason and Revolution* (New York, 1954), and *One Dimensional Man* (Boston, 1964). See also William Connolly's discussion of "contrast models" in "The Challenge to Pluralist Theory," Chapter 1 of this volume.

7. Cf. Charles Lindblom, *The Intelligence of Democracy* (New York and London, 1965). Brian Barry's "The Public Interest," this volume, Chapter 7, relates well to the theme of rationality discussed here.

8. I have tried to argue my position in "Political Science and Political Rationality," in David Spitz (ed.), *Political Theory and Social Change* (New York, 1967). In many ways, the present essay is a continuation of that effort.

9. See, e.g., Karl Mannheim, *Diagnosis of Our Time* (London, 1943); note a surprising early parallel: John Stuart Mill, "The Spirit of the Age," *Essays on Politics and Culture*, Gertrude Himmelfarb, ed. (New York, 1962), pp. 1–44.

10. In discussions of the Vietnam War, the diagnosis of crisis has become quite commonplace; see e.g., Theodore Draper, *Abuse of Power* (New York, 1967), and J. William Fulbright, *The Arrogance of Power* (New York, 1966).

11. For a convenient survey, see two excellent mimeographed study-guides available from the "Radical Education Project" (Box 625, Ann Arbor, Michigan): Hal Benenson, "The New Left" and Jim Jacobs, "Power in American Society." Most books reflecting these directions published so far are collections; the most important sources continue to be journals like *Studies on the Left, New York Review of Books, The Nation, The New Republic, Dissent, New Politics, National Guardian,* and so on.

12. To label the style "Platonist" does not deny that this is only one aspect of Plato's complex thought. Cf. David Kettler, "Plato and the Problem of Social Change" (unpublished M.A. thesis, Columbia University, New York, 1953).

13. See, e.g., V. I. Lenin, "What Is To Be Done?" "Two Tactics of Social Democracy in the Democratic Revolution," and "Proletarian Revolution and the Renegade Kautsky," *Selected Works,* Vols. I and III (Moscow, 1960).

14. It would be pedantic to cite sources for these allusions and sketchy interpretations. The comments reflect some thinking about the classical texts brought to a head by the challenge in the winter of 1966 to make this Western tradition relevant to an excellent and

properly impatient group of students, many non-Western, enrolled in a "National Development" course at the Institute for Social Science in the Hague; and I thank the students for their challenges and the Institute for the chance to attempt a response. My reading of J. S. Mill depends heavily on *Representative Government* and on recognition of his direct and indirect debts to David Hume's political essays.

15. Cf. David Spitz, *Patterns of Anti-Democratic Thought* (New York, 1949); C. Wright Mills offers introductory excerpts from socialist critics of Stalinism in *The Marxists* (New York, 1962).
16. George Lichtheim, *The New Europe* (New York, 1963), esp. pp. 175–215.
17. E.g., Malcolm X, *Autobiography* (New York, 1965); Barrington Moore, Jr., *Social Origins of Dictatorship and Democracy* (Boston, 1966); John K. Galbraith, *The New Industrial State* (New York, 1966).
18. Cf. E. V. Walter, "Mass Society: The Late Stages of an Idea," 31: 4, *Social Research* (1964), 391–410, and the literature there cited.
19. See especially the work of Theodore Adorno; cf. David Kettler, *Marxismus und Kultur. Mannheim und Lukacs in den ungarischen Revolutionen 1918/19* (Neuwied/Rhine, 1967).
20. The great day of that confrontation, when the gifted followers of Leo Strauss served as harmless and official dissenters from orthodox political science, seems happily ended. See Herbert Storing (ed.), *Essays on the Scientific Study of Politics* (New York, 1962).
21. Cf. William E. Connolly, *Political Science and Ideology* (New York, 1967), esp. pp. 13–55.
22. Giovanni Sartori, *Democratic Theory* (Detroit, 1962), stresses distinctions between democratic and liberal elements in modern democratic theory; but my views are closer to Franz L. Neumann, *loc. cit.* cf. also Peter Bachrach, *The Theory of Democratic Elitism* (Boston and Toronto, 1967). Robert Dahl, *A Preface to Democratic Theory* (Chicago, 1956), builds a typology quite narrowly based on American traditions and tied to a faulty paradigm of the political theory enterprise.
23. Bertrand de Jouvenel, "The Means of Contestation," *Government and Opposition*, vol. 1, no. 2 (Jan. 1966), pp. 155ff.
24. Walter Lippmann's *The Public Philosophy* (New York, 1965) remains a convenient short statement.
25. E. H. Carr's *The New Society* (London, 1951) epitomizes relevant arguments.
26. The old Liberal interpretation is less likely to influence American national government than local, although there are parallels between it and the "presidentialist" variant of Machiavellian elitism, to be discussed below. The notions of "responsible" authorities, "respectable" publics, and their "law and order" are more prevalent at local levels in the United States; they sweep all before them in the Netherlands, Germany, and in northern Europe generally.
27. A. H. Birch, *Representative and Responsible Government* (London, 1964), pp. 114ff. For an indication of the continued influence of this approach among spokesmen for the Left opposition in Continental socialist parties, see, e.g., Hans van de Doel, et al., *Tien over Rood* (Amsterdam, 1966). A recent American statement growing out of this tradition is James MacGregor Burns, *The Deadlock of Democracy* (Englewood Cliffs, N.J., 1963).

28. Because so much of contemporary political science addresses itself to these contentions, it would be superfluous to cite bibliography. As will be suggested below, modern American pluralism has grown and thrived on the shallowness of the critical diagnosis contained in this account. The description of conditions is accurate enough, by and large, but the explanations and responses to the conditions are radically inadequate.

29. This last point, probably the most interesting of the three, is already implicit in Rousseau and, as noted, was in some measure cautiously taken up by John Stuart Mill. It receives brilliant development in the critique of Hegel's *Philosophy of Right* and in the early contributions to the *Rheinische Zeitung* written by Karl Marx when he was a radical democrat. See Karl Marx, *Frühe Schriften*, Hans-Joachim Lieber and Peter Furth, eds. (Stuttgart, 1962), pp. 110–426, esp. pp. 292ff. and p. 410; useful excerpts are now available in English in Lloyd D. Easton and Kurt H. Guddat, eds., *Writings of the Young Marx on Philosophy and Society* (New York, 1967).

30. Cf. David Kettler, "Nieuwe Voormen voor de Democratie," *De Gids* (June and July, 1967), pp. 3–18. This essay includes an early draft of parts of the present paper, but also attempts to apply the discussion to Dutch conditions.

31. Sartori, *op. cit.*, p. 84.

32. Birch, *op. cit.*, pp. 123 and 126.

33. Still influential and, in important ways, paradigmatic is Karl Mannheim, *Man and Society in an Age of Reconstruction* (London, 1946). Most commonly the charge is implicit in policy-oriented studies in economics, international politics, etc.

34. Charles Lindblom, *op. cit.*, gives an elegant version of the argument.

35. Discussion has also been influenced by Karl Popper, especially *The Open Society and Its Enemies* (Princeton, 1950) and *The Poverty of Historicism* (Boston, 1957).

36. The early statements of this "Kennedy" position are still the most revealing; see the concluding section of Arthur Schlesinger, Jr., *The Age of Roosevelt* (Boston, 1960), Volume III, and James MacGregor Burns, *Roosevelt: The Lion and the Fox* (New York, 1956). As the citation of Burns indicates, the presidentialist argument may be more or less ingenuously combined with the old democratic approach. Another combination common in some recent literature equips the presidency with the most sophisticated problem-solving technology and attaches to it something approaching the old liberal confidence in the elite.

37. See John McDermott, "The Crisis-Managers" [a review of Roger Hilsman, *To Move a Nation*], *New York Review of Books*. IX:4 (September 14, 1967), 4–10.

38. A sober and systematic location of this sort of crisis-leadership within a broader theoretical framework, which nevertheless does not serve to give it any substantial support, is found in Chalmers Johnson, *Revolutionary Change* (Boston, 1966), pp. 71f. A sharply contrasting and more persuasive assessment of the consequences of relying on such leadership instead of revolutionary change is given in Barrington Moore, *op. cit.*, esp. pp. 433–452.

39. See the excellent essay by Sheldon Wolin and John Schaar, "The Abuses of the Multiversity," in Seymour Martin Lipset and Sheldon S. Wolin (eds.), *The Berkeley Student Revolt* (New York, 1966),

pp. 350-363; also Carl Davidson, *The New Radicals in the Multi-versity* (Printed by SDS, March 1968); an important theoretical contribution is Michael Walzer, "The Obligation to Disobey," in David Spitz (ed.), *Political Theory and Social Change* (New York, 1967), pp. 185-202; other essays in that volume also bear on the topics here discussed, especially those in Part II.

40. Richard Falk, "World Revolution and International Order," in *Nomos VIII: Revolution* (New York, 1966), pp. 154-177, and *Law, Morality and War in the Contemporary World* (Princeton, 1963). But compare the troubling problems raised in Franz L. Neumann, "The Change in the Function of Law," *op. cit.*, pp. 22-68.

41. Arthur Waskow, *From Race-Riot to Sit-In* (New York, 1966) is loaded down with some clumsy concepts, but has a number of important suggestions about "creative disorder."

42. Arnold Kaufman develops the case for participation well in "Human Nature and Participatory Democracy," this volume, Chapter 8. Peter Bachrach, *op. cit.*, also makes a strong case for "participatory democracy"; see also Staughton Lynd, "The New Radicals and Participatory Democracy," *Dissent* (Summer 1965), and many other items listed in the study-guides cited in note 11, above.

Selected Bibliography

PLURALIST THEORY

Books

Almond, Gabriel A., and Sidney Verba. *The Civic Culture* (Boston: Little, Brown, 1965).

Bauer, Raymond A., Ithiel de Sola Pool, and Lewis Anthony Dexter. *American Business and Public Policy: The Politics of Foreign Trade* (New York: Atherton Press, 1963).

Bentley, Arthur F. *The Process of Government* (Chicago: University of Chicago Press, 1908).

Berle, Adolf. *The Twentieth Century Capitalist Revolution* (New York: Harvest Books, 1954).

Berle, Adolf. *Power Without Property* (New York: Harcourt, 1959).

Campbell, Angus, Philip Converse, Warren Miller, and Donald Stokes. *Elections and the Political Order* (New York: John Wiley, 1966).

Chambers, William N., and Robert H. Salisbury (eds.). *Democracy in the Mid-Twentieth Century: Problems and Prospects* (St. Louis: The Washington University Press, 1960).

Dahl, Robert. *A Preface to Democratic Theory* (Chicago: University of Chicago Press, 1956).

Dahl, Robert. *Who Governs?* (New Haven: Yale University Press, 1961).

Dahl, Robert. *Pluralist Democracy in the United States: Conflict and Consent* (Chicago: Rand McNally, 1967).

Dahl, Robert, and Charles E. Lindblom. *Politics, Economics and Welfare* (New York: Harper & Row, 1953).

Etzioni, Amitai. *The Active Society* (New York: The Free Press, 1968).

Galbraith, John Kenneth. *American Capitalism: The Concept of Countervailing Power* (Boston: Houghton Mifflin, 1952).

Keller, Suzanne. *Beyond the Ruling Class* (New York: Random House, 1963).

Key, V. O. *Public Opinion and American Democracy* (New York: Knopf, 1961).

Key, V. O. *Politics, Parties, and Pressure Groups* (New York: Thomas Y. Crowell, 1964).

Kornhauser, William. *The Politics of Mass Society* (New York: The Free Press, 1959).

Lindblom, Charles. *The Intelligence of Democracy* (New York: The Free Press, 1965).

Lipset, Seymour M. *Political Man: The Social Bases of Politics* (New York: Anchor Books, 1960).

Mannheim, Karl. *Freedom, Power, and Democratic Planning.* Edited by Hans Gerth and Ernest Branstedt (London: Routledge & Kegan Paul, 1950).

Mannheim, Karl. *Man and Society in an Age of Reconstruction* (New York: Harcourt, 1954).

Monsen, Joseph, Jr., and Mark W. Cannon. *The Makers of Public Policy: American Power Groups and Their Ideologies* (New York: McGraw-Hill, 1965).

Rose, Arnold. *The Power Structure* (New York: Oxford University Press, 1967).

Sartori, Giovanni. *Democratic Theory* (Detroit: Wayne State University Press, 1962).

Schubert, Glendon. *The Public Interest* (New York: The Free Press, 1960).

Schumpeter, Joseph. *Capitalism, Socialism, and Democracy,* 2nd edition (New York: Harper & Row, 1947).

Tocqueville, Alexis de. *Democracy in America.* Edited by Richard D. Heffner (New York: Mentor Books, 1956).

Truman, David. *The Governmental Process* (New York: Knopf, 1951).

Periodicals

Dahl, Robert. "A Critique of the Ruling Elite Model," *American Political Science Review,* LII (June 1958), 463–469.

Dahl, Robert. "Further Reflections on 'The Elitist Theory of Democracy,'" *American Political Science Review,* LX (June 1966), 296–305.

Dahl, Robert. "The City in the Future of Democracy," *American Political Science Review,* LXI (December 1967), 953–970.

Latham, Earl. "The Group Basis of Politics: Notes for a Theory," *American Political Science Review,* XLVI (June 1952), 376–397.

Mayo, H. B. "How Can We Justify Democracy?" *American Political Science Review* LVI (June 1962), 555–556.

McClosky, Herbert. "Consensus and Ideology in American Politics," *American Political Science Review,* LVIII (June 1964), 361–382.

McClosky, Herbert, Paul Hoffman, and Rosemary O'Hara. "Issue Conflict and Consensus Among Party Leaders and Followers," *American Political Science Review,* 44 (June 1960), 406–427.

Merelman, Richard M. "On the Neo-Elitist Critique of Community Power," *American Political Science Review* LXII (June 1968), 451–460.

Neubauer, Deane. "Some Conditions of Democracy," *American Political Science Review*, LXI (December 1967), 1002–1009.

Prothro, James, and Charles Grigg. "Fundamental Principles of Democracy: Bases of Agreement and Disagreement," *Journal of Politics,* 22 (1960).

Truman, David. "The American System in Crisis," *Political Science Quarterly* (December 1959), 481–497.

CRITIQUE OF PLURALIST THEORY

Books

Bachrach, Peter. *The Theory of Democratic Elitism: A Critique* (Boston: Little, Brown, 1967).

Baran, Paul and Paul Sweezy. *Monopoly Capital—An Essay on the American Economic and Social Order* (New York and London: Monthly Review Press, 1966).

Connolly, William E. *Political Science and Ideology* (New York: Atherton Press, 1967).

Coser, Lewis. *The Functions of Social Conflict* (New York: The Free Press, 1956).

Dewey, John. *The Public and Its Problems* (New York: Holt, 1967).

Domhoff, William. *Who Rules America?* (Englewood Cliffs, N.J.: Prentice-Hall, 1967).

Galbraith, John Kenneth. *The New Industrial State* (Boston: Houghton Mifflin, 1967).

Hacker, Andrew (ed.). *The Corporation Take-over* (New York: Harper & Row, 1964).

Horowitz, Irving Louis (ed.). *The New Sociology* (New York: Oxford University Press, 1965).

Kariel, Henry. *The Decline of American Pluralism* (Stanford: Stanford University Press, 1961).

Kariel, Henry. *The Promise of Politics* (Englewood Cliffs, N.J.: Prentice-Hall, 1966).

Kolko, Gabriel. *Wealth and Power in America: An Analysis of Social Class and Income Distribution* (New York: Praeger, 1962).

Lenski, Gerhard. *Power and Privilege: A Theory of Social Stratification* (New York: McGraw-Hill, 1966).

Marcuse, Herbert. *One Dimensional Man* (Boston: Beacon Press, 1964).

McConnell, Grant. *Private Property and American Democracy* (New York: Knopf, 1966).

McCoy, Charles A., and John Playford (eds.). *Apolitical Politics: A Critique of Behavioralism* (New York: Thomas Y. Crowell, 1967).

Meisel, James (ed.). *Pareto and Mosca* (Englewood Cliffs, N.J.: Prentice-Hall, 1965).

Michels, Robert. *Political Parties* (New York: The Free Press, 1949).

Mills, C. Wright. *White Collar* (New York: Oxford University Press, 1951).

Mills, C. Wright. *The Power Elite* (New York: Oxford University Press, 1959).

Mills, C. Wright. *Power, Politics, and People: The Collected Papers of C. Wright Mills.* Edited by I. L. Horowitz (New York: Ballantine Books, 1961).

Nieburg, H. L. *In the Name of Science* (Chicago: Quadrangle Books, 1966).

Presthus, Robert. *The Organizational Society* (New York: Vintage Books, 1962).

Reagan, Michael D. *The Managed Economy* (New York: Oxford University Press, 1963).

Schattschneider, E. E. *The Semi-Sovereign People* (New York: Holt, 1960).

Wolff, Robert Paul, Herbert Marcuse, and Barrington Moore, Jr. *A Critique of Pure Tolerance* (Boston: Beacon Press, 1965).

Periodicals

Bachrach, Peter. "Elite Consensus and Democracy," *Journal of Politics*, 24 (August 1962), 439–452.

Bachrach, Peter, and Morton Baratz. "Decisions and Nondecisions: An Analytical Framework," *American Political Science Review*, LVII (September 1963), 632–642.

Bay, Christian. "Politics and Pseudo-Politics: A Critical Evaluation of Some Behavioral Literature," *American Political Science Review*, LIX (March 1965), 39–51.

Davis, Lane. "The Costs of Realism: Contemporary Restatements of Democracy," *Western Political Quarterly*, 17 (1964), 37–46.

Duncan, Graeme, and Steven Lukes. "The New Democracy," *Political Studies*, 11 (June 1963), 156–177.

Green, Philip. "Science, Government, and the Case of RAND: A Singular Pluralism," *World Politics*, XX (January 1968), 301–326.

Horowitz, Irving L. "Consensus, Conflict, and Cooperation: A Sociological Inventory," *Social Forces*, 41 (December 3, 1962), 177–188.

Lowi, Theodore. "American Business, Public Policy, Case Studies and Political Theory," *World Politics*, 16 (1964), 677–715.

Nieburg, H. L. "The Politicization of the Economic System: Convergence of Market Place and Forum," paper given at Midwest Conference of Political Scientists (May 3, 1968).

Walker, Jack. "A Critique of the Elitist Theory of Democracy," *American Political Science Review*, LX (June 1966).

ALTERNATIVE IDEALS AND STRATEGIES

Books

Barry, Brian. *Political Argument* (New York: The Humanities Press, 1965).

Bay, Christian. *The Structure of Freedom* (New York: Atheneum, 1965).

Benn, Stanley, and Richard Peters. *The Principles of Political Thought* (New York: The Free Press, 1965).

Brandt, Richard (ed.) *Social Justice* (Englewood Cliffs, N.J.: Prentice-Hall, 1962).

Flathman, Richard. *The Public Interest* (New York: John Wiley, 1966).

Friedrich, Carl J. (ed.). *The Public Interest*: Nomos V (New York: Atherton Press, 1962).

Fromm, Erich (ed.). *Socialist Humanism* (New York: Anchor Books, 1966).

Harrington, Michael. *Toward a Democratic Left* (New York: Macmillan, 1968).

Howe, Irving (ed.). *The Radical Papers* (New York: Anchor Books, 1966).

Kateb, George. *Utopia and Its Enemies* (New York: The Free Press, 1963).

Kaufman, Arnold S. *The Radical Liberal: New Man in American Politics* (New York: Atherton Press, 1968).

Kolaja, Jiri. *Worker's Councils: The Jugoslav Experience* (New York: Praeger, 1966).

Myrdal, Gunnar. *Beyond The Welfare State* (New Haven: Yale University Press, 1960).

Pranger, Robert J. *The Eclipse of Citizenship: Power and Participation in Contemporary Politics* (New York: Holt, 1968).

Perucci, R., and Marc Pilisuk (eds.). *The Triple Revolution: Social Problems in Depth* (Boston: Little, Brown, 1968).

Runciman, W. G. *Relative Deprivation and Social Justice* (Berkeley: University of California Press, 1966).

Spitz, David (ed.). *Political Theory and Social Change* (New York: Atherton Press, 1967).

Sturmthal, Adolf. *Worker's Councils* (Cambridge, Mass.: Harvard University Press, 1964).

Periodicals

Aranson, Ronald, "The Movement and Its Critics," *Studies on the Left* (January-February 1966), 3–20.

Harrington, Michael. "Strategies For Opposition," *Dissent* (March-April 1968), 119–130.

Kaufman, Arnold. "Radicalism and Conventional Politics," *Dissent* (July-August 1967), 1–8.

Lasch, Christopher. "The Trouble with Black Power," *New York Review of Books* (February 29, 1968), 4–14.

Lipsky, Michael. "Protest as a Political Resource," *American Political Science Review,* LXII (December 1968), 1144–1158.

Rosen, Summer R. "The Case For a Radical Politics," *Studies on the Left* (Summer 1964), 32–38.

Swados, Harvey. "What's Left of the Left," *The Nation, 100th Anniversary Issue* (1965), 108–114.

Walzer, Michael *et al.* "Civil Disobedience and 'Resistance' "—A Symposium," *Dissent* (January-February 1968), 13–25.

Note: Many of the most provocative articles in this field are found in anthologies mentioned above. See, especially, Hacker, *The Corporation Takeover*; McCoy and Playford, *Apolitical Politics*; Howe, *The Radical Papers*; and Spitz, *Political Theory and Social Change.*

Index

anachronism
  of democracy, 222–224
  and medieval theories, 224–225
  in political thought, 222–226
anticipated reaction, 63n
authority, crisis of, 84, 93–94

Bachrach, Peter, on participation, 24
Baran, Paul, and equilibrium theory, 47–48
Bay, Christian, and critical temper, 24
behavioralism, 20
Bell, Daniel, critique of power elite, 131–132
Benn, S. I., on interest, 163
Bentley, Arthur
  influence of, 45–47
  on groups, 41–42, 44
  on interest, 40–41, 42–43, 159, 174
  on knowledge, 39, 49
Berle, Adolf, on pluralism, 11–13

bias, see nondecision process; pluralism
Bridgman, Percy, 40
Brodbeck, May, on prediction, 32n
Burke, Edmund, 4

change
  and liberalism, 234–239
  and new left, 239–245
  strategies of, 26–28, 234–245
class
  and corporate elites, 75
  and pluralism, 12–13, 31n
  see also middle class
conflict
  displacement of, 99
  see also nondecision
concept formation
  in pluralist theory, 21
  see also interest; power; public interest
concern, ambiguities in meaning, 161
  see also interest

257